Inquire

A Student Handbook for 21st Century Learning

Robert King, Christopher Erickson, and Janae Sebranek

Created by

Thoughtful Learning

Distributed exclusively by

ZB **Zaner-Bloser**

Acknowledgments

Inquire is a reality because of the collaborative efforts of our hardworking team of educators, students, researchers, writers, editors, and designers. Their critical and creative thinking, as well as their problem-solving and communication skills, made this resource possible.

The *Inquire* Team

Steven J. Augustyn	Mark Lalumondier	Jean Varley
Tim Kemper	Cindy Smith	Claire Ziffer
Lois Krenzke	Lester Smith	

A special thanks goes to Cindy Smith, project-based instructor at Karcher Middle School in Burlington, Wisconsin. In addition to providing guidance and feedback on *Inquire*, Mrs. Smith graciously allowed the team to field-test the material in her class. Her insights and those of her students greatly improved *Inquire*.

Inquire on the Web

This book is just the beginning! Log on to thoughtfullearning.com to find dozens of downloadable templates and forms, additional models and projects, links to great resources, and much, much more.

Trademarks and trade names are shown in this book strictly for illustrative purposes and are the property of their respective owners. The authors' references herein should not be regarded as affecting their validity. Wikipedia is a registered trademark of the Wikimedia Foundation. Microsoft and PowerPoint are either trademarks or registered trademarks of Microsoft Corporation in the United States and/or other countries.

Copyright © by Thoughtful Learning

Distributed in the U.S.A. exclusively by Zaner-Bloser, Inc., 1-800-421-3018, www.zaner-bloser.com.

ISBN (softcover) 978-1-453110-44-7
1 2 3 4 5 6 7 8 9 10 13880 18 17 16 15 14 13

ISBN (hardcover) 978-1-453110-43-0
1 2 3 4 5 6 7 8 9 10 13880 18 17 16 15 14 13

ISBN (online) 978-1-453110-46-1

Printed in the U.S.A.

SUSTAINABLE FORESTRY INITIATIVE

Certified Chain of Custody
Promoting Sustainable Forestry
www.sfiprogram.org
SFI-01171

Inquire

Inquire is your personal learning guide. It will help you become a better thinker, problem solver, speaker, team player, planner, and researcher in all of your classes. This guide is divided into three parts.

Part I: Building 21st Century Skills

The first part helps you develop the skills you need to succeed in school, in life, and later in the world of work. It covers everything from critical thinking and building strong arguments to using social media and studying for tests.

Part II: Using the Inquiry Process

The second part provides an overview of the inquiry process, including conducting research and presenting what you have learned. To inquire means "to question," and the process of asking questions and searching for answers leads to authentic learning.

Part III: Developing Projects

The third part helps you create all sorts of exciting and meaningful projects—from writing narratives to creating podcasts, from developing brochures to building scale models.

Electronic Aids

The **e-book version** of *Inquire* contains links that make it easy to search for information from part to part. And the *Inquire* Web site contains downloadable planning sheets, additional models, activities, and projects to try! (Go to thoughtfullearning.com.)

Using *Inquire*

The special design of *Inquire* makes it easy to find information from chapter to chapter and within each part. With practice, you will know the best way to turn to the guidelines, models, and tips that you need.

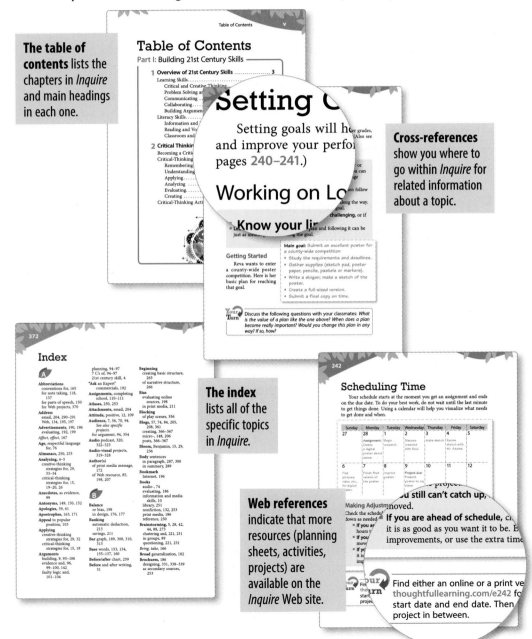

The table of contents lists the chapters in *Inquire* and main headings in each one.

Cross-references show you where to go within *Inquire* for related information about a topic.

The index lists all of the specific topics in *Inquire*.

Web references indicate that more resources (planning sheets, activities, projects) are available on the *Inquire* Web site.

Table of Contents

Part I: Building 21st Century Skills

Part II: Using the Inquiry Process

Part III: Developing Projects

Photos

Cory Militzer: 344 (Rube Goldberg Machine)

Flickr: 127, 230, 331, 341

Public Domain: 11, 367

Shutterstock: v, viii, xi, xii, 4, 11, 16, 17, 24, 33, 35, 38, 40, 45, 53, 60, 65, 69, 80, 82, 85, 96, 103, 108, 121, 123, 130, 135, 136, 141, 148, 151, 152, 158, 162, 165, 167, 170, 174, 175, 176, 177, 178, 179, 180, 184, 186, 188, 190, 193, 194, 195, 196, 202, 203, 205, 206, 210, 213, 215, 224, 226, 229, 231, 233, 234, 240, 243, 244, 246, 249, 250, 251, 252, 258, 263, 264, 267, 268, 273, 274, 276, 284, 285, 287, 289, 291, 293, 295, 297, 299, 303, 305, 306, 308, 309, 311, 312, 313, 315, 317, 318, 320, 321, 323, 325, 327, 328, 330, 331, 333, 335, 337, 339, 341, 343, 344, 346, 347, 349, 351, 353, 355, 357, 358, 360, 361, 363, 365, 367, 369, 371

Wikimedia Commons: 188, 207 (Screen Capture), 360, 365

Why *Inquire*?

What do artists, engineers, scientists, doctors, and students like you have in common? All of you have to ask questions, conduct research, communicate, and collaborate to do your best work. In fact, skills like these are at the core of real learning.

A Handbook for 21st Century Skills

Inquire will help you learn about and practice all of the key learning skills. Here are the main skills covered in the first part of the book:

- Critical and creative thinking
- Collaborating and communicating
- Problem solving and building arguments
- Understanding and using media
- Studying and taking tests

A Handbook for Inquiry and Projects

Inquire also helps you use the inquiry process to solve problems and develop great projects. Here are some of the inquiry-based skills and projects covered in the next two parts of the book:

- Asking questions and planning research
- Creating and presenting projects
- Developing writing and Web projects
- Building audio-visual and graphic projects
- Preparing performing and design projects

A Handbook for All of Your Classes

You can use *Inquire* in all of your classes, in your extracurricular activities, and in life itself. *Inquire* will help you succeed right now and prepare you to learn and succeed for years to come!

Part 1:
Building
21st
Century
Skills

Part I:
Building 21st Century Skills

This section covers all of the important 21st century skills—and more. If you follow the strategies in each chapter, you will become a better thinker and learner now and for years to come. These skills will also help you use the inquiry process and create great projects in Parts II and III.

Chapters in This Section

Chapter 1

Overview of 21st Century Skills

Life in the 21st century is changing quickly. New technology allows you to connect with people around the globe almost instantly. In a way, the whole world has become your neighborhood. Today, being a good neighbor requires 21st century skills. You'll be solving problems, communicating, collaborating, finding information, and much more. *Inquire* can help, and this chapter tells you about the key skills the book covers.

You will learn . . .

- Critical and Creative Thinking
- Problem Solving and Inquiry
- Communicating
- Collaborating
- Building Arguments
- Information and Media Skills
- Reading and Vocabulary
- Classroom and Study Skills
- Workplace Skills

Preparing to Learn

Have you ever heard the term "old school"? It means using an old, traditional way of doing things—like memorizing lists of facts, completing pages of problems, and answering a lot of basic questions. Learning today involves the more active 21st century skills.

21st Century Skills
- Critical and creative thinking
- Problem solving and inquiry
- Communicating and collaborating
- Building arguments

You'll also need strong literacy and life skills.

Literacy and Life Skills
- Information and media skills
- Reading and vocabulary skills
- Study skills
- Workplace skills

 Your Turn Working with a partner or in a small group, list situations in which you have to think critically and creatively. Then list situations in which you need to communicate and collaborate. Afterward, share your ideas with the class.

The well-prepared student . . .
- is curious.
- thinks carefully.
- analyzes information.
- communicates in different ways.
- values teamwork.
- manages time.
- takes control of learning.

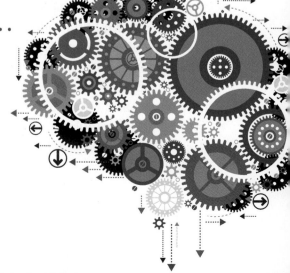

Learning Skills

The next few pages give you a preview of the 21st century skills. Later, you'll find a separate chapter for each skill.

Critical and Creative Thinking

The word *creative* comes from the Latin word *crescere,* meaning "to grow." When you think creatively, you grow or produce ideas. The word *critical* comes from the Greek word *kritikos,* meaning "to judge." When you think critically, you judge or sort through the ideas you have created. (Also see pages **13–26** and **27–40.**)

A **creative thinker** produces many different possibilities and grows abundant ideas. A creative thinker is involved in the following activities:

- imagining
- producing
- gathering
- inventing
- brainstorming
- connecting

A **critical thinker** carefully studies possibilities and ideas, deciding which are the best. A critical thinker is involved in the following activities:

- sorting
- studying
- organizing
- analyzing
- evaluating
- choosing

🔍 In Focus Fossils discovered in Utah tell us that many more huge dinosaurs lived there than was first believed. At one time, scientists thought it was highly improbable for many huge dinosaurs to live in one area: How would they all find enough to eat? But after finding these new fossils, paleontologists (scientists who study fossil remains) have to reconsider that idea. They need to think creatively and critically about the new fossils and what they mean. The scientists will likely come up with a new idea or theory. Many people will believe the latest theory—until some new discoveries cause them to question it.

Your Turn Write down a few examples of creative and critical thinking that you have done lately. Share your examples with the class.

Problem Solving and Inquiry

Every day, you face problems—like deciding what to wear (a simple problem) or figuring out how to earn the money you need for music camp (a not-so-simple problem). When you face a challenging problem, always follow a problem-solving process. (See pages 41–54 for a discussion of this process. Also see pages 219–226 for information about a related process.)

Steps to Problem Solving

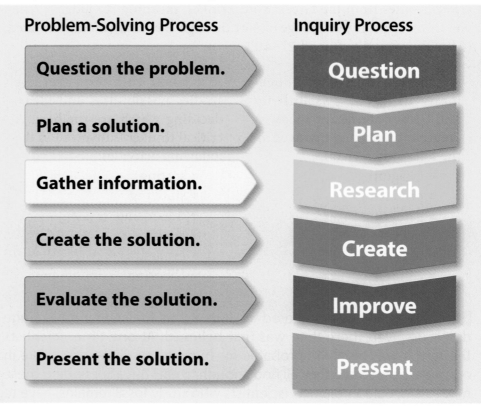

Problem-Solving Process	Inquiry Process
Question the problem.	Question
Plan a solution.	Plan
Gather information.	Research
Create the solution.	Create
Evaluate the solution.	Improve
Present the solution.	Present

Your Turn Imagine your class will plan a butterfly garden next to the school. Here is your problem: You're not sure how to begin. Working as a class or in small groups, use the first three or four steps above to work on solving your problem. Your goal is to plan a butterfly garden.

Communicating

Talking is different from communicating. Often, you talk just to connect with people around you. Spending time with friends and talking about whatever comes to mind is an example. But you communicate to inquire and share ideas. Talking can be easy and casual, while communicating is more purposeful and thoughtful. Do you see the difference? (See pages 55–78 for more information.)

Communication Skills

Basic communication skills include writing, speaking, and listening. Working on these skills is very important, because you need them to share ideas in these different ways:

- Participating in discussions
- Making oral presentations
- Composing emails and messages
- Conducting interviews
- Writing essays and reports

> "We have two ears and one mouth so that we can listen twice as much as we speak."
> —Epictetus
> Greek philosopher

The Parts of Communication

Every type of communication has four parts: purpose, topic, audience, and form. For example, imagine that Carlos is interested in entering an essay contest sponsored by his city's chamber of commerce. Here are the parts of this type of communication.

Purpose: To persuade
Topic: Becoming a pen pal with a senior citizen
Audience: Chamber of commerce officials
Form: Essay

🔍 **In Focus** Students in many countries are required to learn a second language, very often English. That skill plus new technology allows them to communicate with people around the world. By learning another language, you can become a global student.

Your Turn Explain what the quotation above means to you. Afterward, share your thoughts with your classmates.

Collaborating

Collaboration means "working together as a team." (See pages **79–92** for more information.) Consider these two great collaborators:

- **Harriet Tubman** helped many slaves gain their freedom by working together with the Underground Railroad, a secret network of people who helped the slaves during their flight to freedom.
- **Steve Jobs** might have been the brains behind many famous Apple products, but he worked together with the best minds in software and hardware development to revolutionize the world.

Teamwork

Daily life would be very difficult without teamwork. Consider the people involved in producing the food we eat, manufacturing the products we use, building schools, running hospitals, and the list goes on and on. With teamwork being so important, you will need to develop the following team skills:

☑ Being a good listener

☑ Helping as needed

☑ Taking turns

☑ Praising others for their work

☑ Offering advice

☑ Avoiding put-downs

☑ Working toward team goals

Technology and Teamwork

Technology has made it easier to collaborate with others, whether they are near or faraway. You can text, email, chat, blog, and participate in conference calls. Check with your teachers and your school's information specialist for the options available to you.

Your Turn List all the different "teams" you are part of, starting with your family. Keep listing as long as you can. Share your list with the class.

Building Arguments

You know about arguing, getting mad, and raising your voice. But this book will help you build logical, convincing, well-researched arguments about important topics. (See pages 93–106 for more information.)

The Building Blocks

An argument is built with an opinion and supporting facts.

- An **opinion** is a personal view or belief. It can be supported by facts, but it is not a fact itself. Here is an example.

> Our school should start a drama club.
> *(This is a personal view that can be supported with facts.)*

- A **fact** is used to support an opinion. It can be checked for accuracy. Here is an example.

> According to the latest student survey, 45 students expressed an interest in drama.
> *(This is a provable statement that supports an opinion.)*

Weak Arguments

An effective argument presents reasonable information, while a weak argument presents unreasonable or even dishonest information. Here are two examples of weak arguments. (See pages 101–104 for more information.)

> Having a drama club will make our school the best in the state.
> *(an exaggeration that can't be proved)*
>
> Either we have a drama club, or students will revolt.
> *(a statement of two extremes, ignoring anything in between)*

Your Turn Write the first part of a typical argument with a friend. Then rewrite it as a logical argument based on the information shared above. Discuss your work with the class.

Literacy Skills

Learning the three R's—reading, writing, and 'rithmetic—has always been important. And today, you still need these skills in order to understand and use all the information available through new technologies. The next pages preview the key literacy and learning skills covered in this book.

Information and Media Skills

Information comes from many different sources—books, magazines, radio shows, Web sites, and more. Each source has its strengths and weaknesses. For example, books can hold a lot of reliable information about a topic, but the information may be out-of-date. On the other hand, the Internet can easily update information, but it may not be reliable or trustworthy.

Reliability Check

To determine the reliability of a source, ask yourself these questions:

1. **Who created the source?** For a book or magazine, find out who the author is and check his or her credentials. Do the same for the author and sponsor of a Web site.

2. **What is the source's purpose?** Does the information attempt to inform, persuade, or entertain? How does the purpose affect the source's value?

3. **How accurate is the information?** Does the text contain careless errors? Are the facts accurate? (To find out, check with other sources.) Does the information seem complete?

4. **How current is the information?** Check the publication date. This is especially important with technical or scientific material. Older publications may contain out-of-date information.

Your Turn Working with a partner, find one trustworthy online source and one untrustworthy online source. Share your findings with your classmates.

Reading and Vocabulary

You can learn a lot by watching, listening, and doing; but reading remains one of the very best ways to learn. (See pages 131–146 for more information.)

Becoming a Strong Reader

Athletes and musicians practice to improve their skills; so should readers. Reading every day is the best way to improve this important skill. Strong readers do the following:

- ☑ Read for fun.
- ☑ Read to learn.
- ☑ Read with a plan in mind.
- ☑ Think and write while reading.
- ☑ Learn new words.

Note: As you continue to practice your reading, you will naturally increase your vocabulary. And knowing new words will make you a stronger communicator.

🔍 **In Focus** According to his biography, Gary Paulsen was not the best student in school. But once he discovered the library and books, he became a regular reader. In fact, he often spent hours reading book after book. His love of reading, plus many personal adventures, led him to become a writer. He is now the proud author of more than 150 books, including the award-winning *Hatchet, Dogsong,* and *The Winter Room.* Getting hooked on books now (both fiction and nonfiction) will not only help you learn but also take you to places you may never have dreamed of going.

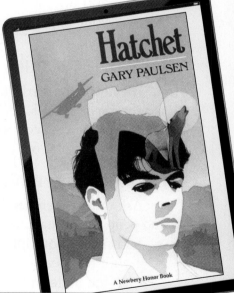

Your Turn Find an interesting nonfiction book or article to read. Then help your classmates decide whether they also want to read it by sharing a few details with them—such as the author, the topic, and a fascinating fact or two.

Classroom and Study Skills

To do your best work in school, you need to get actively involved in the learning process. Do the following:

☑ Keep a positive attitude about school.
☑ Take advantage of every learning opportunity.
☑ Listen well and follow directions.
☑ Practice strong study skills.
☑ Connect new information with things you already know.
☑ Take pride in your work.

Note: Study skills such as taking notes and summarizing will help you understand what you read, get the most out of class discussions, and create accurate lab reports. (See pages **117–130** for more information.)

 Your Turn What kind of a learner are you? Identify one of your strengths and one of your weaknesses. Then discuss your ideas with your classmates.

Workplace Skills

It's never too early to think about summer jobs and community service opportunities. Working teaches the importance of being on time, finishing a job, and cooperating in a group. Working also helps you make career choices later on. (See pages **209–216** for more information.)

Finding Opportunities to Volunteer

Ask family members and friends. They may know of opportunities and people to contact.

- **Consider your interests.** For example, if you like animals, check with the local animal shelter.
- **Check bulletin boards.** People often advertise events, volunteer opportunities, and jobs on bulletin boards in grocery stores.

Your Turn List three or four jobs you would like to try right now. Then list three or four jobs or careers you would like to try as an adult. Share your lists in class.

A bug is a bug is a bug . . . or is it?

Chapter 2
Critical Thinking

Thinking comes naturally. Sometimes your thoughts are simple: *That creepy crawly thing is one big bug!* Other times, your thoughts are more complex: *I wonder what kind of bug that is.* Critical thinking often begins with that sort of curiosity. This chapter explains critical thinking—from basic remembering and understanding to complex analyzing and evaluating.

You will learn . . .
- Becoming a Critical Thinker
- Remembering
- Understanding
- Applying
- Analyzing
- Evaluating
- Creating

Becoming a Critical Thinker

When you think critically, you think things through. For example, if you're getting dressed, you may want to grab your favorite jeans. But then you remember that you have art class and that paint splatters. So you decide to wear a pair of older jeans. That's thinking things through.

A Guide to Critical Thinking

Here are some basic guidelines for becoming a critical thinker.

Concentrate.	Stay focused on the task in front of you.
Question.	Ask *why* and *how* to learn more about a topic.
Take your time.	Don't expect quick solutions or easy answers, especially when a problem or question is challenging.
Look at the whole.	Start by looking at the "big picture." Name the topic, define it, say what it is and is not. Describe it, which means "draw a circle around it."
Look at the parts.	See the pieces that make up the whole. Explore how the pieces fit together. Think about the job of each piece. Take them apart.
Put the parts back together.	Rebuild the whole. Describe what you have discovered. Think about strengths and weaknesses. Summarize the experience.
Share and reflect.	Tell others what you have learned. Think about what it means.

 Think about this idea: "Time given to thought is the greatest time saver of all." Then write down what the idea means to you. Afterward, share your thoughts with your classmates.

Critical-Thinking Strategies

A researcher named Benjamin Bloom created a list of critical-thinking skills, from basic to more complex. The next pages give you specific strategies for thinking at each level. During most of your work, you will move back and forth between the different types of thinking.

Bloom's Thinking Skills

Remembering is recalling basic information.	**You'll learn** how to use questions and topic webs to remember important details (see page 16).
Understanding is knowing what something means.	**You'll learn** a key strategy for finding meaning in what you read (see page 17).
Applying is using information.	**You'll learn** how to set goals and plan a project (see page 18).
Analyzing is looking at the parts of something.	**You'll learn** how to compare, classify, and explore causes and effects (see pages 19–20).
Evaluating is judging the value of something.	**You'll learn** different ways to rate something, including how to use a rubric (see page 21).
Creating is putting ideas together to make something new.	**You'll review** the basic three-part structure and basic patterns to create projects (see pages 22–24).

Remembering

Remembering is identifying the facts about a topic. You can do this by answering basic questions or by forming a topic web.

Answering Basic Questions

To remember information about people, places, and things, answer basic questions about them. Here are questions about a person and event:

Name? Queen Elizabeth

Nationality? British

Occasion? Celebrated her Diamond Jubilee

Importance? Marking her 60th year as queen

Setting? London, England; June 2–5, 2012

Activities? Concert at Buckingham Palace, boat pageant on the Thames River, and Jubilee lunches

Andy Lidstone / Shutterstock.com

Topic Web

You can also record basic facts and details in a topic web. Include as many branches, or arms, as needed. Here's an example of a web that records facts about hermit crabs.

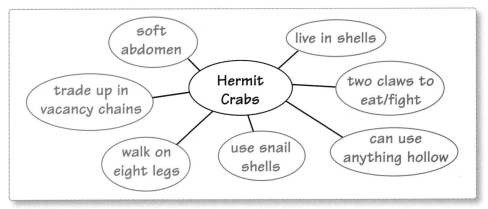

Your Turn Think about a topic you are studying. Create a topic web to explore what you know about the topic.

Understanding

Understanding is figuring something out or being able to explain what something means. You can do this by summarizing or visualizing what you have learned.

Summarizing

To summarize, share the main point and important details about a topic you have learned about. (See pages 288–289 for more information.) The summary below shares the main point about a shell game that hermit crabs "play."

Hermit Crabs Changing Shells

Vacancy chains occur when hermit crabs decide to change shells. (Vacancy means "unfilled" or "unoccupied.") A chain begins when one crab leaves a shell for a bigger one. Another crab may come along and claim the abandoned shell, leaving its shell for some other crab, and so on. Sometimes, the crabs line up in size order near an empty shell. Then, when one crab changes its shell, a chain of swapping begins. This shows that hermit crabs can cooperate for the benefit of all.

Visualizing

You can show that you understand a topic by drawing, graphing, filming, or photographing it. This photo shows a hermit crab with its claws and legs deployed, ready to move.

Your Turn Think about a math, science, or social studies topic you are studying. Create a visual that shows your understanding of the topic. (Review your class notes or textbook for topic ideas.)

Applying

Applying is using what you have learned. It shows deep understanding of information. You can apply by demonstrating your knowledge or by connecting new information to your own life.

Demonstrating

Demonstrate means "to show clearly." When you demonstrate information, you put knowledge into practice. In this math problem example, a student shows the steps in the solution.

Calculating Growth

Problem: Imagine that you are 5 feet 2 inches tall and your uncle is 6 feet tall. Last year, you grew 2 inches. If you continue to grow at the same rate, how many years will it take you to be as tall as your uncle?

Step 1: Write out the measurements in inches:
5 feet 2 inches = 62 inches; 6 feet tall = 72 inches

Step 2: Subtract your height from your uncle's height:
72 inches − 62 inches = 10 inches.

Step 3: Divide the result by the inches you grow per year:
10 inches/2 inches per year = 5 years.

Connecting

When you connect new information to your own experiences, it means more to you. This learning log entry reveals how a student made sense of information by connecting it to her own life.

December 5

I loved learning how hermit crabs hunt for a house. As a crab grows, it moves into a bigger shell. Once the empty shell goes on the market, other crabs look it over to see if it's the right size for them. My family can relate to that. When my mom had twins, our old house became way too small for all of us, so we had to move to a bigger one. But our old house was just the right size for the people who bought it.

Analyzing

Analyzing is carefully studying information—breaking it down, putting the facts and details in order, and comparing them. Graphic organizers can help you analyze.

Using a Time Line

A time line arranges details about historical events, scientific processes, and so on in time order. To create a time line, follow these steps:

1. Gather all the important information.
2. Arrange the main details in time order.
3. List dates on one side and details on the other.

American Revolution
Battles of 1775

April 19 — Lexington/Concord
May 10 — Ticonderoga
May 27 — Chelsea Creek
June 16 — Bunker Hill

Dec. 31 — Quebec

Using a Venn Diagram

A Venn diagram displays the similarities and differences between two topics. To use a Venn diagram, follow these guidelines:

1. Gather the important details about each topic.
2. Draw two overlapping circles.
3. Label each outer part with one of the topics.
4. List the similarities in the overlapping space.
5. List the differences in the outer parts.

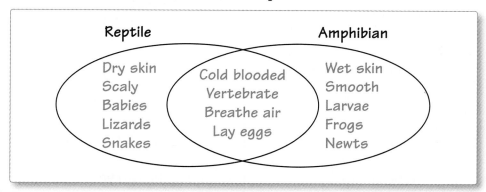

Reptile   Amphibian

Dry skin   Cold blooded   Wet skin
Scaly   Vertebrate   Smooth
Babies   Breathe air   Larvae
Lizards   Lay eggs   Frogs
Snakes   Newts

Using a Line Diagram

A line diagram breaks something down into parts or categories. To use a line diagram, follow these guidelines:

1. Gather information about a topic.
2. Write the topic at the top.
3. List categories below.
4. Add subcategories.
5. Connect the parts with lines.

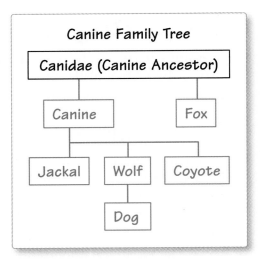

Canine Family Tree

Canidae (Canine Ancestor)
— Canine — Fox
— Jackal — Wolf — Coyote
— Dog

Using a Problem-Solution Chart

A problem-solution chart records the causes and possible solutions to a problem. To use this type of chart, follow these guidelines:

1. Gather details about the problem and study them.
2. Write the problem at the top.
3. List the causes next.
4. Then list possible solutions.

Problem: Some sports can cause concussions.

Causes	Solutions
– Contact sports	– Ban certain sports
– Starting kids too early	– Limit early involvement
– Need for education about head injuries	– Change the sports so they are less violent
– Need for better equipment	– Provide better equipment
– Need for injury-response instruction and training	– Provide injury-response training

Your Turn Think of a topic you are currently studying. Use one of the types of graphic organizers on pages 19–20 to analyze the topic. Share one or more surprising facts with your class.

Evaluating

Evaluating is judging the value or worth of something. Critical thinkers often use a rubric or rating scale to make an evaluation. This rubric uses the goal and objectives for a digital story project.

Name: _Akyra Jones_   Project: _Bicycling in Our Community_

Goal:	Evaluation	Rating			Score
Our team will make a digital story showing bicycling in our community.	The digital story looks great.	**Beat** 60	**Met** (40)	**Didn't** 20	40
Objectives:					
1. All group members will share in the work.	Anna and Shanika did the most work.	**Beat** 10	**Met** 6	**Didn't** (2)	2
2. We'll gather interviews and photos for a digital story.	We used photos, interviews, and music!	**Beat** (10)	**Met** 6	**Didn't** 2	10
3. We'll work in the class, in the city, and at City Hall.	We didn't get a chance to go to City Hall.	**Beat** 10	**Met** 6	**Didn't** (2)	2
4. We'll complete the digital story over the next two weeks.	Our project was done right on time.	**Beat** 10	**Met** (6)	**Didn't** 2	6
5. Our digital story will show how bicycling makes our town a better place.	The story did this.	**Beat** 10	**Met** (6)	**Didn't** 2	6
6. We'll use PowerPoint to put our digital stories together.	We used an even better program so we could add better music.	**Beat** (10)	**Met** 6	**Didn't** 2	10
				Total:	78

Creating

Creating is bringing your thoughts together into an original project you can share. Strong projects are usually built with a three-part structure.

Understanding the Big Picture

Many of your projects—from podcasts to play scripts to posters—will tell a story that has a beginning, a middle, and an ending. The following graphic highlights the main features of each part.

Beginning: Beginnings often do these things:
- Greet the audience (listener, viewer, or reader).
- Provide interesting background information.
- Introduce the topic.

Middle: Middle parts often do these things:
- Support the topic with specific details.
- Present details in a logical order. (See page 23.)
- Lead the audience through an important process.
- Connect the audience to ideas.

Ending: Endings often do these things:
- Summarize the project's ideas.
- Revisit the topic or main point.
- Provide a memorable final thought.
- Encourage the audience to take action.

Your Turn Find an interesting Web page, poster, article, or advertisement. Working with a partner, figure out what is happening in the beginning, middle, and ending parts.

A Closer Look at Structure

Projects that tell a story or explain something usually share most of the facts and details in the middle part. Use one or more of the patterns below to organize information and make it easy to follow.

Organizing Ideas

Organization Pattern	Words Related to the Pattern
Time Order: Arranging details in the order that they happen (*chronological order*)	after, before, during, finally, first, later, next, second, soon, then
Place Order: Placing details by location—from top to bottom, close up to faraway, left to right, and so on (*spatial order*)	above, around, behind, beneath, by, inside, near, off, under, onto, within
Categories: Arranging details by groups, types, or parts (*classification*)	one kind, one type, the first part, another kind, a second type, the next part
Problem-Solution: Explaining a problem first; then exploring possible solutions	at risk, unfortunately, as a result, the reason, one solution, a better solution, please support
Logical Order: Arranging details so that they build on or connect to one another in an understandable way	also, and, another, for this reason, in addition, likewise, next, therefore
Comparison-Contrast **Similarities-Differences:** Sharing all similarities and then all differences **Subject-by-Subject:** Discussing one subject and then the other subject **Point-by-Point:** Looking at one point for both subjects before going to the next point	**Comparing:** along with, also, both, likewise, just as, in the same way, like **Contrasting:** but, by contrast, or, even though, on the other hand, still, yet

Your Turn Name the pattern of organization used for three writing projects in this book. (See pages 283–306.)

Other Project Structures

Sometimes projects involve building various things, each with its own structure. Here are four different structures with four different jobs.

Saxophone

- Reed
- Mouthpiece
- Neck
- Thumb hook
- Body
- Keys
- Bell
- Bow

Scooter

- Hand grips
- Steering column
- Deck
- Rear fender brake
- Wheels

Rain Barrel

- Downspout
- Filter
- Overflow
- Barrel
- Slab
- Spigot

Suspension Bridge

- Tower
- Suspension cable
- Main cable
- Deck
- Anchor
- Pier

Your Turn Draw a picture or find a photo of a common object (such as a toothbrush or an umbrella). Then label its main parts. Afterward, share your work with your classmates.

Critical-Thinking Activities

The activities that follow will help you to practice critical thinking.

Learning the Basics

Asking questions helps you to identify and remember the basic facts about a topic. Here are key questions about a famous monument, the Statue of Liberty.

Name?	Statue of Liberty
Location?	Upper New York Bay on Liberty Island
Importance?	The statue stands for freedom, awareness, and democracy in the United States and around the world. It also shows the friendship between the U.S. and France.
Description?	The 152-foot statue sits on a 150-foot pedestal. It is made of copper on the outside and wrought iron on the inside. The statue is modeled after the Roman goddess of liberty.

 Your Turn Identify the key facts and details about an event or a place by answering basic questions about it. Afterward, share your work with your classmates.

Writing One Sentence

One of the best ways to check your understanding of new information is to summarize it. State the main point in a single sentence. To do so, you must think critically about the subject and what it means to you.

Our best advice: After your teacher introduces a new topic, summarize the main point in a single sentence.

Your Turn For two or three days, practice summarizing in at least two of your subjects. In each case, write your single sentence at a natural stopping point—after your teacher finishes talking about a topic or at a break in your research.

Organizing Your Thinking

Graphic organizers help you analyze information. The following problem-solution chart analyzes a community issue.

Problem: The community art contest may be canceled.

Causes	Solutions
— The coordinator is a volunteer.	— Form a community art committee.
— City hall has budget limits.	— Raise money for the contest.
— Judges are hard to find.	— Advertise for judges.
— Some art teachers don't promote the contest.	— Promote the contest in the schools.

Our best advice: Use graphic organizers to think critically about important information. Arranging information with an organizer naturally helps you understand and remember it.

 Your Turn Team up with a classmate to identify a problem in your school or community. Then analyze the problem by filling in a problem-solution chart. (Put a star next to your best solution.) Afterward, share your work with your classmates.

Celebrating Critical Thinkers

Great thinkers often make important remarks, like the following quotation from Benjamin Franklin: "An investment in knowledge always pays the best interest." What do you think he meant? Here is one idea: The time you spend learning today will help you think more clearly tomorrow. If you Google "quotations about critical thinking" or "thinking quotations," you will find many quotations like this one.

Our best advice: It is interesting and helpful to read famous quotations about thinking. Read and reflect on them from time to time.

Your Turn Working alone or with a partner, find a quotation about thinking. Make a poster that includes the quotation and display it in your classroom.

Wow! How'd you come up with that idea?

Chapter 3
Creative Thinking

Creative thinking is original thinking. When you look at information in new ways, experiment with materials, and develop unique solutions or projects, you are thinking creatively. This chapter offers strategies for unlocking your creativity in all of your subjects and projects.

You will learn . . .

- Becoming a Creative Thinker
- Remembering
- Understanding
- Applying
- Analyzing
- Evaluating
- Creating

Becoming a Creative Thinker

Creative thinking can open your mind to new and varied ideas. For example, you may see an old lawn mower and wonder, "What stories could this contraption tell?" Or you may spread peanut butter on bread and wonder, "How would this stuff taste on a hamburger?" Creative thinking is mind expanding.

A Guide to Creative Thinking

Here are some basic guidelines for becoming a creative thinker.

Question.	Ask *why* and *why not* about things around you. Ask creative questions (see page 235).
Wonder.	Watch for possibilities and opportunities. Experiment, take risks, and try something new.
Wander.	Make unusual connections and find solutions that others haven't considered.
Play.	Treat a topic like a game that you want to win. Gather a team around you to help you win.
Create.	Produce many ideas. Try many possibilities. Work fast and make more than you need.
Reimagine.	Brainstorm ways to make your creations even better.
Exceed.	Go beyond "good." Make your work fantastic, magnificent, world-shaking, unbelievable, awesome.

Your Turn Discuss these questions in class:
- Why are artists and musicians considered creative?
- What other activities require creativity?
- What did Albert Einstein mean when he said, "Imagination is more important than knowledge"?
- How can creative thinking work with critical thinking?

Creative-Thinking Strategies

In the last chapter, you learned about Benjamin Bloom's levels of thinking. (See page 15.) In the next pages, you'll learn creative-thinking strategies for each level of thought.

Bloom's Thinking Skills

Remembering
is recalling basic information.

You'll learn
how to recall details by using thought traps and sensory charts (see page 30).

Understanding
is knowing what something means.

You'll learn
to develop ideas with creative comparisons and before-and-after writing (see page 31).

Applying
is using information.

You'll learn
how to use ideas by writing riddles and poems (see page 32).

Analyzing
is looking at the parts of something.

You'll learn
to use paper-ball analysis and "what if" questions (see pages 33–34).

Evaluating
is judging the value of something.

You'll learn
how to create a pro-con chart and think metaphorically (see pages 35–36).

Creating
is putting ideas together to make something new.

You'll learn
about the many different ways that you can create projects (see pages 37–38).

In Focus For any project, you will use many different types of creative and critical thinking.

Remembering

Remembering is the process of identifying and recalling information. The creative-thinking strategies below can strengthen your memory.

Thought Trapping

Start a "thought trap" by writing the main point about a topic. Then list key details and "trap" the details by repeating the main point.

Amelia Earhart

a brave pioneer female pilot
- first flying lesson in 1921
- set women's records for flying at high altitudes
- in 1928 flew across Atlantic with a pilot and copilot
- then first woman to solo this flight
- showed a woman could do it just as well as a man
- in 1937 took final challenge to fly around the world
- lost radio contact over the Pacific
a brave pioneer female pilot

Sensing a Subject

You can fill in a sensory chart to help you remember details about an event or experience. This chart lists details about a farmers' market.

Farmers' Market

sights	piles of peppers, potatoes, onions, tomatoes; shuffling shoppers; farmers bagging produce
sounds	performer sings "This Land Is Your Land"; farmer says, "This corn was just picked this morning"; a shopper asks how to store tomatoes
smells	freshly popped kettle corn, ripe melons, sun block
textures	smooth eggplant, bumpy squash, crusty bread
tastes	rich, tangy tomatoes; sugary honeydew melon

 Your Turn Create a thought trap and sensory chart for a current topic.

Understanding

Thinking creatively about topics can help you understand them better. Here are two creative strategies for you to try.

Making Creative Comparisons

To deepen your understanding, compare a topic to something completely different, as in the following examples.

Comparison 1:	**Comparison 2:**
If Amelia Earhart were an animal, she would be an eagle because she was happiest when she was flying and in control of everything.	If Amelia Earhart were a color, she would be red because it represents strength and danger, and Earhart showed a lot of courage.

Before-and-After Writing

Before studying a topic, write what you already know about it. After studying, write what you learned. Compare the two writings.

Before:	**After:**
A couple of times I flew kites with my dad on windy spring days. We flew the diamond-shaped ones with cloth tails. The tail stopped the kite from spinning out of control. One time, we got the kite to stay way up in the air for a long time. Other times, it kept dropping and even crashed. . . .	Kites originated in China and have been around for thousands of years. They have been used for fun, for festivals, for science experiments, and for military reasons. Ben Franklin used a kite for his electricity experiment, and the Wright brothers used kites to study flight. . . .

Your Turn

Use this sentence starter to write a creative comparison.

If _____ were a (color, animal, or food), it would be _____ because _____.

Applying

Thinking creatively can help you use information in new and interesting ways. This page talks about two creative applications.

Thinking Poetically

One creative way to apply information is to write a poem about it.

■ Terse Verse

A terse-verse poem uses the fewest words possible to explain something. This kind of poetry usually rhymes, and the title is important:

Raisin	Coleslaw	Pedicure
Out of shape	Ravaged	Nail gloss
Grape	Cabbage	And toe floss

■ Concrete Poetry

A concrete poem uses a shape to express its meaning:

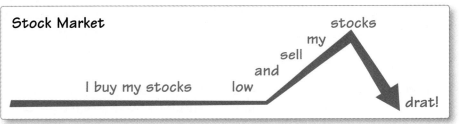

Writing a Riddle

Writing a riddle helps you apply information creatively. A riddle, like a puzzle, shares a question or statement that the reader must figure out.

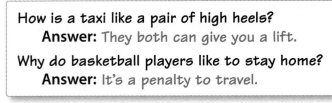

How is a taxi like a pair of high heels?
   Answer: They both can give you a lift.

Why do basketball players like to stay home?
   Answer: It's a penalty to travel.

Your Turn Write a poem about a topic you are currently studying. Afterward, share your work in class.

Analyzing

Analyzing a topic may sound like a controlled, uncreative activity. But creative thinking is very useful in an analysis. Here are two ways to analyze creatively.

Paper-Ball Analysis

Roll a piece of paper into a loose ball. Write the numbers **1**, **2**, **3**, **4**, and **5** (which correspond to the directions below) on five fairly flat surfaces of the paper ball. Toss the ball in the air, catch it, and briefly write or discuss your topic based on the number you see first. Repeat this process two or three times.

1. **Compare it.** What is the topic similar to?
2. **Contrast it.** What is it different from?
3. **Break it down.** What are its main parts?
4. **Connect it.** What other things can you link to the topic?
5. **Rank it.** How would you rate its importance or value?

Example paper-ball analysis of a kite:

(3) Break it down. What are its main parts?

A diamond kite is made of two thin wood poles with notches at the ends. The poles form a frame in the shape of a small "t," and the frame is covered by colorful plastic or paper. At each of the four points of the "t," a string fitting into the notch attaches the cover to the frame. When everything is connected, the cover stretches over the frame. A tail made of steamers, ribbon, crepe paper, or bits of cloth is usually attached to the bottom point. A towline is connected to another string stretched between the top and the bottom of the kite.

Your Turn Try paper-ball analysis the next time you need to analyze a topic you are studying in class or researching for a project.

Asking "What If" Questions

Asking and answering "what if" questions creatively will give you new insights about topics. Here's an example:

What if all timing devices stopped working?

- Officials wouldn't know when a football or basketball game was finished.
- Your principal wouldn't know when to start and stop the school day.
- Your mother wouldn't be able to schedule doctor and dentist appointments.
- Your family wouldn't know when to ring in the new year.
- Your parents couldn't complain that you were late for supper.
- You couldn't follow the baking directions on a frozen-pizza wrapper.
- Everyone would have an excuse for not paying taxes on time.
- You may lose track of what day it is.
- Daylight savings time would become obsolete.
- You would have to use the sun and the moon to tell time.
- Sundials would sell out fast!

Your Turn On your own or with a partner, answer either of the following "what if" questions in many different ways. Afterward, share your work with your classmates.

- What if the world suddenly ran out of oil?
- What if robots started thinking for themselves?

Special Challenge: Create one or two of your own "what if" questions about a topic you are studying.

Evaluating

There are many different ways to rate the value of something. For example, judges of a diving competition evaluate a diver's performance and then give that diver a score. These two pages share creative strategies that you can use for evaluating.

Creating a Pro-Con Chart

You can evaluate something by using a pro-con chart. This type of chart lists the positives (pros) and the negatives (cons) about a topic or idea. Follow these steps:

1. **Learn as much as you can** about the topic or idea.
2. **Label the chart.**
3. **List the pros** on one side.
4. **List the cons** on the other side.

Pro-Con Chart:

Using City Buses	
Pros	Cons
– cheaper than buying a car	– not always on time
– conserves gasoline	– can take a long time
– friendly to the environment	– stops may be spread out
– reduces traffic	– some passengers may be
– can read or text while riding	rude
– adds some exercise to	– must follow the bus schedule
your day	– some bus stops are not nice
– see the city	– worry about missing the bus

Your Turn On your own or with a partner, create a pro-con chart to evaluate another community-related topic. Afterward, share your work in class.

Using Metaphors

A reviewer might say that a book "crackles with electricity," or that the characters "leap off the page to shake your hand." Of course, these things don't actually happen. The reviewer is using metaphors to evaluate the writing. You also can use metaphorical thinking to evaluate books, movies, video games, and many other things:

Metaphorical Thinking

Metaphor	Definition	Example
Simile	comparing using *like* or *as*	Each sentence unfolds like a flower greeting the sun.
Metaphor	comparing without *like* or *as*	This novel is a cold drink on a hot day.
Personification	giving human traits to nonhuman things	The band's new album yearns for distant horizons.
Exaggeration	describing a minor thing in a major way	The lead singer's voice can strip paint.
Understatement	describing a major thing in a minor way	At the top of the roller coaster, I voiced my misgivings.
Irony	showing how something has the opposite result that it should	I fertilized the life out of my garden.
Sarcasm	saying the opposite of what you mean	The soup's scalding temperature soothed my tongue.
Word play	using language in a special, often humorous way	The rousing chorus at the end of the play woke me up.

Creating

With creative thinking, you can develop projects that are new and original. We create in many different ways, as shown in the following mind map.

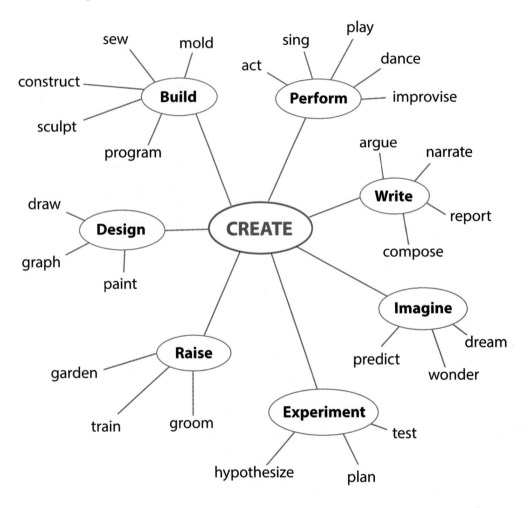

 Your Turn Review the mind map above. Try to think of two other ways that we create things. Select two ways you tried in the past. Select two ways you would like to try in the future.

Previewing Projects

Inquire offers many project ideas. Here are a few that are included in this text. (See pages 281–370.)

Lab Reports ────────

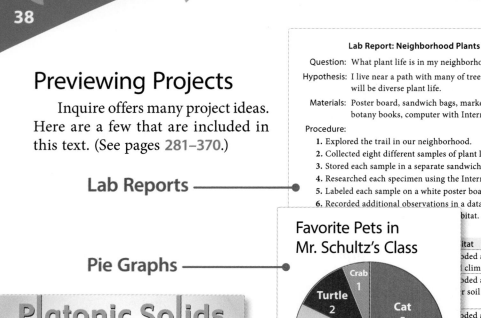

Lab Report: Neighborhood Plants

Question: What plant life is in my neighborhood?

Hypothesis: I live near a path with many of trees, so there will be diverse plant life.

Materials: Poster board, sandwich bags, marker, ruler, botany books, computer with Internet

Procedure:

1. Explored the trail in our neighborhood.
2. Collected eight different samples of plant life.
3. Stored each sample in a separate sandwich bag.
4. Researched each specimen using the Internet.
5. Labeled each sample on a white poster board.
6. Recorded additional observations in a data table

Pie Graphs ────────

Favorite Pets in Mr. Schultz's Class

Crab 1
Turtle 2
Parakeet 2
Hamster 3
Cat 5
Dog 4

Total Pets: 17

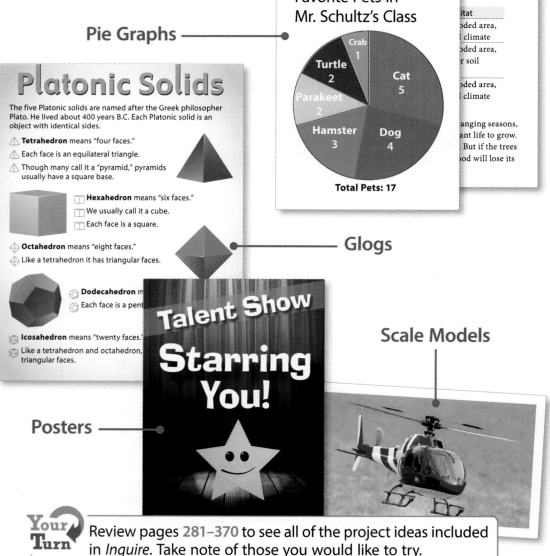

Platonic Solids

The five Platonic solids are named after the Greek philosopher Plato. He lived about 400 years B.C. Each Platonic solid is an object with identical sides.

⚠ **Tetrahedron** means "four faces."
⚠ Each face is an equilateral triangle.
⚠ Though many call it a "pyramid," pyramids usually have a square base.

▱ **Hexahedron** means "six faces."
▱ We usually call it a cube.
▱ Each face is a square.

◇ **Octahedron** means "eight faces."
◇ Like a tetrahedron it has triangular faces.

⬡ **Dodecahedron** m
⬡ Each face is a pent

⬡ **Icosahedron** means "twenty faces."
⬡ Like a tetrahedron and octahedron, triangular faces.

Glogs ────────

Scale Models ────────

Talent Show
Starring You!

Posters ────────

Your Turn Review pages **281–370** to see all of the project ideas included in *Inquire*. Take note of those you would like to try.

Creative-Thinking Activities

The activities listed below will give you practice in creative thinking.

Presenting Me!

Creative thinking doesn't involve right or wrong answers. It doesn't involve being overly precise either. Instead, creative thinking pushes the boundaries and may even be a little wild and goofy.

Our best advice: Think of ways to be creative when you have free time in school or at home. For example, write diary entries as if you were the pencil or the computer keyboard, or draw pictures as if you were an owl or an orca whale.

 Your Turn Introduce yourself in a creative way by answering the following questions:

1. Write your name backward (and pronounce it).
2. Give your address 20 years from now.
3. Name the most important thing that will ever happen to you.
4. Identify three things that you never want to do.
5. Name the famous person that you are most like and tell why you are alike.

Having Fun

Thinking and learning can definitely be fun. Letting loose and taking risks can unlock your best ideas.

Our best advice: Invent and play new games, role-play different characters during discussions, compose music, create play scripts, and act them out. Activities like these will make you think in new and original ways.

Your Turn On your own or with a partner, try one of the creative activities identified above. Create a brief play script about a topic you are studying, invent a new game, or write a song.

Mind Map

Mind mapping can unlock many creative ideas. To get started, write a topic in the middle of your paper. Then make a cluster of related ideas around it. As you write each new word, circle it and connect it to the closest related word. Keep writing until you've filled a good portion of your paper. (See page **37** for an example mind map.)

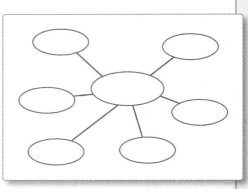

Our best advice: Use clustering for different purposes—to search for a project idea, to gather ideas about a topic, to review information for a test, or to think of things to do with a friend.

Your Turn Create a mind map starting with one of these topics: books, bats, bandages, or blueberries. Write related words quickly to unlock your ideas.

Special Challenge: Put a star next to the idea in your cluster that especially interests you. Then use this idea as a starting point for a story or discussion with a classmate.

Saying It in Pictures

Artists may be some of the most creative people around. Activities like doodling, sketching, taking pictures, or painting can put you in a creative frame of mind and help you think in new ways about a topic.

Our best advice: As you work on a new unit or project, sketch or doodle to explore your thoughts about the topic. Also consider making art a part of your finished projects.

Your Turn Sketch at least three of the ideas that you clustered in the "Your Turn" activity above. Don't think too carefully about your drawings. Instead, sketch loosely and see where the drawing takes you.

Chapter 4
Problem Solving

Life has its problems—everything from getting stains out of your favorite T-shirt to raising your grades to designing a poster for a class project. To solve a problem, you need to understand it. Start by answering the 5 W's about it. Then follow the process laid out in this chapter to find the best solution.

You will learn . . .
- Solving Problems
- Problem Solving in Action
- Using the Scientific Method
- Problem Solving in Math

Solving Problems

When you solve a problem, you work back and forth between critical and creative thinking, following a process like the one below:

Problem-Solving Process

Critical Thinking	Creative Thinking

Question the problem.
- Answer basic questions about the problem.
  - Explore causes and effects.

Plan a solution.
- Brainstorm solutions and pick one.
- Set a goal and plan the tasks and time.

Gather information.
- Look for resources and conduct research.
  - Arrange teams and collect tools.

Create the solution.
- Put your solution together in a first form.
  - Try it out and see if it works.

Evaluate the solution.
- Check the solution against your plan.
- Decide how you can improve your solution.

Present the solution.
- Put your solution to work, solving the problem.

 Your Turn Suppose that a friend's mom has taken you and your friend to a huge water park. Somehow, you got lost; neither your friend nor the mom are anywhere in sight, and walking around looking for them is not working. Without a cell phone, how will you find your friend and his or her mom? Come up with solutions and discuss them with your classmates.

Problem Solving in Action

The following pages explain the problem-solving process in action.

Questioning the Problem

Answering the 5 W's is one way to review a problem. (Add *how?* if it fits the situation.)

The Problem

Who?	many students
What?	don't know how to apologize
Where?	at Steel School
When?	after saying something hurtful
Why?	They forget about the feelings of others.

 Working alone or with a partner, identify a problem related to something you would like to do, such as staying with your grandmother for the summer or buying a new bike.

Exploring Causes and Effects

Completing a cause-effect chart can help you analyze the problem.

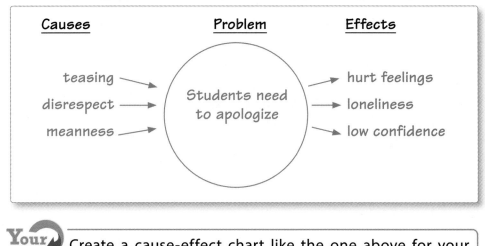

Causes	Problem	Effects
teasing	Students need to apologize	hurt feelings
disrespect		loneliness
meanness		low confidence

 Create a cause-effect chart like the one above for your problem.

Planning a Solution

Brainstorming is a good way to think of many possible solutions. The list below was created by a team of students. They put a star (*) next to the most promising solutions and then evaluated them.

Problem: <u>Many students don't know when or how to apologize.</u>

Possible solutions:
- Think before you speak.
- Think of others.
- Have "mean police."
- Tag hurtful comments.*
- Get a counselor.*
- Teach how to apologize.*
- Show self-control.
- Remember differences.

Your Turn Brainstorm a list of possible solutions for your problem. Keep listing ideas for as long as you can, and mark the most promising ideas.

Picking an Idea

In order to choose the best solution, you must consider your options. Here's how the team rated their top three solutions, chose the best one, and even decided how to improve it.

Solutions	Evaluation	Improvements
Tag hurtful comments.	That's a start, but it doesn't tell students how to apologize.	
Get a counselor.	Students need to know how to solve conflicts on their own.	
Teach how to apologize.	This is the best solution, but it needs one change.	Let's also teach when to apologize.

Your Turn Create a chart like the one above to evaluate your two or three most promising ideas. Then choose the best solution and make any necessary improvements.

Setting a Goal

Planning includes stating the goal (what will be done to solve the problem) and figuring out how to achieve it. Here is an example plan.

Goal: _Teach students when and how to apologize._

Tasks:

1. **Teach when to apologize.**

   Students need to recognize how and why certain comments and actions are hurtful, disrespectful, or mean.

2. **Teach how to apologize.**

   After a time-out period, the person who apologizes should
   - address the other person by name,
   - make eye contact,
   - explain why he or she is apologizing,
   - sincerely express regret, and
   - discussion the problem if necessary.

3. **Teach how to accept an apology.**

   The person who receives the apology should
   - make eye contact,
   - listen carefully,
   - discuss the problem if necessary, and
   - accept the apology if possible.

4. **Evaluate apologies.**

   Students should create a rubric for evaluating and improving apologies.

Your Turn

Referring to the best solution you devised in the previous "Your Turn" activity, write a goal and the steps you will take to achieve it. Use the example above as a basic guide.

Creating the Solution

Once you have planned your solution, you should create it. The students working on apologies created a group of scenarios to help students practice giving and receiving apologies.

Apology Scenarios

- **Scenario 1:** Ross laughed at a new student because he didn't know how to throw or catch a football. As it turns out, the new student came from another country and had never played football before.

- **Scenario 2:** Jill told a classmate to mind her own business when she tried to talk with Jill's friends at the lunch table.

- **Scenario 3:** Donald talked out of turn three or four times on the day that the class had a substitute teacher. He didn't follow the substitute's directions, either. The sub noted Donald's behavior in her report.

- **Scenario 4:** In the band room, Larissa told Chelsea she shouldn't be playing first clarinet because Chelsea wasn't very good. Another band member told the director about Larissa's comment.

- **Scenario 5:** Matt tripped Joe in the hall, which made Joe drop his books and skin his knee. A hall monitor reported this to a teacher.

- **Scenario 6:** Anna, Yvonne, and Thomas worked hard on a science project, while Chuck contributed very little. The three felt it was unfair that Chuck earned the same grade that they did, and they told him so.

 Your Turn

If your class needs to work on apologizing, ask for permission to practice in small groups, using these scenarios.

Decide on the best way to test the effectiveness of your solution. If it is possible, practice your solution with scenarios like those above.

Evaluating the Solution

This rubric can be used to rate both practice and actual apologies. The rubric lists an overall goal and specific objectives. The person who fills out the rubric evaluates and rates the goal and objectives.

Project Rubric

Name: _Devon_   Project: _When and how to apologize_

Goal:	Evaluation	Rating			Score
Make an effective apology.	The apology was effective.	**Beat** 60	**Met** (40)	**Didn't** 20	40
Objectives:					
1. Take a time out.	The person should have waited a little longer.	**Beat** 10	**Met** 6	**Didn't** (4)	4
2. Make eye contact.	The eye contact was good.	**Beat** 10	**Met** (6)	**Didn't** 4	6
3. Refer to the receiver by name.	The person referred to the receiver.	**Beat** 10	**Met** (6)	**Didn't** 4	6
4. Explain the reason for the apology.	The explanation was very clear and helpful.	**Beat** (10)	**Met** 6	**Didn't** 4	10
5. Sincerely express regret.	The apology was sincere.	**Beat** 10	**Met** (6)	**Didn't** 4	6
6. Discuss the problem, if necessary.	Both sides discussed the issue and forgave.	**Beat** 10	**Met** (6)	**Didn't** 4	6
				Total:	78

 Your Turn Create a rubric to evaluate your solution. (Download a template at **thoughtfullearning.com/e47**.)

Improving and Presenting the Solution

After evaluating the solution, you can think of ways to make it more effective. For example, students delivering apologies may need to sound more sincere or make better eye contact. Here is an effective apology using the planned solution:

An Apology in Action

Scenario:
During recess, Josh was getting too physical while playing soccer. Mrs. Ketter, a teacher's aide, told him to settle down. Josh yelled, "What do you know!" Later in the day, Mrs. Ketter asked the principal to talk to Josh about his behavior, and the principal told Josh to apologize to the aide.

Josh (making eye contact): Mrs. Ketter, I need to talk to you about what happened on the playground yesterday.

Mrs. Ketter: I've noticed that you always play by the rules, Josh, so what you did yesterday surprised me.

Josh: Well, the other team was bragging how good they were, so I really wanted to score a goal before the bell rang. That's why I started pushing guys out of my way. I really lost it. I'm sorry for how I acted and for talking back to you.

Mrs. Ketter: I accept your apology. Do you think you'll be able to play soccer without having more trouble?

Josh: It'll be hard if the other team starts bragging again.

Mrs. Ketter: If they do, how will you handle it?

Josh: I'll ignore them and keep my cool.

Your Turn Based on your rubric (page 47), make changes to improve your solution.

Using the Scientific Method

The scientific method is a unique version of problem solving. You will use the scientific method to design an experiment or complete a project in science class. Here are the basic steps:

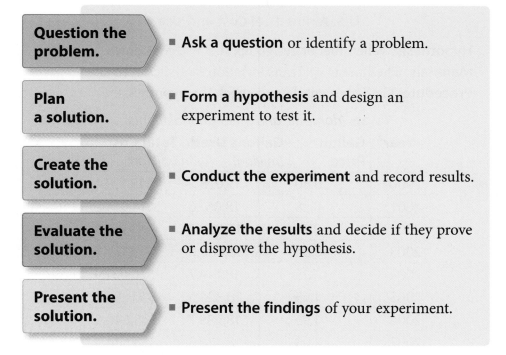

Question the problem.

- **Ask a question** or identify a problem.

Plan a solution.

- **Form a hypothesis** and design an experiment to test it.

Create the solution.

- **Conduct the experiment** and record results.

Evaluate the solution.

- **Analyze the results** and decide if they prove or disprove the hypothesis.

Present the solution.

- **Present the findings** of your experiment.

Forming a Hypothesis

A **hypothesis** is a general explanation of a science question or problem. The statement *Many ferns seem to grow well in shaded areas* is an example hypothesis. Here is the same hypothesis stated more formally:

> If ferns grow well in shaded areas, then providing shade will improve the health of this fern.

An "If . . . then . . ." statement like this can serve as a starting point for an experiment to test the hypothesis.

 Your Turn Think of a science-related problem and form a hypothesis using an if-then statement. Think how you could test it.

Thinking Deductively

To think deductively, you begin with a general idea (hypothesis) and gather specific evidence to prove or disprove it. The lab report below uses deduction to analyze fuel use by U.S. airlines.

U.S. Airline Fuel Cost and Use

Hypothesis: When fuel prices go up, fuel use goes down.
Materials: The Bureau of Transportation Statistics Web site
Procedure: Gather recent data to check the hypothesis.

Totals *(domestic and international flights)*

Year	Gallon Price	Gallons Used (million)	Total Cost (million)
2000	0.80	19,026.2	$15,199.4
2001	0.78	18,067.6	$14,014.2
2002	0.71	16,858.7	$11,937.7
2003	0.84	16,868.0	$14,153.7
2004	1.15	18,144.7	$20,831.9
2005	1.65	18,324.5	$30,283.7
2006	1.95	18,239.7	$35,640.6
2007	2.09	18,426.8	$38,584.9
2008	3.06	17,978.4	$54,968.4
2009	1.89	16,234.0	$30,682.9
2010	2.23	16,302.6	$36,418.4
2011	2.86	16,385.7	$46,881.4

Conclusion: From 2003 to 2007, fuel prices went up each year, but so did fuel use. In 2008, fuel prices rose nearly one dollar per gallon, and fuel use did drop a little. In 2009, fuel prices dropped more than a dollar per gallon, but fuel use dropped as well. Higher fuel prices don't mean lower fuel use.

Your Turn How could you test the hypothesis you created on page 49?

Thinking Inductively

To think inductively, you begin with specific details and work toward a general theory. The following lab report uses inductive thinking to create a general theory about airline fuel use.

Airline Fuel Use
(Bureau of Transportation Statistics)

Monthly Fuel Use by U.S. Airlines *(million gallons)*

	2009	2010	2011
January	1,338.9	1,282.7	1,314.4
February	1,291.2	1,148.4	1,193.5
March	1,382.8	1,351.9	1,415.0
April	1,353.0	1,311.3	1,374.5
May	1,377.4	1,393.6	1,401.8
June	1,443.1	1,427.7	1,452.2
July	1,521.0	1,506.7	1,510.7
August	1,428.1	1,478.6	1,464.7
September	1,281.1	1,354.6	1,323.2
October	1,324.8	1,370.7	1,338.8
November	1,229.9	1,303.6	1,269.7
December	1,334.8	1,372.6	1,326.2

Observations: Each year, fuel use was highest in the summer. For example, in 2011, 3,922.9 million gallons were used during the winter (January–March), 4,228.5 million gallons during the spring (April–June), 4,298.6 million gallons during the summer (July–September), and 3,934.7 million gallons during the fall (October–December). Each year, July had the most fuel used.

Theory: Fuel use is highest in summer due to vacation travel.

Your Turn When is the least fuel used? What theory could explain that difference? Share that theory and any others with your class.

Problem Solving in Math

Math also uses the problem-solving process. Here is an example math problem and how the problem-solving process leads to a solution.

Write the following numbers in scientific notation.

1. 650,000   **2.** 7,480,000   **3.** 86,700,000

Question the problem.

What exactly is scientific notation? It is using the power of 10 to express a number. 210,000 in scientific notation is 2.1×10^5

Plan a solution.

To use scientific notation, take a large number and move the decimal to the left until only one number appears above it. Then multiply that number by 10 to the power of the times you moved the decimal.

Create the solution.

650,000 becomes 6.5×10^5
7,480,000 becomes 7.48×10^6
86,700,000 becomes 8.67×10^7

Evaluate the solution.

Check your answers with multiplication:
6.5×10^5 (or 100,000)
$6.5 \times 100,000 = 650,000$

Present the solution.

650,000 in scientific notation is 6.5×10^5
7,480,000 in scientific notation is 7.48×10^6
86,700,000 becomes 8.67×10^7

Your Turn

Use scientific notation to write the population of the United States: 315,000,000 people.

Use the problem-solving process for a new type of problem you are learning about in math. Explain each step you take.

Solving Word Problems

The same steps can help you solve a word problem or a mathematical problem in real life.

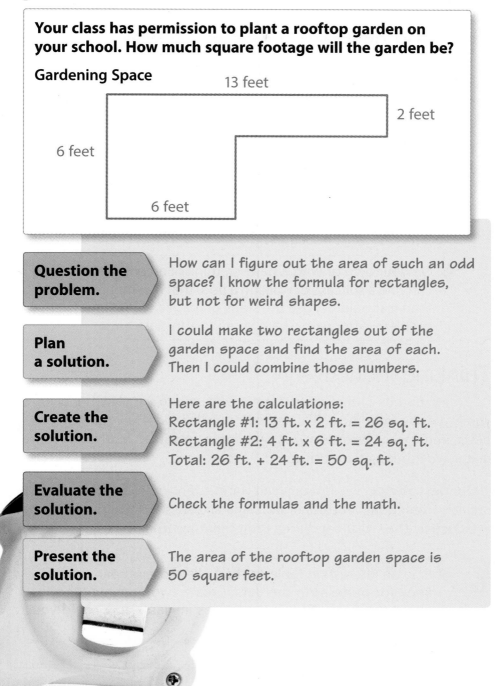

Your class has permission to plant a rooftop garden on your school. How much square footage will the garden be?

Gardening Space

13 feet

2 feet

6 feet

6 feet

Question the problem.

How can I figure out the area of such an odd space? I know the formula for rectangles, but not for weird shapes.

Plan a solution.

I could make two rectangles out of the garden space and find the area of each. Then I could combine those numbers.

Create the solution.

Here are the calculations:
Rectangle #1: 13 ft. x 2 ft. = 26 sq. ft.
Rectangle #2: 4 ft. x 6 ft. = 24 sq. ft.
Total: 26 ft. + 24 ft. = 50 sq. ft.

Evaluate the solution.

Check the formulas and the math.

Present the solution.

The area of the rooftop garden space is 50 square feet.

Problem-Solving Activities

Use these activities to practice your problem-solving skills. Then get ready to apply these skills to the problems that come your way.

Providing Relief

Many of the conveniences we take for granted were invented to solve a problem. Putting wheels on suitcases is a perfect example. It happened because one man hated carrying his luggage so much that he designed the suitcase on wheels. Many people today wheel their luggage around airports.

Our best advice: Be on the lookout for problem-solving opportunities in school and at home. Then use the steps on page **42** to solve these problems. Who knows? You may come up with an idea that helps a lot of people.

 Your Turn On your own or with a partner, think of a common task (like carrying a suitcase or walking a dog) that is sometimes harder than it should be. Use the steps on pages **42–48** to solve the problem. Afterward, share your work in class.

Thinking Inductively

You can study a list of specific facts and details to see what fun theories you can draw from them. This process is called inductive thinking. You never know what theories you might come up with. Then you can use deductive thinking to test them.

Our best advice: The Internet and your textbooks are full of tables and charts containing all sorts of facts and statistics. To practice thinking inductively, see what conclusions you can draw from the data you find.

Your Turn Find an interesting table or chart like those on pages **50–51**. Look for patterns in the data. Create two or three theories about the data. Discuss your ideas in class. How could you test one of your theories?

Chapter 5
Communicating

When you answer the phone, you might ask, "Who is it?" Well, it could be anyone—a family member, classmate, teacher, or neighbor. Whoever it is, being able to connect with the person is important. Strong communication skills give you that connection. Learning to speak effectively, listen carefully, and write well will help you share ideas, participate in groups, and much more.
This chapter shows you how.

You will learn . . .

- Understanding Communication
- Speaking
- Listening
- Writing
- Communicating Online
- Using Appropriate Language

Understanding Communication

Any important speaking or writing situation includes these elements: *purpose, topic, audience,* and *form.* Keep them in mind as you communicate. Below, you'll find three sample communication situations and the elements of each.

- Suppose your mom is out of town on business, but you want to email her about school.

  Purpose: to share information
  Topic: how school is going
  Audience: your mother
  Form: email message

- Imagine you've been assigned to demonstrate a new Web site in science class and lead a discussion.

  Purpose: to demonstrate and lead
  Topic: new Web site
  Audience: science classmates
  Form: 3- to 4-minute demonstration and discussion

- Let's say you and a friend are creating a comedy routine about succeeding in school.

  Purpose: to entertain
  Topic: "tips" for succeeding in school
  Audience: classmates
  Form: comedy script

Your Turn Identify the elements—*purpose, topic, audience,* and *form*—in the situation below. Afterward, discuss your ideas in class.

You've completed a group project about the future of recycling, and you need to introduce the project to judges at your school's learning fair.

Special Challenge: Create one or two of your own communication situations and exchange them with a partner. Identify the four elements of each other's situations. Afterward, discuss your ideas together.

The Range of Speaking and Writing

The following chart shows many ways to communicate. The ways become more formal and complex as you go down.

Types of Communicating

Casual and Simple

Formal and Complex

- friendly talk
- texting
- personal emails
- blogs
- class notes
- class discussions
- business emails
- business letters
- informational speeches
- stories/songs
- podcasts
- essays/reports
- persuasive speeches
- project presentations

Your Turn In small groups or as a class, discuss the chart by answering these questions:

- What general observations can you make about the information in this chart?
- Why is texting simpler than writing a school-related email?
- Why is participating in a class discussion simpler than delivering a persuasive speech?
- What types of speaking and writing demand that you identify the purpose, topic, audience, and form?
- Do you disagree with or question any part of the chart? Explain.

Speaking

Talking can be easy and spontaneous. Without thinking too deeply, you just let the words flow. Speaking is usually more careful. You wouldn't deliver a classroom speech without preparing. The following pages deal with speaking to one person, in groups, and to large audiences.

One-on-One Conversations

It's not easy to speak one-on-one with your principal or with a local business owner, is it? To be at your best, you need to plan ahead. Here are a few guidelines.

Before

Study the situation. Know the purpose, topic, audience, and form of the conversation. Are you asking for information or sharing it? What is your topic? With whom will you speak? Will you speak in person or by phone?

Learn about your audience. Know how to pronounce the person's name. Learn how to address him or her properly (Ms. Jones, Officer Williams, Senator Traber). (See page **76** for help.)

During

Make eye contact. Show your interest in the person's ideas by nodding your head, smiling, and so on.

Speak clearly and politely. Pronounce words clearly and keep your voice at a reasonable level.

Stay calm. Pace yourself. Sit up straight. Avoid bouncing your leg, slouching, or leaning.

Remember your purpose. Are you asking for information, providing information, or sharing an opinion? When you finish, thank the person.

After

Think about the conversation. Did you share or get the information you needed? Were you polite? Did you thank the person?

What to Say

The following tips will help you to be courteous and confident during conversations with adults.

■ Introducing Yourself

Do say: "Thank you for meeting with me, Senator Traber" or "It's nice to meet you, Senator Traber."

Don't say: "How's it going, Senator?" or "What's up?"

■ Ending a Conversation

Do say: "Thank you for your time, Dr. Nichols."

Don't say: "Thanks, Doc" or "I'm out of here."

■ Asking for Help

Do say: "Mr. Larsen, could you please help me with this?"

Don't say: "Hey, I need some help."

■ Apologizing

Do say: "I'm sorry, Ms. Ritter. I shouldn't have said that."

Don't say: "Forget what I said."

■ Asking for Information

Do say: "Could you please explain the new requirements?"

Don't say: "What's with these new requirements?"

■ Adding to the Conversation

Do say: "Ms. Cole, isn't it also important that . . . ?"

Don't say: "Here's what I think" or "Listen to this . . ."

■ Disagreeing

Do say: "Mr. Peters, I'm not sure I agree with that."

Don't say: "You're wrong!" or "What are you talking about?"

Your Turn Write a short conversation between a student and an adult (teacher, counselor, or coach) and use a few of the "Don't say" examples above. Exchange papers with a partner and change "Don't say" remarks into "Do say" remarks. Afterward, share your work.

Speaking in Group Discussions

Often you need to speak to more than one person, whether to team members or classmates. Follow these tips when speaking to a group.

Before

Remember the situation. Think about the purpose and the topic of the discussion. What do you hope to learn? Research the topic if necessary.

Know your group members. Plan to use each member's name as you talk together. (Say, "Sam, what do you think?" or "Please repeat your point, Julie.")

Assign roles. Decide who will lead the discussion and who will take notes.

During

Make eye contact as you speak and listen. Doing so shows your interest in the topic and other people's ideas.

Be polite. Ask and answer questions in a courteous way. Always wait for a good time to speak. Don't interrupt someone who is talking.

Remain calm and be patient. Avoid tapping a pen or pencil or slouching in your chair.

Provide helpful information. Explain your ideas clearly. If possible, make your points with the help of visual aids.

Be fair. Encourage everyone to participate, and be careful not to do all of the talking.

After

Think about the discussion. What worked well? What didn't work so well? Did the group meet its goal?

What to Say

In order to have an effective discussion, you must respect and value each speaker's contribution, even when you disagree in some way. Instead of saying something like "That's stupid" or "Get real," respond in the following ways:

- **Be positive and helpful:** "I like the bright colors and clear labels in your graph."
- **Begin your remarks with "I," not "You":** "I wonder if that other chart should be redone."
- **Compliment good ideas:** "Raymond, that background music will add something really special to our presentation."
- **Apologize for mistakes or hurtful comments:** "Sorry, I spoke too quickly and didn't let you finish your idea."
- **Comment on the ideas and work (not on the people):** "I wonder if our introduction is clear enough."
- **Respond in ways that make everyone feel important to the team:** "Let's all talk about the voice-overs. Who should do them?"

Dealing with Interruptions

If someone interrupts you during a discussion, you might let the person speak before returning to your point. You could also say, "Please, let me finish" and then go on. Avoid getting angry. If someone is constantly interrupting, ask a teacher or team leader for help.

Your Turn Team up with two or three classmates to discuss the quotations below. Decide what they mean, how they relate to group work, and whether you agree with them. Afterward, share your ideas in class.

> "The older I grow, the more I listen to people who don't talk much."
>
> —Germain G. Glien

> "The kindest word in all the world is the unkind word, unsaid."
>
> —Author unknown

Speaking to a Large Group

When you speak to a large group, follow the guidelines below. (Also see page 64.)

Before

Study the situation. Know the purpose, topic, audience, and form of your speech. With a clear goal in mind, decide how to deliver your ideas.

Plan the speech. Either write it out word for word or list the main ideas on note cards. Prepare slides, graphs, photos, or other visuals to present the information.

Practice. Repeat your speech over and over until you can deliver it smoothly, without hesitating or stumbling. As you practice, remember to speak clearly enough for the audience to understand your ideas.

During

Make eye contact. Even if you are reading your speech, look out at your audience often.

Try to appear calm and confident. Avoid nervous actions like fumbling with papers, looking down too much, or shuffling your feet.

Check your speed. Don't speak too quickly or too slowly.

Cover all the information you planned to share. Also be certain your charts and graphs are clearly visible to the audience. At the end, ask for and answer questions from the audience.

After

Review your speech. Either use a checklist to evaluate it (see page 66) or freewrite about how things went. Did the speech go as planned? What went wrong, if anything? What would you do differently next time?

 Your Turn Which would you rather do: (1) deliver a speech to your class or (2) deliver a speech electronically to many students in different schools? List the pluses and minuses for each. Discuss your answers.

What to Speak About

You'll speak about different topics in different classes. Four types of speeches appear below, with sample topics.

- An **informative speech** explains an interesting topic to the audience and includes plenty of important facts and details.

Social Studies:	A skilled trade in early America
Science:	The causes of ocean currents
Math:	An introduction to Roman numerals
The Arts:	An introduction to folk art

- A **persuasive speech** provides evidence to support a claim or an opinion. To be convincing, the evidence must be strong and logical. (See pages **94–100** and **350–351** for more.)

Social Studies:	Promoting a local Native American exhibit
Science:	Improving a severe-weather warning system
Math:	Connecting math to the real world
The Arts:	The need for a drama club

- A **demonstration speech** shows how to do or make something. It requires the necessary materials and a clear explanation of the steps in the process.

Social Studies:	Making johnnycakes
Science:	Designing paper airplanes
Math:	Using a scatter plot to make predictions
The Arts:	Playing beginner chords on a guitar

- An **entertainment speech** is a mini-performance in which you share a personal story, read aloud, deliver funny facts, and so on. Plenty of practice is necessary for this kind of speech to be successful.

Social Studies:	Role-playing a historical figure
Science:	Reading aloud an article about current medical news
Math:	Sharing some funny facts or jokes about math
The Arts:	Reading aloud a series of poems

Overcoming Stage Fright

If speaking in front of a large group makes you feel nervous, you are not alone. Just about everyone gets "the jitters." The tips that follow will help you control your nerves during speeches and presentations.

■ Choose a topic that interests you.

Liking your topic and knowing a lot about it can calm your nerves. It's always easier to talk about something you care about.

■ Practice, practice, practice.

Professional performers rehearse over and over again before taking the stage. You must do the same. Practice in front of a mirror as well as in front of one or two friends or family members.

■ Look and feel ready to speak.

Wear comfortable clothes on the day of your speech, but avoid T-shirts and shorts for most speaking situations. To boost your confidence, imagine yourself giving your speech without a glitch. Finally, take a few deep breaths right before you begin.

■ Start out strong.

Doing well on the first part should settle your nerves and help you get through the rest of your speech.

■ Focus on your speech.

Concentrate on the information you are sharing, not on your audience's reaction.

In Focus You might make a mistake or two, so don't freeze if it happens. As you practice, pay special attention to parts that make you stumble, and think of ways to get through them.

 Your Turn Discover how one of your favorite performers (athlete, actor, musician) deals with nervousness. Share your findings in class.

Respecting Listeners

Some listeners may need to read your lips because of hearing problems, so always look at your audience and speak clearly. Also remember that good visuals will help the entire audience.

Using Sign Language

Perhaps you have seen someone signing a speech for those who have hearing impairments. It is interesting to note that American Sign Language is considered a separate language, not simply a visual form of English. Here are the signs for the letters of the alphabet. (For more information, go to **thoughtfullearning.com/e65**.)

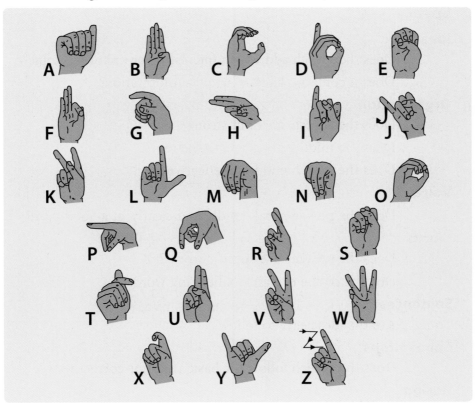

Your Turn Find an interesting six- or seven-letter word in another chapter in this book. Learn how to sign this word using the letters in the chart above. Sign the word for your classmates.

Evaluating Speeches

Use the following checklist to evaluate speeches and presentations.

Speech Checklist

Speaker: _____ Date: _____

Speaker

_____ Is the speaker well prepared?

_____ Is the speaker knowledgeable about the topic?

Speech

Ideas

_____ Does the speech address an interesting or important topic?

_____ Does it contain plenty of quality information?

Organization

_____ Does the speech start out strong?

_____ Does the middle part explain the topic?

_____ Does the speech end in an effective way?

Voice

_____ Does the person speak loudly and clearly, at a good pace?

Words

_____ Does the speaker use specific words?

_____ Does he or she explain challenging words?

Sentences

_____ Are the ideas easy to follow?

Conventions

_____ Does the speech follow the basic rules for correctness?

Design

_____ Are charts and graphs helpful?

 Evaluate a speech. (Go to thoughtfullearning.com/e66.)

Parts of a Speech

The following note cards show parts of a PowerPoint presentation in which the speaker shares interesting facts and details about the state capitol building in Lansing, Michigan.

The **first card** contains the opening, word for word.

Opening (show first slide)

"Wow!" That's usually what people say when they see a state capitol for the first time. They are magnificent, standing bigger and higher and brighter than everything around them. Each capitol is a shrine representing all that is important about a state. Our capitol in Lansing, Michigan, is a great example. The details of this building are truly amazing.

Dome (show slide)

- tan, then bright white, then off white
- forms highest point (267 feet)
- inner dome looks like a starry sky

The **middle cards** list main points only.

Rotunda (show slide)

- first floor
- circular room in center of capitol
- gives view of the dome
- rotunda floor—976 pieces of glass (from above, the floor seems to sink into a bowl)

The **last card** contains the closing, word for word.

Closing (show last slide)

A National Historic Landmark is a special building, site, or structure that is recognized by the United States government for its historical importance. The Michigan capitol is one of the buildings to receive this great honor. Please visit our capitol as soon as you can to see firsthand the magnificent details that make it so special. You will not be disappointed.

Listening

Just because you hear someone doesn't mean you are listening to the person. Listening requires focus. When you listen to a speech or other presentation, you need to work hard to keep your focus. Follow these guidelines:

Before

Be prepared. Know what topic is being discussed. Also be ready to take notes, ask questions, and offer your own thoughts.

During

Pay attention to the speaker, including his or her hand movements, tone of voice, and facial expressions. These signals help you understand what is being said.

Listen for signal words like *first, as a result,* and *by contrast.* Words such as these show how ideas are connected together.

Stay focused. Watch the speaker and avoid daydreaming.

Take notes, but only on key points. If you take too many notes, you will miss some of the speaker's ideas.

List questions you would like to ask the speaker, but wait until a good time to ask them.

After

Review your notes or discuss the information with another listener.

Use one or more active learning strategies from the facing page.

 Your Turn Listen to a speech online using the guidelines above. (Your teacher will recommend one for you.) Then, as a class, discuss what you learned.

Learning Through Listening

To understand new information, you need to apply it. The following active learning strategies will help you apply information from speeches and presentations.

- **Write freely about the information** in a learning log or blog. Explore your thoughts about the ideas. (See pages **120–121** and **366–367**.)

- **Think critically about the topic.** Make comparisons, look for causes and effects, identify steps, and so on. (See pages **13–26**.)

- **Think creatively about the topic.** Ask and answer creative questions about it: What color comes to mind when you think of the topic? Why? What type of music is it like? Would the topic make a good friend? (See pages **27–40**.)

- **Discuss the topic** with classmates, friends, and family members. Discussions help you better understand the information.

- **Teach someone else about the topic.** Explaining a topic to another person lets you sort out your own thinking.

- **Learn more about the topic.** Research the topic to see what else you can discover out about it.

Discuss this Turkish proverb: "If speaking is silver, then listening is gold." What does the proverb mean to you? Do you agree with it? Why or why not? What personal experiences have you had that show this proverb to be true?

Writing

Good writing does not happen all at once. Instead, it goes through a series of steps called the writing process. Only then is it ready to share. The guidelines below explain this process and show you how to use it. (Also see the chart on the next page.)

Before
> **Study the assignment.** To get started, think about the purpose, topic, audience, and form of the writing assignment.

During
> **Prewriting:** Choose a topic that interests you. Then collect details about it and make a plan for organizing the information.
>
> **Writing:** Write a first draft using the details you've collected and your organization plan. Don't try to get everything exactly right. Just get your thoughts down.
>
> **Revising:** Read your first draft, focusing on the ideas, organization, and voice. Change any parts that are unclear, incomplete, or out of place.
>
> **Editing:** Check your revised writing, focusing on words and sentences. Edit for grammar, spelling, punctuation, and capitalization errors. Make corrections.
>
> **Publishing:** Create a final copy to share.

After
> **Evaluate your work.** Use a checklist (see page 72), or simply ask yourself what works well and what you need to improve in your next assignment.

In Focus When you respond to a writing prompt on a test, you may have just a short amount of time to complete your work. Use the first few minutes for prewriting, most of your time for writing, and the final minutes for revising and editing.

Writing in Action

This graphic shows how the writing process works. The arrows show that you can move back and forth between the steps rather than following them straight through to the end. For example, you may discover that you need to gather more information about your topic (prewriting) after doing some writing or revising.

The Writing Process

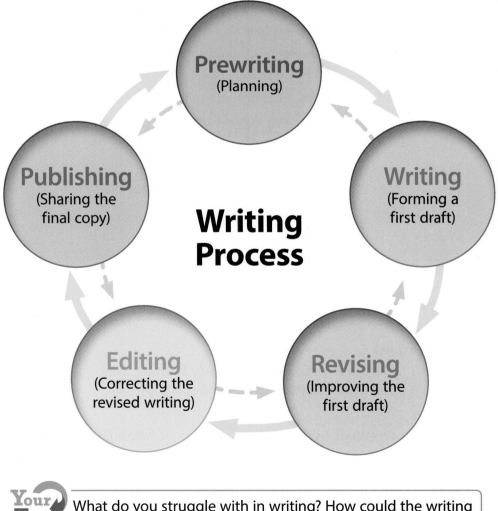

Writing Process

Prewriting
(Planning)

Writing
(Forming a first draft)

Publishing
(Sharing the final copy)

Editing
(Correcting the revised writing)

Revising
(Improving the first draft)

Your Turn What do you struggle with in writing? How could the writing process help you succeed? Share your thoughts in class.

Evaluating Writing

The checklist below will help you evaluate informational paragraphs, essays, and reports.

Writing Checklist

Writer: _____ Date: _____

Ideas

_____ Does the writing explore an interesting topic?

_____ Does it contain plenty of quality information?

Organization

_____ Does the writing start out strong?

_____ Does the middle part explain the topic?

_____ Does the writing end in an effective way?

Voice

_____ Does the writer seem knowledgeable about the topic?

_____ Does he or she sound interested?

Words

_____ Does the writer use specific words?

_____ Does he or she explain any challenging words?

Sentences

_____ Are the ideas easy to follow?

Conventions

_____ Does the writing follow the basic rules for grammar, punctuation, capitalization, and spelling?

Design

_____ Are visuals (photos, graphs, drawings) helpful?

Your Turn Use the checklist above to evaluate the writing on the next page as well as your future writing projects. (Go to **thoughtfullearning.com/e72** to download the checklist.)

Example Report

The beginning introduces the topic.

The middle explains the topic.

The ending provides important final thoughts.

Helping the Needy

What is the best way to feed those who are hungry in Africa? For decades, the answer seemed to be to send food. Now, efforts are shifting toward helping Africans develop the vast resources of their continent.

Africa has enough fertile land, fresh water, and mineral wealth to support its population. According to a World Health study, if the land were used properly, African farming could feed everyone on the continent and Europe (World Health). Sadly, much of this land goes unused or is exploited by those outside Africa.

What causes these problems? In some places, governmental instability, social unrest, and tribal warfare prevent the resources from being used (Kohl, p. 43). African nations need help from the world community to prevent warlords and corporations from taking power. In other places, stable governments need to make agricultural production a priority.

There's reason for hope. Not long ago, India suffered a hunger crisis, but now it produces enough food for its population. This change came about through a stable government that has focused on developing farming and food production. African governments can do the same.

The best way to help the hungry people of Africa is to provide food for today, promote stability for tomorrow, and plan agriculture for the future ("Aid," p. 12). If this type of relief continues, the hungry people of Africa will be able to help themselves. Currently, they have the resources and the will to do so. All that they need now is the chance.

Communicating Online

Technology provides many communication opportunities both in school and at home. (Also see pages 359–370.)

- **Blogs** are online journals that you can add to and readers can comment on.

- **Comic-book software** lets you arrange photographs or drawings in comic-book style and add speech bubbles.

- **Fan-fiction sites** allow users to share their stories. Often these stories are interactive, with one writer starting a story and others continuing it.

- **Music-mixing programs** let you record and edit your own songs on a computer.

- **Online word processors** allow you to create and edit documents on the Web with other people.

- **Photo-sharing sites** let users post photos to the Web for other people to view. Some of the sites share photos only with the poster's friends and family. Other sites make photos available for anyone to view and use.

- **Podcasting sites** let people post audio files for others to listen to. Podcasts may include music, lessons, commentary, or even audiobooks.

- **Slideshow software** allows users to create and display multimedia presentations. Classrooms and businesses alike use these programs to present reports to an audience.

- **Social-network sites** let people view text and photos posted by friends and family. They also may list recommended books, movies, and music and provide games and quizzes.

- **Video-editing software** lets you import recorded video into your computer, edit it, and post it to sharing sites.

- **Wikis** are projects written and edited by a community of people. Your class might create a wiki about its town history, for example.

Your Turn Go online to find examples of two or more of the technologies listed above. Share these examples with your classmates.

Using Appropriate Language

When you speak and write in formal situations, you should follow the rules of Standard English. The chart below shows how to switch from informal English to Standard English. (Also see pages 161–172.)

When you want to . . .	don't say . . .	do say . . .
1. form a plural	10 mile	10 miles
2. show repeated action	He always be early.	He always is early.
3. show ownership	My friend car . . .	My friend's car . . .
4. use a third-person singular verb	The customer ask . . .	The customer asks . . .
5. express negatives	They don't never . . .	They don't ever . . .
6. refer back to a pronoun	He sees hisself . . .	He sees himself . . .
7. use a pronoun subject	Them are . . .	Those are . . .
8. use the past tense of *do*	He done it.	He did it.
9. refer to a subject	My teacher he assigned . . .	My teacher assigned . . .
10. use *a* or *an*	I need new laptop. She had good day.	I need a new laptop. She had a good day.
11. use past-tense verbs	Carl finish his . . .	Carl finished his . . .
12. say *is not* or *are not*	The company ain't . . .	The company isn't . . .

Using Fair Language

Always show respect when speaking with or about others. This chart will help you refer to people and groups in the polite, proper way.

When referring to race, say . . .

- American Indians, Native Americans, or tribe names *(Hopi, Inuit)*
- Asian Americans *(not Orientals)* or nationalities *(Japanese, Chinese)*
- Hispanic, Latino, or nationalities *(Mexican, Cuban)*
- African American *(black is preferred by some)*

When referring to age, say . . .

- Older adults, older people *(people 70 or older)*
- Women, men, adults *(people 30 or older)*
- Young adults *(late teens and 20s)*
- Young people, adolescents *(people between 13–19)*
- Girls, boys *(people 12 or younger)*

When referring to adults, say . . .

- Mr. Nelson *(an adult man)*
- Ms. Brand *(an adult woman)*
- Mrs. Larson *(an adult woman who is married)*
- Miss Long *(an adult woman who is single)*

When referring to adults with titles, say . . .

- President Obama
- Rabbi Gould
- Mullah Abdul
- Dr. Monk

When referring to disabilities, say . . . . Don't say . . .

- disabled . . . . *handicapped*
- a person with autism . . . . *an autistic*

When referring to inclusive gender, say . . . . Don't say . . .

- police officer . . . . *policeman*
- chair . . . . *chairman*
- postal worker . . . . *postman*
- he or she . . . . *he*

Communication Activities

Use these activities to practice your communication skills.

Sharing a Story

One way to practice speaking is to retell personal stories about your own or others' experiences. You may speak from memory, use notes, or have the story written out word for word.

Our best advice: Start by sharing your own personal stories with a partner or small group of classmates. As you become more comfortable, increase the size of your audience. Make it your goal to eventually share a story in front of the entire class.

 Your Turn Choose an interesting personal story that someone else told you or that you read. Plan to share it with a partner or small group. Either speak from notes or from the written text of the story.

Listening for Directions

Do you consider yourself a good listener? Are you someone who can pick out and remember the key points of a speaker's message? Most students could probably use more practice in this area. Effective listening requires a lot of concentration. (See pages **68–69**.)

Our best advice: Make a special point of listening whenever your teacher, coaches, or classmates are sharing important information. Becoming a good listener will make you a better learner.

Your Turn Team up with three or four students. To begin, write down the directions from your bedroom to the refrigerator (or some other object) in your house. Then whisper what you have written to one of the students, who in turn must whisper the directions to the next student, and so on, until the last person receives the message and repeats the directions out loud. Are they accurate? If not, review the guidelines for listening and try again with other directions.

Writing Practice

Writing is both a physical and a mental activity. You must write the words on paper or type them on a keyboard. So until you master the physical part of writing, you will not feel comfortable writing.

Our best advice: Practice your handwriting or keyboarding as often as you can. Writing in a personal journal or learning log is a comfortable way to practice since you usually don't have to turn that writing in to anyone. (See pages **120–121**.)

 Pretend that you are a famous person. Then write one or two journal entries (or blog postings) as if you were that person. For each entry, write for at least five minutes, recording your ideas freely and rapidly. Afterward, share your work in class.

Following the Standard

You learned on page **75** that Standard English is used in school assignments and all important forms of communication. So always carefully check your grammar, punctuation, mechanics, and spelling before you share your writing.

Our best advice: Keep your audience in mind. If you are texting or emailing a friend, you can write in a more relaxed way, without worrying so much about the rules. But if you are writing a classroom report, you must follow the rules that apply to this more formal situation.

Your Turn Write two notes or email messages describing what you are studying in one of your classes. (Each note should be five or six sentences long.) In the first note, write to your best friend. In the second note, write to your principal. Afterward, ask yourself these questions: How are the messages different? Which one should follow the rules of Standard English? Why?

How should we
do this?

Chapter 6
Collaborating

The word "we" is probably the most important part of the question at the top of this page. When we collaborate, or work together, we can accomplish important things. So whether you need to rescue a cat, plan a fund-raiser, or cook supper with your family, collaboration is key. This chapter will help you be a good team member in many different situations.

You will learn . . .

- Being a Good Team Member
- Understanding Diversity
- Making Groups Work
- Collaborating Online
- Conducting Meetings
- Brainstorming
- Group Problem Solving
- Resolving Conflicts

Being a Good Team Member

A team is only as good as its members. Everyone has to do his or her job in order for the team to succeed. Follow the guidelines below.

Tuning In

Group members need to share common goals and work toward achieving them. Here are ways that you can tune in during group work.

- **Listen carefully.** Think about what others are saying before responding.
- **Add your own thoughts.** However, don't interrupt someone else.
- **Focus on your group's goals.** Help the group decide on goals and work to help accomplish them.
- **Focus on ideas instead of personalities.** Keep your common interests in mind.
- **Focus on solutions rather than problems.** Instead of saying, "We never get any help," say, "How can we make sure that we get enough help?"
- **Make decisions together.** Do this after everyone has had the chance to contribute ideas.

Your Turn In a small group, discuss how teamwork would be involved in the situations listed here. (Follow the guidelines above.)
1. Creating a YouTube video
2. Holding a bake sale
3. Putting on a holiday concert
4. Earning a black belt
5. Building a doghouse

Doing Your Part

If each team member does his or her part, the group can accomplish its goals. Here are some good reminders:

- **Respect your teammates.** Show that you value the contribution of each team member.
- **Be fair.** Don't dominate the discussion. Instead, get everyone involved.
- **Deal with problems and move on.** For example, if the group is talking about too many things at once, you could say, "Guys, we need to focus on one thing at a time."
- **Offer your help.** Once the group decides on a next step, ask how you can help.

In Focus Because of technology, team members can work from different locations. Working in online groups is becoming more common. (See pages 84–85 for ideas.)

Understanding the Roles

These are the three main roles within a group:

- **The leader** controls the team, getting everyone to work together and handling any problems.
- **A note taker** writes down important information besides sharing his or her own ideas.
- **The other group members** offer ideas, ask questions, and work together.

Your Turn With a partner, create a poster about teamwork. Include a message or statement like "Teamwork takes a team to the top." Add a drawing or photo that illustrates the idea. (See pages 334–335.)

Understanding Diversity

Diversity means "being different from one another." A diverse group might include people from different countries or those who speak different languages or enjoy different foods or music. Diversity can make life rich and interesting in school, at home, and in the community. To welcome people from many backgrounds, you should do the following:

- **Value different cultures.** Become friends with students from other countries or backgrounds and learn about their cultures.

- **Realize that some students may need encouragement.** Students from other countries may feel uncomfortable talking in groups because they don't understand the language as well as the others do. Be patient, and encourage them to share their thoughts.

- **Work together.** Be sure everyone knows and understands the group's purpose, has a role, and receives the help he or she needs.

- **Deal with problems.** Be friendly and positive even when problems do arise. Work together to solve them. (See page **90**.)

In Focus Working with students from other countries or cultures will help you understand your world better. In fact, today's technology is making worldwide collaboration easier and more common. You may already have had the opportunity to take part in group discussions with students from countries around the world.

Your Turn Think of a country you know about and would like to visit. Then compare it to your own country in three or four ways. (For example, in your country, you may have easy access to the Internet, while students in another country may not.) Afterward, share your ideas in class. Discuss how the differences between the two places may affect group work involving students from both countries.

Making Groups Work

A team needs to know its goal and have a plan to reach it. A goal is a simple statement of what you hope to achieve. After setting up a goal, you can create objectives by answering the 5 W's about it.

Goal:	We want to create a green space out of the vacant lot next to the school.
Who is involved? (Team)	Jackie James, Ross Hermann, Susie Park, Larissa Kapinski, and Daniel Williams
What are we doing? (Project)	Making a proposal to create a green space
Where? (Setting)	In an empty lot near our school
When? (Deadline)	During the spring semester, to be completed by April 16
Why are we doing it? (Purpose)	To provide a place for students to study nature

Knowing the Project

Big Projects: Some projects, like the one described above, require a lot of planning and time. After setting up a goal and objectives, teams need to list the tasks they need to accomplish, the time each task will take, and the tools they have to do the work. Chapter 19 outlines this process. Chapters 24–29 explain step-by-step how to develop long-term projects.

Small Projects: Some projects, like making a decision, may require just a discussion. (See pages 89–90 for information about solving minor problems or making decisions.)

Your Turn Think of an interesting group project you would love to work on. Working alone or with a partner, set a goal and objectives for this project. Then share your ideas in class.

Collaborating Online

You may have communicated electronically with students from other schools in your district or county. You may also have used the Internet to work on projects with students in a different state or country. If so, you already know the power of online collaborating.

Online Options

The chart below lists types of online collaboration. Each type allows you to work with students at a distance.

- **Wikis** are Web pages that allow a group of students to write, edit, and save text. Visitors to wikis can edit or add to the text. (See pages **205** and **366–367**.)

- **Blogs** are sites on which you can write personal thoughts and ideas, share links to other blogs, and post videos and music. Blog readers can react to blog posts. (See pages **205** and **366–367**.)

- **Chat** services let you communicate with one or more people in real time—without delays. (See pages **202–203**.)

- **Email** allows members of a group to communicate from any location. (See pages **204** and **290–291**.)

- **VOIP** (Voice Over Internet Protocol) connects students in different schools by voice and video calls. You can send files, participate in discussions, and share screens. Check with your teacher for information about VOIP in your school. (See page **203**.)

- **Online forums,** or message boards, give you a chance to discuss topics by posting messages on threads. A thread is a group of comments about a single topic. (See page **207**.)

Your Turn Write down two or three comments or questions about the list of options above. Share them in a class discussion about online collaboration.

Netiquette

Netiquette refers to the right way to behave online. When you collaborate online, be polite. Use the information that follows to guide your behavior.

- **Respect others.** Avoid sending hurtful comments or messages.

- **Respect cultural differences.** Make a point of learning about the differences between cultures and respecting group members from different backgrounds. (See page **82**.)

- **Honor everyone's input.** Don't change the group's plan without discussing it with everyone.

- **Honor everyone's right to privacy.** Do not give out passwords or personal information online. Share information only if group members, your teacher, and a parent/guardian agree to it.

- **Give credit for Web information.** If your group decides to use information from another Web site, put the information in your own words and provide a link to the site. Before using a picture or graphic from a Web site, check with your teacher to make sure it is okay to use. Always give credit to the photographer or designer. (See page **255**.)

Your Turn With a partner, look online for other netiquette tips to share with your class.

Conducting Meetings

A meeting is a discussion held by a group for a common purpose—such as a student council discussing a school fund-raiser. The guidelines below explain the typical steps followed during a meeting.

Meeting Guidelines

1. The adviser or leader of the group announces the meeting ahead of time so that people can plan to attend.

2. The leader (or someone assigned) creates an agenda and time schedule for the meeting. An agenda lists the ideas and actions to be discussed.

3. To get started, the leader calls the meeting to order, and the secretary, or recorder, reads the minutes from the last meeting. Minutes record the actions of a meeting. (See page 87.)

4. Old business is discussed before new business. (Old business includes topics from the last meeting that are still being discussed.)

5. Rules, such as *Robert's Rules of Order,* are followed to keep discussions orderly. Here are the basic rules. (Check online for more details.)
   - The leader introduces each new point of discussion on the agenda.
   - He or she also calls on each person who wants to speak. This prevents everyone from speaking at the same time.
   - Once a topic has been thoroughly discussed, the leader asks for a yes or no vote on an action or on a decision to postpone action until another time.

6. After the agenda has been covered (or time has run out), the leader ends the meeting and informs everyone about any next steps.

Minutes

The minutes below were taken during a student council meeting and follow the guidelines on page 86.

Parkview Student Council Minutes
Thursday, February 21, 2013

The **beginning** identifies the date and the students at the meeting.

Present: Larry Smith, Missy Uhen, Josie Hernandez, Bobbie Jones, Si Pak, Katie Dey, Jesse Williams, Candice Baker, Jon Palermo, Maya Fischer, Ms. Peterson

13:101 Larry called the meeting to order. The agenda was approved.

Old Business

13:102 The Feb. 7 meeting minutes were accepted.

In the **middle**, each topic is identified with the year and item number.

13:103 The council discussed motion 13:98 and voted to sponsor an art contest.

New Business

13:104 Jon Palermo argued for the computer lab to be open during lunch and after school:
1. Students need more computer time.
2. Students need practice with computers.
A motion to consider this idea passed.
Jon Palermo and Katie Dey will investigate this idea and report next meeting.

Next Meeting

In the **ending**, actions for the next meeting are identified.

13:105 We will discuss the library checkout system.
13:106 The next meeting is scheduled for March 7 at 12:30 p.m. (Library Meeting Room).

Submitted by Josie Hernandez, secretary

Brainstorming

Brainstorming is a strategy for gathering ideas. One person asks a question or presents a problem, and everyone tries to come up with as many answers or solutions as possible. They create a "storm" of ideas.

Brainstorming Guidelines

1. **Begin** brainstorming with a goal in mind. For example, you may need ideas for a project on transportation.

2. **Choose** one person to lead the brainstorming and another to list the ideas.

3. **Write** down all the ideas shared. If they are coming too quickly, slow things down so no ideas are lost.

4. **Display** the ideas so everyone can see them. This will help group members think of even more ideas.

5. **Keep** the brainstorming going for as long as you can. The best idea may be the next one.

Sample Brainstorming

Here are the ideas listed by one group for a learning fair project about transportation.

Ideas for a Transportation Project

light rail	in-line skating lanes	electric cars
bullet trains	river ferries	hybrids
city bikes	alternative buses	student scooters
bike trails and lanes	city trolleys	automated walkways

 Your Turn With two classmates, brainstorm even more ideas for a transportation project. (The sky's the limit!) Afterward, share your ideas in class.

Group Problem Solving

Groups solve problems using the same process that individuals use. Imagine that your school needs new playground equipment. Here is a process that your student council might use:

Problem-Solving Guidelines

1. **Examine the problem** by asking the 5 W's.

   > **Who?** Your school
   > **What?** Needs new playground equipment
   > **Where?** On the playground
   > **When?** As soon as possible
   > **Why?** Because the old equipment is worn out

2. **Analyze the problem,** looking at causes and effects.

   > **Causes:** Old or missing equipment and a lack of funds
   > **Effects:** Overcrowding on equipment and student boredom

3. **Brainstorm ideas** to solve the problem.

   > Hold a swing-a-thon with the PTO; get business sponsors for each new piece of equipment; sell the old equipment for scrap; hold a playground design contest.

4. **Evaluate ideas** to find the best one. Which idea would best address the causes and eliminate the effects?

5. **Plan the solution** by defining your goal and listing the tasks, time, tools, and teams to make the goal a reality.

6. **Apply your solution** to the situation.

7. **Evaluate the solution** against your goal.

8. **Make improvements** to perfect your solution.

9. **Present the solution**, improving your school or community.

Your Turn Identify a problem in your school and follow steps 1–5 to find a solution. Share your ideas with the rest of the class.

Resolving Conflicts

It is not unusual for a group to disagree as they work on a project. Some conflicts may be easy to resolve, while others may require careful attention. Consider the following conflict:

> Imagine that three students—Jenna, Hallie, and Beth—are in charge of making posters to advertise their school's cultural fair. Jenna wants to make two big posters, one for each main entrance to the school, and Hallie wants a series of small posters to display around the school. Beth sees value in both ideas, but she knows they don't have the time to do both. Unfortunately, Jenna and Hallie don't want to give up their ideas.

To resolve this conflict, the girls must (1) practice good group skills, (2) explore the situation and possible solutions, and (3) agree on the best solution.

In Focus Conflicts can be resolved only when group members treat each other with respect. Always concentrate on the problem, not on your personal feelings.

Finding a Solution

Here are three ways that this group can resolve their conflict.

1. **Work it out** among themselves.
2. **Have a teacher or adviser guide them** as they work on a solution.
3. **Ask a teacher or an adviser to make the decision** for them.

Your Turn With a partner or in a small group, resolve the conflict described above. Discuss the problem, consider possible solutions, and choose the best one.

Collaboration Activities

The four activities that follow will help you work in groups. After finishing them, think of others to try.

Heading West

Form a group of three or four students and pretend that you live in an isolated area in the U.S. or Canada. A severe winter blizzard is heading your way, and you must decide to either stay put in your cabin with its limited provisions or to set off for the nearest town that is offering food and shelter to people.

Our best advice: Work with partners or in small groups as often as you can to become a strong team member.

 Use the group skills on pages 80–81 as you form your plan. Write it out, stating what you will do first, second, third, and so on. Afterward, share the plan in class.

Getting to Know You

Write down two facts that reveal your family's background, customs, or culture. For example, your great-great-grandfather ran a hot-dog stand when he first came to this country from Poland; or your family visits your grandmother's house in North Carolina every summer. (You may need help from an older family member with this.)

Our best advice: Learning about and sharing your own background stories will show you how you and your classmates are all from unique cultures. Remember to celebrate the diversity in your classroom as often as you can.

 Complete this activity after your have discussed "Understanding Diversity" on page 82 in this chapter. Share your discoveries with your classmates.

Connecting Online

Correspond with a classmate about a topic you are currently studying. Start by writing an email to the classmate. Ask your partner to respond by the next day. Continue your email discussion for a week or so.

Our best advice: Learn how to work with others electronically. Sharing email messages is a good starting point. Also try the other options listed on pages **84–85**. (Ask your teacher or school's technical person for help.)

 As you send messages back and forth, remember to react to your partner's questions and statements. In this way, you will each learn more about the topic. Write emails of at least four or five sentences.

Group Design

With a partner, create a poster that shares an important message about working in groups. Review this chapter for ideas, and remember to share the work equally. Include one main idea plus a visual—a drawing, photo, or graphic—in your poster.

Our best advice: Working in a group involves more than simply discussing a topic. Often, you will create something together. Be prepared to share the duties so that each of you can contribute something unique.

 As you create your poster, remember that it must share important information and be visually appealing. (See pages **334–335** for information about poster making.) Afterward, evaluate the posters in class.

Chapter 7

Building Arguments

When you build an argument, you use evidence to make a point. Strong evidence will convince others to believe you. Perhaps you've heard of Sherlock Holmes. He always managed to find the facts and build logical arguments that solved crimes and amazed his friends. This chapter will show you how to use reason and evidence to build strong arguments.

You will learn . . .

- Planning an Argument
- Separating Opinions from Facts
- Using Strong Evidence
- Avoiding Faulty Logic

Planning an Argument

Building a strong argument takes careful thinking and planning. The 7 C's of building an argument outline the steps that you should follow.

The 7 C's of Building an Argument

1. **Consider** the situation.
2. **Clarify** your thinking.
3. **Construct** a claim.
4. **Collect** evidence.
5. **Consider** key objections.
6. **Craft** your argument.
7. **Confirm** your main point.

1. Consider the situation.

To get started, answer these questions: *What is my topic? What is my position about the topic? What is my purpose? Who is my audience? What action do I want my audience to take?* Doing this will get you thinking about your argument.

> **Topic:** Our district might cut recess from the school day.
>
> **Position:** Our school district should keep recess.
>
> **Purpose:** To argue that cutting recess will do more harm than good
>
> **Audience:** Students
>
> **Action:** Get students to share their concerns with their parents; I want parents to talk to teachers and school board members about saving recess.

Your Turn List rules you would like to add, modify, or remove from your school. Perhaps your library needs a no-talking rule, or the current rule is too strict or not strict enough. If you were to write about the rule, how would you define your topic, position, purpose, and audience? What action would you want people to take?

2. **Clarify** your thinking.

Next, be sure that you feel strongly about your position. Ask yourself these types of questions: *Why do I feel the way I do? What evidence do I have to support my position? Have I thought about everyone affected by it?* You may also want to create a pro-con chart to help you look at both sides of the issue.

Pro	Con
The proposal will . . . • give more class time. • save money spent on recess attendants. • cut down on visits to the nurse.	The proposal will . . . • cut time for exercise. • take away the chance to hang out with friends. • take a lot of fun out of school. • make some people burn out.

 Write your position and use the questions above to think about it. Then create a pro-con chart to deepen your thinking.

3. **Construct** a claim.

Once you are clear about your position, state it as a claim that you will prove in your argument. You can use this formula to write your claim. (Also see pages **300–301** for more information.)

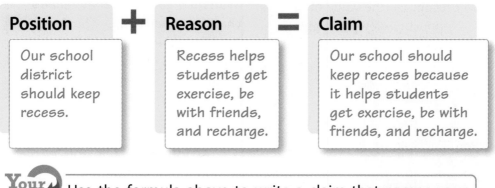

Position

Our school district should keep recess.

+

Reason

Recess helps students get exercise, be with friends, and recharge.

=

Claim

Our school should keep recess because it helps students get exercise, be with friends, and recharge.

Use the formula above to write a claim that names your position and your reason for it.

4. **Collect** evidence.

A strong claim needs strong supporting evidence. Facts, statistics, examples, quotations, and graphics support claims in different ways. (See pages **98–99** for more information.)

Your Turn Gather evidence to support your claim. Try to collect at least two or three different types. (If you have trouble collecting evidence, rethink your claim.)

5. **Consider** key objections.

People have different opinions, so you need to consider opposing points of view. If you disagree with an opposing viewpoint, you can argue against it (counter it). If you can't argue against it, you can concede it (recognize it has some value).

- **To counter an objection,** point out its weakness, but do so in a fair and reasonable way. Keep the tone positive.

The school board says that removing recess will increase class time and improve test scores. However, students in Finland score higher on tests than students in the U.S., and Finland has more recess time.

- **To concede an objection,** recognize the value of an opposing viewpoint and move on.

The nurse reports that more students get injured at recess than at other times. That's true, but the benefits of exercise outweigh the risks of injury.

Your Turn List two objections to your claim. Write a response to each one, either countering it or conceding it.

6. **Craft** your argument.

In the beginning part of your argument, introduce your topic and claim (main point). In the middle, present your evidence and deal with any important opposing arguments. In the ending, re-emphasize your claim and, if necessary, ask the audience to act on it. (See below.)

Be sure to include convincing facts and details. Also try to appeal to your audience's sense of fairness and common sense.

> **Fact:** Students now get a 15-minute recess break in the morning and in the afternoon.
>
> **Fairness appeal:** Is this really too much time outside?
>
> **Commonsense appeal:** Students need to be refreshed and alert to do their best learning. That is the purpose of recess.

 Put together your argument.

7. **Confirm** your main point.

End your argument by stating your main point in a way that your audience will be sure to remember.

> **Final appeal:** We need to save recess because it gives students exercise, lets them be with friends, and refreshes them to learn.
>
> **Call to action:** Please talk to school board members to let them know you want to keep recess.
>
> **Final word:** If students and parents make their feelings clear, we can save recess in our schools.

 Develop the final part of your argument using the example above as a guide.

Separating Opinions from Facts

Your main point in an argument expresses an opinion, but it should be supported by facts. Be sure that you understand the difference.

Opinions

An **opinion** is a personal view or belief. An opinion may be supported by facts, but it is not a fact itself.

| The use of thin plastic bags should be greatly reduced. | ▶ | (a personal view that can be supported) |

Caution: Opinions that include words like *all, every,* or *always* or words that end in *-est (best, hardest, strongest)* may be hard to support.

| The government should ban all plastic bags. | ▶ | (a personal view that may be hard to support) |

Facts

A **fact** is information that can be checked for correctness. In arguments, facts are used to support claims or opinions.

| Plastic bags litter even remote areas like Antarctica. | ▶ | (a statement that can be checked for correctness) |

Caution: Supporting facts must be accurate and reasonable.

| Jute shopping bags are the only answer to the problem. | ▶ | (an unreasonable statement, providing no real support) |

 Your Turn Decide which statements are opinions and which are facts:
1. Doctors have the most important job in the world.
2. Doctors diagnose illnesses and prescribe medicines.
3. Nursing care is more important than doctor visits.

Using Strong Evidence

The word *evidence* comes from a Latin word meaning "obvious to see." Strong evidence helps someone see the value of a claim or opinion. Some of the important types of evidence are listed below.

- **Facts** are provable statements, and **statistics** are facts that contain numbers.

   Plastic bags are made from oil. *(fact)*

   An Irish tax on plastic bags caused their use to drop by 90 percent. *(statistic)*

- **Examples** show how something works or what happens.

   Plastic bags put many marine animals at risk. *(main idea)* For example, leatherback turtles mistake plastic bags for jellyfish and eat them.

- **Reasons** tell why something is the case.

   Plastic litter harms the environment because it takes a long time to break down and it poisons the soil and water.

- **Definitions** explain new words or concepts.

   The North Pacific Subtropical Gyre, a slow-moving path of currents, is home to the Great Pacific Garbage Patch. Floating plastic makes up a major part of the garbage in the Patch.

- **Quotations** are specific words spoken or written by experts and people in authority.

   "Prohibiting single-use plastic bags in our city will improve the environment," stated Mayor Josh Seikert.

- **Anecdotes** are stories that help explain a main idea.

   One South Sea adventurer made a surprising discovery while exploring a remote island. As he walked toward a hidden beach, he could hear an odd sound and was shocked to see "mountains" of plastic bottles washing up on shore. The sound came from the bottles bumping into one another.

Your Turn

On page 96 you were asked to collect at least two types of evidence to support your claim. Collect one additional type from the list above.

Using Levels of Evidence

A thoughtful argument will contain different levels of detail. One sentence may state a main point, and the next may clarify the point. A third sentence may give an example of the ideas in the second sentence. Each new level of detail makes your argument clearer and more convincing.

Main Point: Some Africans have put discarded plastic bags to good use.

Level 1: They gather thousands of used bags and make products out of them.

Level 2: The products include hats and bags that they weave out of the plastic.

 Your Turn From the evidence you have gathered on pages 96 and 99, write a main point about your topic and support it with a level 1 and level 2 detail. Use the example above as a guide.

Using Quotations

Quotations are the words of others used to explain or support a main point in an argument. A quotation can be the spoken words of an expert or authority, or it can be an idea found in a book, magazine, or Web site. Here are some guidelines for using quotations.

- **Include quoted material** to support your own ideas.
- **Identify the speaker or source** of the quoted material.
- **Place quotation marks around direct quotations**—the exact words as you heard or found them.

> "Prohibiting single-use plastic bags in our city will improve the environment," stated Mayor Josh Seikert.

- **Do not use quotation marks when you use your own words** to explain what you heard or read:

> Mayor Josh Seikert agrees that a single-use policy will reduce waste in the city.

Avoiding Faulty Logic

While effective evidence strengthens an argument, untrue, incomplete, or exaggerated evidence weakens it. The next four pages show examples of weak or faulty evidence. By studying them, you will know what to avoid in your own arguments.

Distorting the Issue

The two examples that follow twist or distort the facts.

■ Exaggerating the Facts

> There is no problem in the world more serious than the overuse of plastic bags.

The overuse of plastic bags is a serious environmental problem, but it is not the most serious problem in the world. What about world hunger, civil wars, or nuclear meltdowns? Exaggeration weakens an argument.

When you hear a surprising or shocking claim, ask yourself if it is exaggerating the facts.

■ Offering Two Extremes

> Either we completely stop using plastic bags soon, or our environment will never be able to recover.

Are there only two choices, either no plastic bags or a doomed environment? Of course not. What this claim ignores is any middle ground, such as greatly reducing plastic-bag use.

When you see or hear an either-or argument, ask yourself if there are really just two choices to consider. Usually, there are more.

Your Turn Search for an exaggeration or an either-or claim in advertisements. (Political ads have many.) Share what you find with your class.

Drawing False Conclusions

To be convincing, an argument needs to draw a fair conclusion from evidence. Avoid the logic problem that follows:

■ Making a Broad Generalization

> Consumers in the U.S. have no idea what trouble they are causing when they use plastic bags.

This statement wrongly groups all U.S. consumers together when, in fact, many consumers are well aware of the environmental troubles caused by plastic bags. In other words, the statement is too broad or inclusive (global). A more specific conclusion would be more convincing.

When a claim groups everyone together, be immediately concerned about its accuracy. Feel more confident about claims that use qualifiers such as *some*, *many*, or *most*.

Misusing Evidence

Some claims misuse evidence, which makes it difficult for the reader or listener to make an informed decision about the topic.

■ Telling Only Part of the Truth

> Substituting paper bags for plastic ones is a great idea because it will help save our environment.

A statement like this tells only half of the truth. Yes, using paper bags may save the environment from so many discarded plastic bags. But it causes another problem: destroying many trees for the paper.

Whenever you are not sure about the truthfulness of a claim, ask yourself if it is telling you the whole story.

 Your Turn Write your own broad generalization or half-truth about a food-related topic. Then share it with the class for discussion.

■ Appealing to a Popular Position

> Clearly, a ban on plastic-bag liners in garbage cans is a great idea because so many people at the environmentalist club support the idea.

The popularity of an idea isn't necessarily proof that it is a good idea. A claim may be misleading or faulty no matter how many people like it.

When a claim asks you to join the crowd, resist. Instead, judge its value for yourself.

Your Turn Think about a new fashion or piece of technology that everyone wants to own. How does popularity pressure you into getting it? How could your reasoning be faulty?

■ Using "If Only" Thinking

> If only plastic bags had never been invented, then our oceans would not be in such trouble.

The problem with an "if only" claim is that it cannot be tested. The situation didn't happen, so we can't know the result.

When you hear such a claim, ask yourself if there is other evidence to back it up. If not, don't accept it.

Your Turn Write your own version of an "if only" claim related to another environmental issue. Then share it with the class for discussion. Consider whether this claim can be tested.

Misusing Language

Statements that include name calling or threatening words mislead the reader or listener rather than make a logical claim.

■ Name Calling

> Many people are really selfish and irresponsible, so they should be fined for using so many plastic bags.

Calling people names often means that the speaker or writer does not have enough strong evidence to support the claim.

When a claim engages in name calling, ask yourself if the person is being reasonable about the topic.

 Find an example of name calling made by a politician or some other person in the news. Share your example with your class for discussion.

■ Using Threatening Language

> People who throw away plastic bags shouldn't be surprised to find their garbage cans emptied on their lawns.

No matter how strongly you feel about a topic, it is never okay to threaten people in order to get your way.

When a claim uses threatening language, keep your distance. The person or group making the claim is not being reasonable.

 With your classmates, discuss different examples of threats and why they are a misuse of language. Agree as a group not to tolerate the use of threatening language.

Argumentation Activities

Use these activities to help you practice different parts of arguments. (Also see the guidelines for a persuasive essay on pages **304–306**.)

Could you support this claim?

As you learned on page **95**, a claim states a position (opinion) that someone tries to prove in an argument. A claim containing a qualifier such as *usually* or *many* is generally more supportable than a claim containing inclusive words such as *all* or *none*. Such words leave no room for exceptions, so they make a claim difficult to support.

Identify each of the claims below as effective or ineffective. Remember that effective claims often contain a qualifier and thus seem reasonable. Ineffective claims leave no room for exceptions and usually seem unreasonable.

- Everyone agrees that our school should reduce recess time.
- Using cell phones should never be allowed during school.
- Students generally benefit from art classes.
- No one reads print newspapers anymore.
- Some dog owners need training more than their dogs do.

Comparing Notes

An argument is only as good as the evidence that supports the claim. Evidence, as you have learned, comes in many shapes and sizes. (See pages **98–99**.) Think of the supporting facts and details as the main ingredients in an argument.

Our best advice: Learn as much has you can about the different types of evidence. This knowledge will help you develop strong arguments and evaluate the arguments of others.

In your social studies or science textbook, find examples of these four types of evidence: a fact, a statistic, an example, and a definition. Identify the page number for each example so that you can share your discoveries with your classmates.

I object!

An argument should address an issue that prompts differing opinions. Otherwise, there is nothing to argue about. As you build an argument, keep the differing viewpoints in mind.

Our best advice: Early in your planning, create a pro-con chart like the one on page **95** to help you identify key points on both sides of an issue. In your argument, counter or concede any key opposing viewpoints. (See page **96**.)

In one paragraph, support your opinion about a television show. (Include at least two or three types of evidence.) In a second paragraph, develop a differing opinion about it.

Special Challenge: Combine the two paragraphs. In your rewrite, counter or concede the opposing viewpoint.

Consider the situation.

When talking or texting with friends, you may exaggerate or distort the truth about many topics. This is only natural. However, such comments will not be suitable in many other situations.

Our best advice: Learn to recognize settings when it is okay to exaggerate or use fuzzy logic and situations when you should be more level-headed and thoughtful in your comments. For example, speak freely and easily at the lunch table, but not when giving an oral report. Then you should be at your logical best.

Think of something you really like. Write a paragraph about it as if you were sharing your ideas with your best friends. Then rewrite the paragraph as if you were reporting on the subject for your class. Afterward, exchange your work with a classmate for discussion. Check each beginning paragraph for examples of faulty logic (see pages **101–104**).

How come the trip
home is the best part
of my school day?

Chapter 8

Succeeding in School

If you have ever asked the question above, something is certainly missing from your school experience. We want to help. Learning can be exciting and fun, believe it or not. This chapter will show you how to improve your attitude, set doable goals, and much more.

You will learn . . .

- Preparing to Learn
- Creating a Positive Attitude
- Completing Assignments
- Maintaining a Daily Planner
- Setting Goals
- Planning Your Time
- Managing Stress

Preparing to Learn

When you are ready to learn, there's a good chance that you will learn. These guidelines will show you how.

- **Get plenty of rest.** With enough sleep, you will be alert and able to learn. With too little sleep, you will find it very hard to concentrate in class.

- **Eat the right foods.** Eating fruits, vegetables, and other healthy food keeps your brain working right so you can think clearly.

- **Get enough exercise.** Being active increases the blood flow to your brain, keeping you alert.

- **Take an interest in your classes.** Find something that interests you in each class. It will make learning much easier.

- **Discuss class work with other classmates.** Collaborating not only makes learning enjoyable but also helps you understand the information better.

- **Get into the right mind-set.** Being relaxed and stress free will help you focus on your work. (See page 114.)

In Focus Practice the four C's—**c**ritical thinking, **c**reative thinking, **c**ollaborating, and **c**ommunicating—to be a strong student. Refer to the four chapters in this book that cover these important skills.

Your Turn Write your own definition of success. Then copy the first dictionary definition for the word "success." Compare the two definitions. Which makes the most sense to you? Why?

IMPOSSIBLE

Creating a Positive Attitude

Being positive means being optimistic or hopeful. These tips will help you be positive about school.

- **Work on your attitude.** Staying positive is not always easy, so make a special effort to look for the good in whatever you face.
- **Set learning goals.** Decide what you want to achieve in a particular class or assignment. (See page 112.)
- **Do your best work.** Feeling good about your performance will help you remain positive.
- **Avoid bad influences.** Even when your friends suggest doing the wrong things, don't do them.
- **Stay on course.** Don't give up, especially if a subject is hard for you. What you learn in one course will connect to others.
- **Adjust your goals as needed.** Change is part of life. If you must adjust a learning goal, do so, and then keep working.

"Success" Stories

The famous people listed below have done some great things. But did you know that they also failed along the way?

Walt Disney created an entertainment empire, but only after one newspaper fired him because he "lacked imagination and had no good ideas." He also started a number of businesses that failed.

Albert Einstein, a scientific genius who established the theory of relativity, didn't speak until he was four and did not read until he was seven. Later, he was asked to leave a technical school.

Emily Dickinson is one of the most recognized poets in American history, but her work went unnoticed during her lifetime. Even so, she wrote more than 1,500 poems.

Oprah Winfrey became one of the most successful television personalities in the world, but not before being fired as a reporter because someone said she was "unfit for TV."

Completing Assignments

To be a successful student, carefully complete your assignments and turn them in on time. Also remember to plan enough time for each assignment. Quality work cannot be rushed.

Being Prepared

- **Understand the assignment.** What is its purpose? What must you do? And when is the work due?
- **Decide how much time you will need** to complete the assignment.
- **Choose the best spot to do your work**—the library, study hall, or someplace at home.
- **Select the best time of day to do homework.** You can't do your best work late at night.
- **Collect the necessary materials**—pen, paper, laptop, textbooks, dictionary, and so on.

In Focus Use a daily planner like the one on the next page if you have trouble keeping track of homework assignments. Write down basic directions for each assignment—what work you must complete, when it is due, and what materials you need.

Working Smart

- **Review the directions** to make sure you understand them.
- **Take short breaks** when you are working on long assignments. With your family's help, create a quiet space at home to complete your work.
- **List any questions** you have about the assignment. Then ask for help.
- **Use good reading and study strategies.** (See pages 118–121 and 132–144.)
- **Take pride in your work,** making it neat and accurate.
- **Turn your assignments in on time,** unless you have permission to extend the due date.

Maintaining a Daily Planner

You can organize your daily tasks by creating a daily planner. The planner can be used as a personal reference, so you can make sure you all your homework is done in time. Here is an example daily planning sheet.

Daily Planner

Date: Thursday, January 17, 2013

School Work

Subject	Assignment	Due date	Progress
Language Arts	Read chapters 4–5 of the *Golden Compass*. Prepare for review questions.	Tomorrow	
Science	Test tomorrow. Study, study, study!	Tomorrow	
Social Studies	Work on the Abraham Lincoln research project.	February 8	
Math	Review notes about dividing by 10's. • Answer questions 1–8 on page 24.	Tomorrow	✓
Other	No homework		

After-School Activities

Choir practice

Long-Term Goals

• Run 3 miles non-stop
• Learn Spanish

Your Turn As a class, discuss the tips on page 110 and the planner above. What tips have you used before? What else can you suggest?

Setting Goals

Setting goals will help you complete big projects, get better grades, and improve your performance in sports and other activities. (Also see pages **240–241**.)

Working on Long-Term Goals

- **Know your limits.** Are you able to build your own computer or remove all plastic bags from the world? Probably not, but you can learn how computers are put together, and you can encourage people to stop using plastic bags.
- **Be prepared.** Schedule time to work on your goal and then follow the schedule. (See the next page.)
- **Keep working.** Take small steps as well as big steps along the way. Every meaningful action will help you reach your goal.
- **Change your plan if your original goal is too challenging**, or if it is too easy.
- **Learn from each project.** Making a plan and following it can be just as meaningful as reaching the goal.

Getting Started

Reva wants to enter a county-wide poster competition. Here is her basic plan for reaching that goal.

> **Main goal:** Submit an excellent poster for a county-wide competition
> - Study the requirements and deadlines.
> - Gather supplies (sketch pad, poster paper, pencils, pastels or markers).
> - Write a slogan; make a sketch of the poster.
> - Create a full-sized version.
> - Submit a final copy on time.

Your Turn Discuss the following questions with your classmates: *What is the value of a plan like the one above? When does a plan become really important? Would you change this plan in any way? If so, how?*

Planning Your Time

Give yourself enough time to reach your goal, and use a weekly planner to make the best use of the time you have. Here is part of Reva's plan for creating a poster for the competition.

Weekly Planner

Time of Day	Activities	Comments
Date: Wednesday 3/20		
After school	Study the requirements and deadlines.	I've got one week.
Evening	Discuss them with Mom; list questions for Ms. Jeagar.	I need to think of a safety theme.
	Check my supplies.	I need new markers and poster paper.
Date: Thursday 3/21		
After school	Discuss the competition with Ms. Jeagar.	
	Ask about supplies.	Get stiff poster board.
Evening	Buy needed supplies and brainstorm for slogans.	
Date: Friday 3/22		
After school	Begin sketching.	Use the slogan "Speak Up for Safety."
Evening	Show Mom; finalize my idea.	

🔍 In Focus Every part of your plan must point toward your goal. (In the next few days, Reva would need to work on a full-sized version of her poster, make a final copy, and submit it on time.)

Managing Stress

The students in the following scenarios are under stress. Stress can cause you to feel nervous, get headaches and stomachaches, or have trouble sleeping.

Susie's grandmother is coming to live with Susie's family for the rest of the year. This means Susie must give up her bedroom and share a room with her older sister. *How will I be able to study or get enough rest with my sister bothering me?* Susie wonders.

Charles loves playing Pee Wee football, but his mom has warned him that if he gets a low grade in any class, he will have to quit the team. Charles is having trouble in his reading class, and he worries every day about getting a poor progress report.

The band at TJ's school is getting ready for its spring concert. TJ really wants to get a solo part, and the director will make her choice after listening to a few of the students play the piece. TJ worries, *How will I ever be able to play better than everyone else at the audition?*

What You Can Do

Here are three ways to deal with a stressful situation.

- **Ask for help.** Talk about the situation with someone you trust.
- **Step away from the situation.** Play with a friend, watch a movie, or get some exercise. This will clear your head and prepare you to face the situation again.
- **Solve the problem.** Consider your problem carefully, think of possible solutions, and try one of them to see how it works. See pages 42–48 for help.

Your Turn Team up with a partner and discuss what advice you would give to Susie, Charles, and TJ.

School-Success Activities

The next two pages provide activities that will prepare you to succeed in school. After trying them, think of other activities and continue practicing.

Preparing to Succeed

Just hoping it will happen will not help you succeed in school. Success requires preparation. Among other things, you must be alert, well rested, and eager to learn.

Our best advice: During the school week, be sure to get enough sleep and exercise, and take care to eat right. If you do these things, you will be ready to learn in school.

Your Turn List each guideline from page 108 (get plenty of rest, eat the right foods, etc.) on a piece of paper. Then rank your performance concerning each tip on a scale of 1 to 5, with 1 meaning poorly prepared and 5 meaning well prepared. Afterward, explain in a paragraph what you have learned about yourself.

Success Stories

Everybody likes to hear about people who have succeeded in spite of problems and failure. Four such stories were included on page 109. History is full of such examples, and others frequently show up in the news media or are shared on Internet social media sites.

Our best advice: During the year, be on the lookout for other success stories that you can share with your classmates. These stories can inspire you and your classmates to become better students, athletes, artists, musicians, and so on.

Your Turn Share a success story with your classmates. For ideas, search the Internet; look in newspapers, magazine, and books; or ask family members.

Dealing with Stress

On page 114, you read three brief stories about students facing stressful situations. Studying stories like these may help you deal with stress in your own life, both inside and outside school.

Our best advice: Do whatever you can to manage stress before it hurts your school performance. Ask for help when you need it.

 Your Turn Think of a book you have read recently or a movie you have seen in which a character faces a stressful situation. In a brief paragraph, explain the character's situation and how he or she dealt with it. Be prepared to share your ideas about this character in class.

Goal Making

Many coaches ask their players to list goals at the beginning of the year. At different points during the season, the players read over their goals to see what progress they've made. Such personal goals usually hold great importance.

Our best advice: Set a few goals for your work in school and other activities at the beginning of the year. With these goals in mind, you can focus your efforts and work toward something definite.

Your Turn List two or three goals that you would like to achieve in your schoolwork or in other activities you care about. At different points during the year, reread your goals to see what progress you've made.

Do squirrels really store food to last through the winter?

Chapter 9
Improving Study Skills

Squirrels work hard to store for the future. In the same way, you can "store" information you'll need later by taking classroom notes and using learning logs. Classroom notes and learning logs help you to understand new subjects, remember important facts, and get ready for tests. This chapter talks about all of this, plus tips for taking tests, and more.

You will learn . . .

- Taking Classroom Notes
- Using a Learning Log
- Preparing for Tests
- Using Test-Taking Skills
- Answering Objective Questions
- Responding to Prompts

Taking Classroom Notes

Note taking is an excellent way to connect with the subjects you are studying. Reserve notebook space for each of your classes, and use the tips below to guide your note taking.

- **Take neat, orderly notes.** The next page shows one way to organize your notes.
- **Label your notes** at the top with the topic, the date, and a page number to keep them in order.
- **Include important information** that your teacher puts on the board or emphasizes during class.
- **Listen carefully for clues** such as "There are four types of . . ." or "Please remember that . . ."
- **Pay attention to new words.** Guess how to spell them if you're not sure. Then circle those words and remember to check their spelling and definition later.
- **Write just the key words or phrases.** If you try to write down everything, you won't be able to keep up. So concentrate on key words and phrases, and capture other ideas in your own words as much as possible.
- **Use pictures, abbreviations, and your own shorthand.** For example, you can use + for "and," u for "you," and # for "number."
- **Read your notes after class** and highlight important facts and details. Fill in any ideas you missed. Reviewing your notes after class will help you to remember what you have learned.

In Focus If picking out the main ideas in a lecture is hard for you, ask for permission to record it. Also take notes. Then check your notes against the recording to see if you missed any important points.

Your Turn Discuss the following questions with a group or in class:
- Why is it important to take neat, orderly notes?
- Why is it important to read over your notes?
- Besides the tip above, how can technology help you with your note taking?

Sample Note Page

The notes below are organized using two-thirds of the page for class notes and one-third for reactions, comments, questions, and extra information.

Europe Exploration (cont'd.) Oct. 2	Page 8
— growth of cities, commerce, and trade led to exploring	
— Renaissance: period of scientific inquiry	
— people interested in outside world	
— rivalries grew between some Euro. nations and Italy	
— trade with the East (India + China)	
— other nations looked for trade routes to compete	What other nations?
— Portugal led, exploring around W. Africa	
— Vasco da Gama finally sailed to Calicut	
— Portugal became wealthy/powerful	
— Columbus wanted to sail west to reach Asia	
— Spain, not Port., interested	Was
— after 6 yrs, earned a command	Columbus
— left with 3 ships in 1492	famous in
— Oct. 12, land sighted	Spain at
— thought it was Asia	the time?
— returned with no riches	
— made 4 trips	

Causes	Effects
— age of inquiry	— reached N.A. continent
— looking for trade routes	— more knowledge of world
— searching for riches	— weakened Native Amer. people + culture
— spreading Christianity	— began exploration of N.A.

Using a Learning Log

While taking notes helps you remember information, writing in a learning log helps you make sense of it. Reserve part of your notebook for learning-log entries, and follow these guidelines.

- **Label and date your entries.**
- **Write often** when studying important subjects.
- **Explore your thoughts and feelings** in the log.
  - Write nonstop for 3 to 5 minutes at a time.
  - Make connections between your notes, your reading, and your own ideas.
  - Ask and answer questions.
  - Pay special attention to challenging concepts.
- **Review your writing** to see if it has helped you understand the information better.

Learning-Log Strategies

Here are four ideas for learning-log entries.

- **Summing up:** Summarize what was covered in a lesson, lab, or class period. Consider what it means and its importance.
- **Predicting:** Between sections in your reading, write to guess what may happen next.
- **Dialoguing:** Make up a conversation between you and another person about the subject.
- **Question of the day:** Answer questions like "What if?" or "Why?" about the subject.

Your Turn Review the guidelines above and the learning-log entry on the next page. Then write an entry about a current math or science subject.

Learning-Log Entry

After a class discussion about the events that led up to European exploration, a student explored his thoughts in this entry.

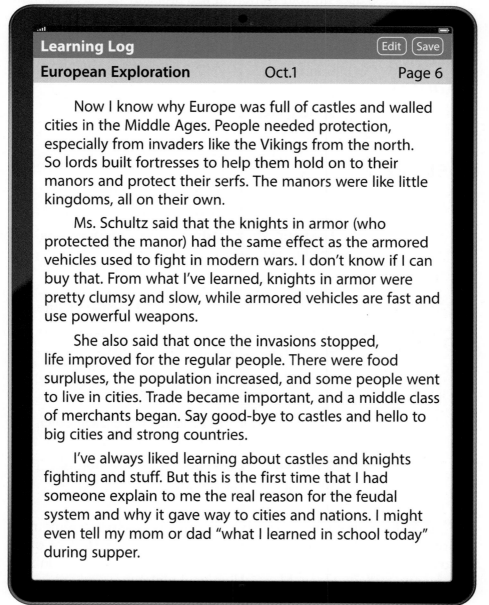

Learning Log [Edit] [Save]

European Exploration   Oct.1   Page 6

Now I know why Europe was full of castles and walled cities in the Middle Ages. People needed protection, especially from invaders like the Vikings from the north. So lords built fortresses to help them hold on to their manors and protect their serfs. The manors were like little kingdoms, all on their own.

Ms. Schultz said that the knights in armor (who protected the manor) had the same effect as the armored vehicles used to fight in modern wars. I don't know if I can buy that. From what I've learned, knights in armor were pretty clumsy and slow, while armored vehicles are fast and use powerful weapons.

She also said that once the invasions stopped, life improved for the regular people. There were food surpluses, the population increased, and some people went to live in cities. Trade became important, and a middle class of merchants began. Say good-bye to castles and hello to big cities and strong countries.

I've always liked learning about castles and knights fighting and stuff. But this is the first time that I had someone explain to me the real reason for the feudal system and why it gave way to cities and nations. I might even tell my mom or dad "what I learned in school today" during supper.

In Focus Blog about your subjects with classmates. Their reactions to your postings can help you understand the information better.

Preparing for Tests

Think of a test as a chance to show what you know. If you pay attention in class and keep up with your work, you will probably have a lot to show. The next few pages explain how to prepare for tests.

Getting Started

Know what the test will cover (topics and information).

Know the form of the test (multiple choice, short answer, essay).

Getting Organized

Make a list of what will be covered on the test.

Organize your notes and handouts.

Get any notes that you may have missed.

Find out which pages in your textbook you need to review.

Getting to Work

Skim all of the material to get the big picture.

Write down questions you need answered.

Review the material more carefully.

Use study aids like graphic organizers or flash cards.

Explain things out loud (or write them down) if that helps you remember.

Study with a classmate or family member. This can help you stay on task.

In Focus Use memory aids such as acronyms to help you remember important facts. Acronyms are spelled with the first letters of other words. **ROY G. BIV**, for example, represents the colors in the rainbow: **r**ed, **o**range, **y**ellow, **g**reen, **b**lue, **i**ndigo, and **v**iolet.

Using Test-Taking Skills

It helps to have a plan in mind when taking a test. Consider these points for what to do before, during, and after.

Before
Come prepared with the right materials and supplies.
Listen carefully to your teacher's directions.

During
Skim the test to get an idea of what you'll be doing.
Carefully follow the directions for each section.
Watch for key words—*always, only, all, never*—in each question.
Answer the questions you are sure of; then move on to the others.
Check the clock occasionally and use your time wisely in order to complete the test.

After
Double-check your work before turning in your test.

Discuss the following questions about preparing for tests:
- Which point above is the most important, and why?
- What other points would you add?
- What should you do if you are not sure of the directions?
- What should you do after your test is handed back to you?

Answering Objective Questions

Objective tests ask you to answer true/false, matching, multiple-choice, and fill-in-the-blank questions. The guidelines that follow will help you answer objective questions.

True or False

Decide if a statement is true or false.

- **Read each statement carefully.** If any part is untrue, then the entire statement is false.
- **Watch for key words** such as *all, every, always,* and *never.* Not many things are *always* true or *never* true.

> <u>False</u> **All** states have county governments.
>
> *(Some states, such as Connecticut, do not have county governments.)*

- **Also watch for words that mean "not,"** and carefully decide how the word affects the meaning of the statement.

> <u>False</u> A U.S. citizen **cannot** live under more than one level of local government.
>
> *(A citizen can be governed by multiple forms of local government.)*

Matching

Connect a word or phrase in one list to a word or phrase in another.

- **Read the directions carefully.** Sometimes choices can be used more than once or not at all.
- **Review both lists before answering.**

> 1. <u>c</u> public works
> 2. <u>a</u> urban planning/zoning
> 3. <u>b</u> emergency management
>
> **a.** deciding how land can be used
> **b.** preparing for and responding to disasters
> **c.** maintaining a city's systems, such as sewer and water

Multiple Choice

Decide which of several answers is correct.

■ **Watch for special answers** that say all responses are correct or none are correct.

> Local governments come in different forms, including . . .
>   **a.** County governments
>   **b.** Township or town governments
>   **c.** Special-purpose governments
>   **d.** All of the above

■ **Watch for words like *not*,** which can completely change the meaning of a question.

> Which statement is **not** true about municipal governments.
>   **a.** States can place restrictions on municipal governments.
>   **b.** A municipal government may contain several departments.
>   **c.** Municipal governments deal with the population of a county.

Fill in the Blank

Write the missing words in a sentence or a paragraph.

■ **Notice the number of blanks.** Usually, each blank stands for one word or answer.

> When Europeans first settled in the United States, only __property__ __owners__ could vote on proposals.
>
> In many states, the two basic tiers of local governments include __county__ and __municipal__ governments.

■ **Watch for articles right before blanks.** The article *a* tells you the next word begins with a consonant sound. The article *an* tells you it begins with a vowel sound.

> A __municipal__ government deals with roads and services in a city.

Responding to Prompts

You may be asked to respond to a prompt by writing a paragraph or short essay. A prompt usually includes three parts that can help you plan your answer: **(1)** It gives background information about the *topic*, **(2)** it tells you to use a particular *form* of writing, and **(3)** it names the *purpose* of your writing.

Sample Prompt

> We've been studying the Great Lakes, and some college students visited the class to speak about Lake Michigan. In a paragraph, explain why these lakes are such a valuable resource. Include at least three or four specific examples.

Your Turn Number and state the three parts of this writing prompt.

Purpose Words

To plan your answer, you need to find the purpose word in the prompt. In the prompt above, you are asked to explain something. Here is a list of common purpose words.

Compare: Show how two things are alike and different.

Contrast: Show how things are different.

Define: Tell what a word or subject means, what category it belongs to, or what it is used for.

Describe: Identify what something or someone looks like, sounds like, feels like, and so on.

Evaluate: Give your viewpoint about the value of something.

Explain: Show how something works or how it happened.

Persuade: Convince the reader to agree with your viewpoint or opinion.

Prove: Show that something is true or false, strong or weak, and so on.

Summarize: Present the main points in a clear, concise form.

Planning and Writing a Response

Planning a response is similar to planning any piece of writing, except for one important point: You have less time.

- **Follow all of the directions supplied by your teacher.** (Notice how much time you have to write your answer.)

- **Consider the parts of the prompt.** You need to know the topic, the form, and the purpose of your writing. (See the previous page.)

- **Write a topic sentence or a thesis statement** for your response, depending on whether you are writing a paragraph or a brief essay. Here is an example topic sentence for a response to the prompt on the previous page.

  > The Great Lakes are one of our most valuable natural resources because they supply so much fresh water.

- **Make a quick list of supporting ideas.**

  - drinking water
  - electrical power
  - recreation
  - commercial shipping

- **Write your response,** starting with your topic sentence. Then include the ideas from your quick list. Add details as needed. End with a closing sentence.

- **Reserve time to review your response** to make sure that your ideas are clear and accurate.

In Focus If you have 30 minutes to complete your response, divide your time this way: 5 minutes for planning, 15 to 20 minutes for writing, and 5 minutes for reviewing.

From Flickr by NASA Goddard Photo and Video

Sample Response

The response below answers the prompt about the Great Lakes. It includes four examples to explain their value.

Prompt

We studied the Great Lakes in chapter 4 of our geography books and watched a documentary about them. In an expository paragraph, evaluate the importance of the Great Lakes as a natural resource. Provide at least three supporting details.

Response

Topic sentence

The Great Lakes are a valuable natural resource because they supply so much fresh water. In fact, the Great Lakes supply 95 percent of the fresh water in the United States. As a result, the drinking water that they supply is their greatest value. In addition, coal-burning and nuclear power plants located on the Great Lakes provide many cities with electricity. How would we ever live without electricity? These lakes also serve as a great source of recreation because many people boat, fish, and swim on them. Recreation and tourism dollars are a great source of income for Great Lakes cities. Finally, huge commercial vessels transport coal, iron ore, and other materials from city to city and lake to lake. Because the Great Lakes are so valuable, citizens must be careful to protect them now and in the future.

Body (supporting sentences)

Closing sentence

Your Turn Using the three-part structure on page 126, write a prompt about a subject you are currently studying. Exchange your work with a classmate and respond to each other's prompt. Discuss the results.

Study-Skills Activities

Use these activities to practice the study skills covered in this chapter.

Listening and Taking Notes

Taking effective class notes requires you to practice good listening skills. As the guidelines on page 118 suggest, always listen for clues like "Remember that . . ." or "The key to this experiment is . . . ." Important information is sure to follow.

Our best advice: To learn the most, take notes regularly in your classes, following the guidelines on page 118. *Remember:* Classroom note taking requires careful listening.

Your Turn Take notes as a partner reads a page from an article supplied by your teacher. Listen carefully and write down the main points. Then reverse roles, reading from a different article. Afterward, discuss the process.

Creating a Conversation

Writing in a learning log is a way of making sense of the subjects you are studying. You can write down your questions, connect the material to familiar ideas, and so on. Page 120 lists strategies for you to try.

Our best advice: Write in your learning log every day, or at least every other day, to discover the value of this activity.

Your Turn Make up a conversation between you and another person (either real or imagined) about a subject you are studying in one of your classes. Keep the conversation going for as long as you can. Use this format:

> **Me:** I learned something really cool today in social studies.
>
> **Older brother:** What might that be?
>
> **Me:** Well, . . .

Test Maker, Test Taker

As you learned in this chapter, each type of objective test question offers a special challenge. For example, you must watch for words like *every, all,* or *never* in true/false questions.

Our best advice: Review pages 124–125 before you take a test with objective questions. And always read each test question carefully.

 Your Turn Write three or four objective test questions about a subject you are studying. Then exchange your work with a partner and answer each other's questions.

A Favorite Prompt

Writing effective responses to prompts takes lots of practice, especially because of the time limit. The key is understanding and following the process described on pages 126–128.

Our best advice: Practice this skill as often as you can because you will be asked to respond to prompts on district and state tests. These practice responses will prepare you for the real thing.

Your Turn Respond to the "practice prompt" below. Before you get started, review pages 126–128. Also ask your teacher how much time you have to complete your response.

Practice Prompt: Think of one of your favorite books, movies, or Web sites. Then describe a specific scene, character, or feature of it in an expository paragraph. Include specific supporting details in your response.

How far is the earth from the moon?

Chapter 10
Reading to Learn

Learning the distance from earth to moon is just one read away. And between books, magazines, and the Internet, you have plenty to read. This chapter will guide you as you learn to read effectively and with purpose—to enjoy yourself, to satisfy your curiosity, and to find good information.

You will learn . . .

- Reading Nonfiction
- Reading Web Sites
- Using Reading Strategies
- Reading Fiction
- Reading Poetry

Reading Nonfiction

Nonfiction sources contain facts instead of made-up stories. Reading nonfiction materials like books, magazines, newspapers, or Web sites is one of the most important ways to learn about new subjects. Use the following plan when you must read nonfiction texts.

Before

Know why you are reading. *(What is your purpose?)*

Skim the selection. Pay attention to headings, bold words, and the beginning and ending parts. *(What is the reading about?)*

Decide when you will read. *(Will you finish the piece in one sitting or in several sittings?)*

During

Use a study-reading strategy such as KWL. (See page 136.)

Take notes. (See page 137.)

Write notes in the margins or highlight phrases, but only if you own the text or are reading a photocopy.

Reread important or challenging parts.

After

Summarize the reading. Focus on its key points. (See pages 288–289.)

Write freely about the piece. *(What did you like about it? How will you use the information?)*

List questions that you still have about the material.

Your Turn One Chinese proverb says, "A book is like a garden carried in a pocket." In a sentence or two, explain what this proverb means. Then, as a class, discuss your explanations.

Nonfiction Page

This page shows a few of the features that are common to nonfiction reading material. (Also see pages 134–135.)

Title
Subtitle
Author

Tour de France
An Introduction to the World's Greatest Cycling Race
By Craig Hill

Cycling has been popular in Europe since the 1800s. Working men everywhere biked to work, and young boys dreamed about cycle racing, much like boys today dream of playing soccer and basketball. The one race that grabbed everyone's attention was the Tour de France, the world's greatest cycling event.

A **heading** tells what will follow.

Early History

The Tour de France was the brainchild of Géo Lefèvre, a journalist with the *L'Auto* magazine. In the early 1900s, popular French magazines sponsored cycle races as a way to boost their subscriptions. Sports enthusiasts would naturally buy the magazines in order to follow the races and the racers.

Lefèvre wanted his magazine to follow this model, and the magazine's editor, Henri Desgrange, agreed. Lefèvre planned to create a very special race, one that was longer and tested riders beyond the limits of other races. The rest, as they say, is history. His race became the "Super Bowl" of cycling.

Bold words share key facts.

The inaugural Tour de France **started on July 1, 1903,** with 60 riders. The race covered **six stages** on six separate days. Because each stage was so challenging, only 21 riders finished. **Maurice Garin won** the first race, averaging over 25 kilometers per hour.

A **heading** predicts special details.

Interesting Facts

The Tour de France places huge demands on the cyclists. Some say that in one race, cyclists exert the emotional and physical energy it takes to participate in multiple Iron Man competitions. The race has changed over time, too. Here are some interesting details about the Tour de France:

Cheating was apparently common in the second Tour de France in 1904. Some riders were physically beaten; others hopped in a car or on a train to gain an advantage. Also, the stages were so long that cyclists rode at night, which made it easier to cheat. Afterward, racing was allowed only during daylight hours . . .

Reading Web Sites

Reading on the Web is a multimedia experience. In addition to reading text, you can follow links to interviews, film clips, maps, and more. Some sites are also interactive, so you can add your own comments or participate in other ways.

Books, newspapers, and magazines are usually reliable, because trained editors check them for accuracy and correctness. Some Web sites, however, may not be checked for accuracy, which can make them less trustworthy. Here are a few points to keep in mind when you use the Web. (Also see page 198.)

What to ask . . .

- **Who is the author?** What experience does this person have? Can you trust him or her?
- **What group or organization sponsors the site?** Can you trust them? Might they have an underlying goal or plan?
- **When was the site last updated?** A site that does not update regularly may share out-of-date information.
- **How accurate is the material?** Compare it to other sources.

What to watch for . . .

- **The site does not name an author or a sponsoring organization.** Without this information, you cannot rely on the accuracy of the material.
- **The writing is hard to follow and contains errors.** Sloppy writing often means sloppy research or sloppy thinking.
- **The information is one-sided.** It does not tell the whole story.
- **The site makes big claims:** "This site will tell you everything you need to know!"
- **The opinions are not supported by facts.** (See pages 101–104.)
- **The language seems unfair, disrespectful, or harmful.**

In Focus Government, education, nonprofit organization, and other professional sites are usually reliable. Their addresses often end with *gov, edu,* and *org.* (See also page 197.)

Web Page

This page shows the typical features of informational Web sites.

The **title** and **introduction** give background information.

Article | Discussion | 🔍 Search

Chickpeas

Chickpeas are an important food source in many parts of the world, including India, Pakistan, Turkey, and Ethiopia. A good source of fiber, protein, and zinc, they are also called garbanzo beans, ceci beans, and chana. Chickpeas have gained special attention in areas that need a durable, sustainable crop. A drought and disease-resistant seed is being grown in Ethiopia.

Contents
Description
History
Preparation
Also see
References

A clickable **contents** list aids navigation.

Description

There are two types of chickpeas: (1) the "kabuli type," large, cream colored, with a regular shape and smooth surface, and (2) the "desi type," irregular and small. Desi color varies from light tan to black, and the plants range from 8 to 20 inches tall. One chickpea pod contains about 2 or 3 beans.

A **graphic** adds interest and clarity.

History

Chickpeas originated in the Middle East 7,500 years ago. Popular with the ancient Romans, Greeks, and Egyptians, they were later introduced to other parts of the world by Spanish explorers. They first appeared in English literature around 600 years ago.

Preparation

Chickpeas are a staple of a vegetarian diet and can be either cooked until soft or roasted until crunchy. They are the main ingredient in hummus, a popular spread, and in falafel, a spicy deep-fried food often served with pita bread. Chickpeas are also used in curries and eaten as a spiced snack.

Related articles provide more information.

Also see

Health benefits of chickpeas
Chickpeas (chana) in India

Information **sources** add authority.

References

Chickpeas, hummus, and falafel
Chickpeas in history

Using Reading Strategies

To understand nonfiction, use active reading strategies such as KWL, note taking, and journal or reading-log entries.

Using KWL

KWL works well when you already know something about the topic. The letters KWL stand for what you *know*, what you *want* to know, and what you *learned*. Here's how the strategy works:

- Name the topic of the reading at the top of your paper. Then make three columns labeled K, W, and L.
- In the first column, write down what you know.
- In the second column, list questions that you hope to answer.
- In the third column, after reading, tell what you learned.

Topic: Ecosystems and the Environment

Know	**W**ant to Know	**L**earned
An ecosystem has something to do with the things in an environment.	What specifically is included in an ecosystem?	An ecosystem is a specific environment and all the living things supported by it.
"Eco" is the first three letters in ecology.	Are the main parts classified in any way?	Biotic factors are the living parts, and abiotic factors are the nonliving parts.
A system means "a how things work together."	What is the difference between ecology and environment?	Ecology studies how living organisms interact in an environment.

Taking Reading Notes

Taking notes is a way of connecting with a text. You can record facts and details, ask questions, or make comments. Use these tips:

- **Use your own words** as much as possible.
- **Write down key phrases** instead of complete sentences.
- **Use abbreviations and symbols**—# for "number," + for "and," w/o for "without," and so on.

Sample Notes

A two-column system uses two-thirds of the page for main notes and one-third for questions and comments.

Introduction of Horses in the Frontier West	March 21
— before horses, Plains and Southwest Indians lived in tribal societies	
— limited hunting and gathering	
— could not travel far	
— Spanish introduced horses in Mexico, early 16th century	
— overpowered natives because of horsemanship	
— first herds in U.S. territory in 1600	
— wild horses in U.S. after Spaniards left New Mexico	
— type of horse thrived in this area	
— small and strong	
— could go long without H_2O	Did Indian
— Apaches first to use horses	children
— rode like Spaniards	get to ride
— improved life	horses, too?

Your Turn Use the two-column notes system for your next reading assignment to see how it works for you.

Writing in a Reading Log

Save space in your notebook for exploring your thoughts and feelings about your reading. This type of writing is especially helpful for understanding long, challenging texts. The following guidelines will help you get started.

- **Label and date your log entries.**
- **Write before, during, and after** your reading.
- **Respond in different ways:** Ask questions, make connections with other ideas, agree or disagree with certain ideas, and so on.
- **Share your reading-log writing** and use it to start conversations with your classmates.

Sample Log Entry

While reading a book about introducing horses to the frontier West, one student responded to the information by writing this log entry.

Introduction of <u>Horses in the Frontier West</u>, March 22, pg. 10

The author said that horses greatly changed the way that Indians lived, and the change was so great, he compared it to the change that computers and the computer chip made in modern life. That comparison really helped me understand how important horses were to Indians in the West.

I never realized that Indians didn't have horses for so long, and that horses made life so different for them. Before horses, they did everything by foot, even hunting buffalo. The only help they had were dogs who could haul small loads. They must have thought that horses were like a miracle sent to them.

Just think of our lives, if we had to walk to do everything and then all of a sudden we had cars, trains, and planes. Wow . . . !

Finding the Main Idea

Your first job when reading your school texts or essays is to pick out the main idea. You will usually find it in the topic sentence of a paragraph and in the thesis statement of an essay.

What the Main Idea Tells You

In *informational* writing, the main idea tells you what the author is going to explain or discuss:

> Horses dramatically changed the lifestyle of Indians in the West.

In *persuasive* writing, the main idea tells you the author's opinion or claim about a topic:

> The Tour de France should be canceled until an effective drug-testing system is in place.

Steps to Follow

Follow these steps to identify the main idea in paragraphs and essays.

1. **Study** the title and the first and last sentence of a paragraph, or the first and last paragraph of an essay.

2. Then **read** the whole paragraph, or the first few paragraphs of an essay.

3. **Look** for the sentence that directs the writing. In a paragraph, it is often the first sentence; in an essay, it is often a sentence at the end of one of the opening paragraphs.

4. **Write down** this sentence.

5. **Read** the paragraph again, or the entire essay, to decide if you have found the correct main idea. The other sentences or paragraphs should support it.

6. *If you have changed your mind,* **write down** the new main idea.

In Focus A paragraph is like a mini-essay. It contains a main idea, supporting details, and a closing thought.

The Main Idea in a Paragraph

The main idea of a paragraph is expressed in the topic sentence, which is underlined in the paragraph below. The remaining sentences in the paragraph provide supporting evidence.

In Focus A main idea has two parts: (1) a topic (peregrine falcon) and (2) an important thought about it (fastest bird in the air).

> The peregrine falcon may be the fastest bird in the air. Its general speed is 40–55 miles per hour, but in pursuit of prey, this falcon can reach a level speed of 65 mph. Then, when it dives (sometimes more than half a mile) to attack its prey, it can reach speeds of more than 200 miles per hour. At that speed, a peregrine falcon can deliver a powerful blow with a half-closed foot. No wonder the Air Force Academy has made the falcon its official mascot.

The Main Idea in an Essay

The main idea of an essay is expressed in the thesis statement, which is underlined in the essay below. The remaining paragraphs in the essay (partially shown) provide supporting evidence.

> Dreams are one of life's greatest mysteries. For centuries, people have tried to figure out why we dream and what our dreams mean. Dream readers even accompanied military leaders during battles. Today, scientists know more, but still not a lot, about dreams.
>
> What scientists do know is that every person dreams every night. In fact, on most nights, people dream several times. . . .
>
> Within five minutes of waking, people forget half of what they have dreamed. Within 10 minutes, they forget 90 percent. . . .
>
> Even with all the breakthroughs in brain science, dreams remain a puzzle to scientists. Why can't people remember dreams . . . ?

Your Turn Use the guidelines on page 139 to find the main idea in paragraphs and essays provided by your teacher.

Identifying Supporting Evidence

An informational text includes supporting evidence to develop its main idea. Identifying and analyzing this evidence will help you understand your reading assignments.

Types of Evidence

Authors use many types of evidence, including facts and statistics, examples, quotations, and definitions. A variety of supporting information can develop the main idea and give the reader a complete picture of a topic. A few types of evidence are examined below. Also see pages 99–100.

Facts and Statistics

Cyclists from France have won the most races with 36 winners.

Examples

The Tour de France places huge demands on the cyclists *(main idea)*. Some say that in one race, cyclists exert the emotional and physical energy it takes to participate in multiple Iron Man competitions *(example)*.

Reasons *(Answering Why?)*

Sports enthusiasts would naturally buy the magazines in order to follow the races and the racers.

Definition

A stage is an individual part of the race, each one carried out on a separate day.

🔍 **In Focus** As an author develops a nonfiction text, he or she will usually include different combinations of supporting evidence. (See the next page.)

Evidence in Action

Parts of nonfiction texts are provided below, with the main ideas and types of evidence labeled in parentheses.

From a Report

Kites have been around for thousands of years, starting in China (main idea). They have been used for fun, for festivals, for science experiments, and for military reasons (facts). Ben Franklin used a kite for his electricity experiment, and the Wright brothers used kites to study flight (examples). Kites need to be light enough to lift up and strong enough to handle high winds (facts). . . .

From an Argument

Eliminating recess would not be a wise move for our school district because it will hurt the students' ability to learn (main idea). Our school administrators say the students need more time on task because we need to improve our performance (fact). But added class time may not be the answer (explanation). Students in Finland outperform students in most countries, and they have more recess time than we do (example). . . .

From an Essay

Africa is a land of many valuable and unused resources, such as farmable land, water, and minerals (main idea). Because of these resources, the African continent should be able to feed all of its people (explanation). In fact, according to a World Health study, if the farmland was used properly, all of Africa, plus all of Europe, could be fed (fact). Sadly, many of the countries in Africa have unstable governments, so there is little or no planning done to use the valuable resources wisely. The leaders spend all of their time trying to stay in power, and the regular citizens fear for their lives either from war or from starvation (explanations). . . .

Your Turn Use the information above and on page 141 to identify the types of evidence used in paragraphs or passages supplied by your teacher. Work with a partner if it is allowed.

Reading Fiction

Fiction is writing that is made up. Although novels and short stories may contain facts, the stories themselves are not real. They are imagined by the author. To get the most meaning out of a book or story, follow the reading plan below.

Before

Learn about the author. Where is the person from? What else has he or she written? Look for this information in the back of the book or online.

Skim the text. Think about the title, review the chapter titles, and read the opening page or two.

Explore your first thoughts in a reading log.

During

Think about the story as you read. What just happened? And what do you think will happen next?

Think about the characters. Why do they act the way they do?

Think about the setting (the time and place of the action). How does it affect the story?

Think about the style. What stands out about the words that the author uses? What confuses you?

After

Consider how the main character changes by the end of the story. Is this change believable?

Decide on the theme or main message in the story. (The theme is like the moral in the story.)

Explore your final thoughts in a reading log.

Your Turn Use the plan above to read your next novel or short story. Afterward, decide if the plan improves your reading experience.

Reading Poetry

A poet named Marianne Moore wrote this definition of poetry: "Imaginary gardens with real toads in them." Poems may come from the writer's imagination, but they are usually rooted in real life. Because poetry is so different from prose, you need to read it in a special way. (Follow the reading plan below.)

Also keep your reading log handy to explore your thoughts and feelings as you read poetry. Doing so will help you understand and enjoy the selection.

Before

Learn about the poet. Where is the poet from? What else has she or he written?

Skim the poem, including the title. What are your first thoughts?

During

Read the poem once for meaning. What does it say to you?

Read it another time for its structure and flow. Is the poem arranged in stanzas? Does the poem flow smoothly from line to line?

Read it a third time for special devices. Does the poet use rhyme, special words, or figures of speech like similes and metaphors?

Reread parts that you really like as well as parts that challenge you.

After

Think about the poem. How do you feel about it? Do you enjoy it more after reading it several times?

Talk about the poem with your classmates.

Your Turn Use the plan above when you read your next poems. Afterward, decide if it improves your reading experience.

Reading Activities

Use these activities to help you practice the strategies included in this chapter.

Worth a Web Visit

As you know, the Web contains many interesting and informative sites. If you search long enough and hard enough, you can learn about almost any topic that interests you.

Our best advice: Take advantage of the Web whenever you need to research a topic for a project or report or to satisfy your curiosity. Remember to check each site for reliability and accuracy before you believe or use the information you find.

Your Turn Find a new Web site that seems especially interesting to you. Then check it for reliability using page 134 as a guide. Share your discoveries with your classmates.

Comparing Notes

Taking notes is one way to identify the important information in a text, including the main ideas and supporting facts and details. In order to be useful, notes must be complete, neat, and easy to follow.

Our best advice: Take notes during your classroom reading assignments. Use the information on page 137 as a guide.

Your Turn Working with a partner, select an article, a Web site, or a chapter to read. Then read it and take notes, following a two-column system. (See page 137.) Afterward, compare notes with your partner. How are they similar and different? What did you learn from the experience?

The Main Idea

Informational texts contain two parts: (1) the main idea (a topic sentence or thesis statement) and (2) supporting evidence. Identifying the main idea and supporting evidence is the key to understanding nonfiction reading material.

Our best advice: Refer to pages 132–135 whenever you are reading a textbook chapter, an essay, an article, or a Web site. The guidelines on those pages will help you find the main idea and supporting evidence in each type of text.

Open to any page in a newspaper and pick one news story to read. Identify the main idea and supporting evidence in the story. If the story is long, work with just the first few paragraphs. Then move on as you have time.

A Novel Approach

Writing can bring understanding as you read. For example, writing about the characters and plot of a novel will help you to comprehend the story's meaning.

Our best advice: Have your reading log handy whenever you are reading fiction or nonfiction. Part of the fun of reading is to interact with the story or text as it unfolds, and a reading log allows you to do this. (See page 138.)

Answer the following questions for the next novel you read:
1. What are you thinking and feeling after reading the first 20 or 30 pages?
2. What are you thinking and feeling after finishing the first half of the book? What do you expect will happen in the second half?
3. What are your thoughts after finishing the book?

Is there a word for
the markings on
a giraffe?

Chapter 11
Improving Vocabulary

Many people refer to the markings on giraffes as spots or patches. There is one kind of giraffe, though, that sports an especially bold pattern of box-like spots. It's the "reticulated" giraffe—now there's a challenging word. Fortunately, this chapter covers five important vocabulary-building strategies that can help you discover the meaning of *reticulated* and any other challenging word you encounter.

You will learn . . .

- Keeping a Vocabulary Notebook
- Using Context
- Using a Dictionary
- Using a Thesaurus
- Understanding Word Parts
- Common Prefixes, Roots, and Suffixes

Keeping a Vocabulary Notebook

A vocabulary notebook is your own personal dictionary. Organizing it subject by subject is a good idea, but feel free to organize your notebook in any way that makes sense to you.

Here are sample entries from a subject-by-subject vocabulary notebook. They include information similar to that found in a dictionary.

Example Words

Math

perimeter (pə-riʹ-mə-tər) ——————————— Pronunciation
- peri (around) + meter (measure) ———— Word parts
- the distance around a closed plane figure —— Definition
- The perimeter of our garden is 50 feet. —— In a sentence
- synonyms: boundary, outline ————— Synonyms
- perimeter of a rectangle formula: P = 2L + 2W

Technology

microblog (mī-kro-blawg)
- micro (small) + blog (online personal writing)
- writing short comments in social media
- Kids in my science club started to microblog about science class.

Social Studies

prejudice (preʹ-jə-dəs)
- pre (before) + jud (judge) + ice (the condition of)
- a negative judgment or opinion made beforehand or without knowledge
- My little sister feels a great prejudice against all bugs.

Your Turn Reserve part of your class notebook for vocabulary study. List new words you need to learn and any words your teacher suggests. For each word, include the type of information shown above.

Using Context

Consider this sentence from a science article: "When the days become shorter, many plants go into dormancy." *Dormancy?* What does that mean? If you don't know, read on. In this case, the next sentence in the article tells you: "A plant that is alive but stops growing during certain seasons is considered to be dormant."

The example above shows how you can figure out the meaning of a word by looking at its context, the words and phrases around the unfamiliar word. Below, you can read about different types of context clues.

■ **Cause and Effect Connections**	In the animal kingdom, *vertebrates* may be in the minority, but their strong internal structure gives them impressive mobility and flexibility.
■ **Definitions Built into the Text**	*Predator* animals, which hunt other animals for food, often have sharp teeth and claws.
■ **Comparisons and Contrasts**	While endothermic animals produce heat within their own bodies, *ectothermic* animals obtain their body heat in a contrasting way.
■ **Words in a Series**	The hawks, falcons, and *shrikes* kept the mice population in check.
■ **Synonyms (words with the same meaning)**	Animals that can *adapt* or change to a new environment will survive.
■ **Antonyms (words with the opposite meaning)**	Fish, being aquatic, live in the water; on the other hand, cats are *terrestrial*.

By yourself or with a partner, define the italicized words above using the clues presented in the sentences. Then check your definitions in a dictionary.

Using a Dictionary

You can always look up new words in either a print or online dictionary. Both types will give you the same information, although the online version may offer an audio pronunciation and hyperlinks to related information.

The key features of a print dictionary are listed below, and a sample dictionary page is included on the next page.

- **Guide words** at the top of the page list the first and last entry on a page. They help you find the page your word is on.

- Each **entry** in a dictionary is in bold type and listed alphabetically.

- The **syllable divisions** show you how to divide a word by syllables.

- **Parts of speech** abbreviations tell how a word can be used. Many words can be used as more than one part of speech.

- **Pronunciations** are included to help you speak the word.

- **Spellings** and **capital letters** are given to help you use words correctly in your writing.

- **Illustrations** offer visual information about words.

- **Accent marks** aid in pronunciation of difficult words.

- **Synonyms** and **antonyms** are provided for some words. (In this way, a dictionary serves as a thesaurus.)

- **Etymology** gives the history of a word. This information will be set off by [brackets].

- A **pronunciation key** serves as a guide to pronouncing words on the page.

Your Turn Look up one word in a print dictionary and in an online version. Identify the similarities and differences in the information you find. Share your discoveries with your classmates.

Dictionary Page

Guide Words —— deep dish
defame

Entry Word ——

Syllable Division ——

deep dish (dēp′dĭsh′) *adj.* Made or used in a deep baking dish.

deep·en (dē′pən) *tr. & intr.v.* **deep·ened, deep·en·ing, deep·ens** To make or become deep or deeper: *More digging slowly deepened the hole. Floodwaters deepened as the rain continued.*

deep-fry (dēp′frī′) *tr.v.* **deep-fried, deep-fry·ing, deep-fried** To fry by immersing in a deep container filled with oil or fat: *deep-fried the chicken wings.*

deep-root·ed (dēp′ro͞o′tĭd *or* dēp′ro͞ot′ĭd) *adj.* **1.** Firmly implanted below the surface: *a deep-rooted oak.* **2.** Firmly fixed; deep-seated: *deep-rooted beliefs.*

Part of Speech ——

deep-sea (dēp′sē′) *adv.* Of or relating to deep parts of the sea: *a deep-sea diver.*

deep-seat·ed (dēp′sē′tĭd) *adj.* **1.** Deeply implanted below the surface: *a deep-seated infection.* **2.** Firmly fixed; deeply rooted; strongly entrenched: *a deep-seated problem of long standing.*

Spelling and Capitalization ——

Deep South A region of the southeast United States, usually made up of the states of Alabama, Georgia, Louisiana, Mississippi, and South Carolina.

deep space *n.* **1.** The regions of space that are beyond the gravitational influence of Earth. **2.** The regions of space that are beyond our solar system.

deer (dîr) *n., pl.* **deer** Any of various hoofed mammals, such as the elk and the white-tailed deer, that chew their cud and usually have antlers in the males. [First written down before 899 in Old English and spelled *dēor* (meaning beast).]

Etymology ——

■ *These sound alike:* **deer, dear** (loved one).

deer mouse *n.* A North American mouse having tan or brown fur, white feet, large ears, and a long tail.

Illustration ——

deer·skin (dîr′skĭn′) *n.* **1.** The skin of a deer. **2.** Leather made from this skin. **3.** A garment made from such leather.

deer mouse

de-es·ca·late (dē-ĕs′kə-lāt′) *tr.v.* To reduce the scale, size, or intensity of: *Calm words de-escalated the crisis.* —**de-es′ca·la′tion** *n.*

Spelling of Verb Forms ——

de·face (dĭ-fās′) *tr.v.* **de·faced, de·fac·ing, de·fac·es** To mar or spoil the surface or appearance of; disfigure: *deface a poster with a crayon.* —**de·face′ment** *n.*

de fac·to (dĭ făk′tō *or* dā făk′tō) *adj.* **1.** Existing in fact but not by official recognition: *housing practices that resulted in de facto segregation.* **2.** Exercising power though not legally established: *a de facto government.*

Pronunciation ——

def·a·ma·tion (dĕf′ə-mā′shən) *n.* The act of making a statement that will damage a person's reputation; slander or libel: *defamation of a person's character.* —**de·fam′a·to′ry** (dĭ-făm′ə-tôr′ē) *adj.*

Accent Marks ——

de·fame (dĭ-fām′) *tr.v.* **de·famed, de·fam·ing, de·fames** To attack or damage the reputation of by slander or libel: *He defamed her good name by spreading false rumors.*

Using a Thesaurus

Always use the best words in your messages. For example, if you are describing a roller coaster, you could say that the cars *race* down the steep slope. It may be more effective, however, to say that they *rip* or *roar* down the slope. A thesaurus is a dictionary of synonyms and antonyms, and it can help you find the best words to use. You'll find both print and online thesauruses.

Print Version

Some thesauruses are organized alphabetically like a dictionary. Others have an index, and you must look up your word there to find which page to turn to. Many words have several different meanings. For example, the word *hit* can mean "strike," "collide," or "accomplish." Look for a synonym with the right meaning for your purpose. (The synonyms for *hit* listed below mean "strike.")

Word Entry

Parts of speech

Entry word ——————→ **hit** *v.* **1** *She hit a double down the left field line.*

Explanations and synonyms ——————→ bang, bat, hammer, knock, poke, punch, rap, slam, slap, strike, swat, whack *n.* **2** *The hit down the line drove in two runs.* blow, clip, knock, lick, poke, punch, rap, slam, slug, stroke, swat

Antonyms ——————→ **antonym:** miss, whiff, fan, strike out

Online Version

You also have many online thesauruses to choose from. Usually, you enter your word in the blank space, click the search box, and wait for synonyms and antonyms to appear. See the example online entry at the left.

Word entry: hit

Part of speech: *verb*

Definition: *strike*

Synonyms: bang, bat, hammer, knock, poke, punch, rap, slam, slap, strike

Your Turn The verb *find*, meaning "to discover," is used often. Use a thesaurus to find two or three synonyms for this verb.

Understanding Word Parts

Words are made up of word parts called prefixes, suffixes, and roots (or base words). For example, the word *microcosm* is made up of two word parts—*micro + cosm*. If you know the meaning of the prefix *micro* (it means "small") and the root *cosm* (it means "world" or "universe"), then you can figure out what *microcosm* means—"a miniature world or universe." (See pages 154–158 for a list of common word parts.)

Example Words

The examples below explain other words and their parts.

Trans·port

Transport combines
- the prefix *trans*, meaning "across"
- and the root *port*, meaning "carry."

So *transport* means "to carry across."

Pre·dic·tion

Prediction combines
- the prefix *pre*, meaning "before,"
- the root *dic*, meaning "say" or "speak,"
- and the suffix *tion*, meaning "act of."

So *prediction* means "the act of saying what will happen beforehand."

Semi·month·ly

Semimonthly combines
- the prefix *semi*, meaning "twice" or "half,"
- the base word *month*, meaning "a unit of about 30 days,"
- and the suffix *ly*, meaning "recurring."

So *semimonthly* means "recurring twice a month."

 Your Turn Choose a computer- or technology-related word. Then, using the glossary on pages 154–158 and a dictionary, identify and define the word parts that make up the word. Afterward, share your work with your classmates.

Common Prefixes, Roots, and Suffixes

The next pages list common prefixes, roots, and suffixes. When you are not sure of a new word, try to figure out its meaning by studying its parts.

Prefixes

Prefixes come before roots, or base words, to form new words. A list of common prefixes follows.

ambi, amphi *(both)* amphibious *(on both land and sea)*

ante *(earlier)* antedate *(to be of an earlier date)*

anti *(against)* antibiotic *(a substance fighting against disease)*

astro *(star)* astronomer *(studier of the stars and planets)*

auto *(self)* autocrat *(ruler with unlimited self-rule)*

bi *(two)* bisect *(to cut into two equal parts)*

circum *(around)* circumvent *(to avoid or get around something)*

dia *(through, across)* diameter *(a straight line passing through the center of a circle)*

epi *(upon, above, outer)* epicenter *(the point of the earth directly above the focus of an earthquake)*

ex *(out)* excavate *(to dig or hollow out)*

extra *(outside, beyond)* extrasensory *(outside the normal range of the senses)*

fore *(before, earlier)* foresee *(to see or know before)*

hemi *(half)* hemisphere *(half of a sphere or half of the human brain)*

hyper *(over)* hypercritical *(overly critical)*

in, im *(not)* improbable *(not probable)*

inter *(between)* interstate *(connecting or between two states)*

intra *(within)* intranet *(a network within the private control of a person)*

macro *(large)* macroclimate *(the climate of a large area)*

mal *(bad, poorly, or wrongly)* malformed *(poorly formed)*

micro *(small)* microcircuit *(a very small circuit)*

mono *(one)* monopoly *(control by one group)*

non *(not)* nonflammable *(not easily set on fire)*

over *(above, more, or too much)* overcharge *(to charge too much for something)*

poly *(many)* polygraph *(an instrument measuring many body actions)*

post *(after)* postwar *(a period of time after a war)*

pre *(before)* predict *(to make known before or in advance)*

re *(again, back)* readjust *(to adjust again)*

semi *(half or occurring twice)* semiautomatic *(partly automatic)*, semimonthly *(occurring twice a month)*

sub *(under)* subway *(an underground railroad)*

trans *(across, beyond)* transatlantic *(crossing the Atlantic Ocean)*

tri *(three)* triad *(a group of three)*

un *(not)* unreal *(not real)*

under *(below)* undercurrent *(a current beneath a surface)*

uni *(one)* unicellular *(having one cell)*

Roots

Roots serve as the base or starting point for most words. A list of common base words follows.

alter *(other)* alternative (*a different choice*)

anni, annu, enni *(year)* anniversary (*yearly event*), annual (*once a year*), biennial (*lasting two years*)

anthrop *(human being)* anthropologist (*someone who studies the development of humans*)

aster *(star)* asteroids (*irregularly shaped bodies orbiting the sun*)

aud *(hear, listen)* audiology (*the study of hearing*)

bibl *(book)* bibliography (*list of books*)

bio *(life)* biosphere (*the part of earth in which living things exist*)

chrom *(color)* chromatic (*of or relating to colors*)

chron *(time)* chronology (*the science dealing with the order of events*)

cise *(cut)* incise (*to cut into or mark*)

claim *(cry out)* proclaim (*to announce or declare*)

cor, card *(heart)* coronary, cardiac (*relating to the heart*)

corp *(body)* corporation (*relating to a business group or body*)

cosm *(universe, world)* microcosm (*a miniature world*)

cred *(believe)* incredible (*unbelievable*)

cycl, cyclo *(wheel, circular)* cyclical (*occurring in cycles*), cyclone (*strong circular wind*)

dem *(people)* epidemic (*an outbreak of a disease spreading among the people*)

dent *(tooth)* dentist (*a person trained to work on teeth*)

derm *(skin)* epidermis (*outer layer of skin*)

dic, dict *(say, speak)* dictate (*to say or read aloud to be recorded or written by another*), contradict (*to speak against*)

dynam *(power)* dynamic (*marked by intensity and power*)

equi *(equal)* equilateral (*having all sides equal*)

fact *(do, make)* manufacture (*to make things*)

fin *(end, ended)* final (*occurring at the end*)

flex *(bend)* reflex (*bending back*)

flu *(flowing)* fluid (*a substance that flows easily*)

fort, forc *(strong)* fortify (*make strong*), forceful (*strong, full of force*)

fract, frag *(break)* fragile (*easy to break*), fracture (*a break*)

gen *(birth, produce)* genetics (*study of birth traits*)

geo *(earth)* geology (*study of the structure of the earth*)

grad *(step, go)* gradual (*step by step*)

graph *(write, written)* autograph (*a person's own signature*)

greg *(group, herd)* congregate (*to come together in a group*)

hab, habit *(live)* habitat (*the area in which animals or plants normally live*)

hetero *(different)* heterogeneous (*consisting of parts that are not alike*)

homo *(same)* homogeneous (*of the same or similar kind*)

hum *(earth)* humus (*earth or dirt*)

hydr, hydro, hydra *(water)* hydroelectric (*generating electricity using water*), hydrant (*an upright pipe fitted with a valve to draw water*)

ject *(throw)* eject (*to throw out or force out*)

leg *(law)* legislator (*a member of a government body that makes laws*)

liber *(free)* liberation (*the process of setting free*)

log *(word, study, speech)* logic (*the study of thinking and reasoning*)

lum *(light)* illuminate (*to provide with lights*)

magn *(great)* magnify (*to make something appear larger*)

man *(hand)* manacle (*handcuffs*)

mania *(insanity)* pyromania (*insane urge to start fires*)

medi *(middle, between)* median (*located in the middle*)

mega *(great)* megabit (*one million bits*)

mem *(remember)* memorial (*something that serves as a remembrance*)

meter *(measure)* thermometer (*an instrument that measures temperatures*)

migra *(wander)* migrant (*a creature that travels*)

mit, miss *(send)* transmit (*send across*), missile (*suited for launching or sending off*)

mob, mot *(move)* mobilize (*to move or gather together*), promotion (*moved ahead or advanced*)

mort *(death)* mortal (*subject to death*)

nat *(to be born)* native (*belonging to by birth or origin*)

neur *(nerve)* neurology (*study of the nervous system*)

nov *(new)* novice (*a person new to an activity*)

numer *(number)* numeral (*a symbol or mark representing a number*)

omni *(all, completely)* omnipotent (*all-powerful*), omnivore (*an organism that eats both plants and animals*)

onym *(name)* synonym (*a word having the same meaning as another word*)

pac *(peace)* pacifist (*a person who believes in peace*)

pater, patr *(father)* patriarch (*father and head of family or clan*), paternal (*characteristic of a father*)

ped *(foot)* pedestrian (*foot traveler*)

pend *(hang, weigh)* pendant (*a hanging ornament, often linked to a necklace*)

phil *(love)* philosophy (*love of wisdom*)

phobia *(fear)* arachnophobia (*fear of spiders*)

phon *(sound)* telephone (*an instrument that sends sounds*)

photo *(light)* photoelectric (*electrical effects caused by light*)

pop *(people)* populate (*to supply with people*)

port *(carry)* portable (*easy to carry*)

proto *(first)* prototype (*an original or first example of something*)

psych *(mind, soul)* psychology (*the study of mental processes*)

rupt *(break)* interrupt (*to break into a conversation*)

sci *(know)* scientist (*someone who is an expert in a scientific field*)

scope *(see, watch)* microscope (*an instrument that magnifies objects*)

scrib, script *(write)* scribble (*to write in a rush*), inscription (*the act of writing, printing, or carving on a surface*)

sen *(old)* senior (*older person*)

sequ, secu *(follow)* sequence (*following of one thing after another*), consecutive (*following in order*)

soph *(wise)* sophisticated (*having acquired more knowledge or refinement*)

spect *(look)* inspect (*to examine carefully*)

sphere *(ball)* hemisphere (*half of the earth*)

spir *(breath)* respiration (*the act or process of breathing*)

strict *(tighten)* constrict (*draw tightly together*)

tag *(touch)* contagious (*transmitted by contact*)

tele *(far)* tel<u>e</u>phone (*an instrument that sends sounds far away*)

tempo *(time)* tempo<u>r</u>ary (*bound by time*)

tend, tens *(stretch, strain)* ex<u>tend</u> (*to make longer*), <u>tens</u>ile (*relating to or capable of being stretched*)

terra *(earth)* <u>terra</u>in (*an area of land*)

therm *(heat)* <u>therm</u>al (*of or relating to producing heat*)

tom *(cut)* ana<u>tom</u>y (*the dissection or cutting of a plant or an animal for study*)

tox *(poison)* anti<u>tox</u>in (*acting against a poison*)

tract *(draw, pull)* at<u>tract</u> (*to cause to draw near*)

typ *(print)* <u>typ</u>ography (*the arrangement and appearance of printed material*)

vac *(empty)* e<u>vac</u>uate (*to remove or make empty*)

vert, vers *(turn)* re<u>vers</u>e (*turn back*), intro<u>vert</u> (*turn inward*)

vid, vis *(see)* <u>vid</u>eo (*visual recording*), <u>vis</u>ible (*possible to see*)

viv *(alive, life)* sur<u>viv</u>e (*to stay alive*)

voc *(call)* in<u>voc</u>ation (*the act of appealing or calling for help*)

vor *(eat)* herbi<u>vor</u>ous (*plant-eating*)

zo *(animal)* <u>zo</u>ology (*study of animal life*)

Suffixes

Suffixes come after base words to form new words. A list of common suffixes follows.

able *(capable of or able)* mov<u>able</u> (*capable of being moved*)

age *(collection, act or result of)* mile<u>age</u> (*the collection or number of miles*), slipp<u>age</u> (*the result of slipping*)

al *(of, relating to)* season<u>al</u> (*relating to the seasons*)

an, ian *(born into, of or relating to)* Afric<u>an</u> (*born into Africa*), Hercule<u>an</u> (*of or relating to Hercules*)

ant *(a person or thing performing an action)* deodor<u>ant</u> (*something that performs or acts against odor*)

ary, ery, ory *(act of or relating to, connect with)* diction<u>ary</u> (*relating to a dictionary*), brib<u>ery</u> (*the act of bribing*)

ate *(characterized by or to act upon)* isol<u>ate</u> (*the act of setting apart*)

cide *(killer of)* insecti<u>cide</u> (*a chemical killer of insects*)

cy *(state, condition, quality)* bankrupt<u>cy</u> (*the state or condition of being bankrupt*)

dom *(condition, state)* serf<u>dom</u> (*the state of being a serf*)

ee *(a person who receives or benefits from)* train<u>ee</u> (*someone who benefits from training*)

en *(to cause to be or resembling)* strength<u>en</u> (*to cause to be stronger*), wood<u>en</u> (*resembling wood*)

ence *(state of or quality)* occurr<u>ence</u> (*the state of having occurred*)

er, or *(a person or thing that does something)* teach<u>er</u> (*someone who teaches*), act<u>or</u> (*someone who acts*)

escent *(beginning to or becoming)* lumin<u>escent</u> (*becoming light*)

ese *(relating to a certain place)* Chin<u>ese</u> (*relating to China*)

ess *(female)* princ<u>ess</u> (*female royalty*)

fy, ify *(to make or cause to become)* simpl<u>ify</u> (*to make simpler*)

ful *(full of)* wonder<u>ful</u> (*full of wonder*)

hood *(condition or quality)* false<u>hood</u> (*the condition or quality of being untrue*)

ic *(relating to, having)* atom<u>ic</u> (*relating to the atom*)

ion, sion, tion *(act of, result of)* forma<u>tion</u> *(the act of forming)*, preci<u>sion</u> *(the result of being precise or exact)*

ish *(of or relating to)* Swed<u>ish</u> *(of or being from Sweden)*

ism *(state of, characteristic, quality)* critic<u>ism</u> *(state of being critical)*

ist *(one who)* lobby<u>ist</u> *(someone who lobbies the government)*

ity *(quality or condition)* clar<u>ity</u> *(the quality of being clear)*

ive *(tending toward or becoming a certain act)* disrupt<u>ive</u> *(tending toward causing trouble)*

less *(without, lacking)* name<u>less</u> *(without a name or an identity)*

ling *(a person connected with, something or someone that is small)* earth<u>ling</u> *(someone connected with the earth)*, duck<u>ling</u> *(a small or young duck)*

ly *(having characteristics of, recurring, or in a specified manner)* brother<u>ly</u> *(having the characteristics of a brother)*, hour<u>ly</u> *(recurring on the hour)*

ment *(act of, state of)* govern<u>ment</u> *(act of governing)*, amaze<u>ment</u> *(state of being amazed)*

ness *(state, condition, quality)* bright<u>ness</u> *(state of being bright)*

ology *(study of)* hyd<u>rology</u> *(the scientific study of water)*

osis *(condition, process)* tubercul<u>osis</u> *(the condition of being tubercular)*

ship *(condition, quality of)* companion<u>ship</u> *(the condition of being a companion or friend)*

some *(apt, like, leading to)* lone<u>some</u> *(leading to loneliness)*

ward *(in a direction, toward)* down<u>ward</u> *(toward a lower place)*

y *(inclined, tending to)* mess<u>y</u> *(inclined to messiness)*

🔍 **In Focus** A word can belong to a family of words, which can help you figure out its meaning. For example, *trouble* means "a state of distress, need, or danger": *The mountain climber was in **trouble** and needed help.* So knowing the word *trouble* gives you a better chance of understanding other words in the same family, like *troublemaker, troublesome, troubleshooter,* or *trouble spot*.

Vocabulary Activities

The activities on the next two pages will help you work on your vocabulary-building skills.

Words at Work

Using context clues helps you (1) define new words and (2) read more effectively. (See page 149.)

Our best advice: Get into the habit of using context clues when you are reading. But also look up difficult words in a dictionary.

 Use context clues to define the italicized words in the following sentences. Then check your definitions against those provided in a dictionary.

1. Humpback whales are very playful. For example, they are often seen *breaching*, lifting their bodies almost completely out of the water.
2. It's hard to say how whales find their destinations. They may rely on hearing sound waves that bounce off the ocean *topography*.

Hail to the Dictionary!

As you learned on pages 150–151, the dictionary shares valuable information about words—meanings, pronunciations, spellings, histories, and more. Whenever you have a question about a word, you can count on the dictionary for an answer.

Our best advice: Always have a dictionary on hand when you are working on a project, reading, or writing.

 Turn to any page of entry words in a print dictionary and answer the following questions:

1. How many of the words are familiar to you?
2. How many of the words are unfamiliar?
3. Name one thing you learned about a familiar word and one thing you learned about an unfamiliar word.

Be Specific

Do not overuse words like *old, pretty, small, big, good, bad,* and *nice.* These words don't say enough, and you can easily replace them with specific, interesting synonyms. Just check a thesaurus. (See page **152**.)

Our best advice: When you revise a report or story, look for words that are too general or overused. Then replace at least some of them with more specific alternatives.

Rewrite each sentence below, substituting a specific synonym for the underlined word.
1. Manny needs to replace his <u>old</u> baseball glove.
2. Every morning, squirrels <u>go</u> across the street.
3. My grandmother <u>goes</u> two miles to the nearest grocery store.
4. On summer evenings, night hawks and bats <u>fly</u> above our neighborhood.
5. Josie painted a <u>pretty</u> mural on the cafeteria wall.

Words Need Roots

The core of a word is its root, which delivers the main meaning. Prefixes and suffixes are very important because they affect the word's meaning. However, without the base word, there is no meaning to affect.

Our best advice: From time to time, study the glossary of prefixes, suffixes, and roots on pages **154–158**. Beginning with the roots, you will learn a lot about the English language.

Along the left-hand margin of a piece of paper, list five roots from pages **155–157**, skipping six or seven lines after each one. Underneath each root, list four words that are formed from it. (Do not list the ones included in *Inquire*.) Then briefly define each word.

Chapter 12
Following Basic Conventions

Before your writing is finished, you need to look at it for conventions—spelling, punctuation, capitalization, word usage, and so on. When you follow basic conventions, you give your reader the best chance of understanding your message. This chapter explains these rules and gives examples of each one.

You will learn . . .

- Using Basic Punctuation
- Following Proper Mechanics
- Understanding Commonly Confused Words
- Using Complete Sentences

Using Basic Punctuation

Punctuation marks serve as road markers to help the reader know when to start, pause, or stop in a piece of writing. The next two pages list 10 essential rules to follow.

Rule 1: Place a period after a statement that expresses a complete thought.	I tried a brussels sprout yesterday**.**
Rule 2: Place a question mark after a sentence that asks a question.	Do dogs ever get colds**?**
Rule 3: Place a single exclamation point after a word, a phrase, or a sentence to show strong emotion.	**Unnecessary:** The Cubs are World Series champs**!!!!!!!!** **Correct:** The Cubs are World Series champs**!**
Rule 4: Use a comma before a connecting word (*and, but, or, nor, yet, so, for*) that joins two or more simple sentences into a compound sentence.	Mountain lions have not been seen in the Midwest for a long time**, but** they are slowly returning.
Rule 5: Place commas between three or more items (*words, phrases,* or *clauses*) in a series.	People share personal messages**,** funny photographs**,** and music playlists on Facebook.

Rule 6: Use commas in large numbers (1,000 and up) but not in years.	Heinz Stücke started pedaling his bike in **1962**. He has traveled **593,625** kilometers, or **368,861** miles, through **257** countries.
Rule 7: Use a semicolon to join two or more closely related simple sentences.	My dentist seems like a nice person; I just don't like his drill.
Rule 8: Use an apostrophe to show possession—add an apostrophe and an *s* to most singular nouns, an apostrophe to plural nouns ending in *s*, and an apostrophe and an *s* to plural nouns not ending in *s*.	**Singular noun:** Jesse**'s** painting captures the storm**'s** fury. **Plural noun ending in *s*:** My textbook**s'** covers need repair. **Plural noun not ending in *s*:** The children**'s** dictionaries are new.
Rule 9: Use quotation marks to set off spoken words in dialogue and for titles of songs, poems, short stories, articles, and specific Web pages. But underline or italicize titles of books, magazines, and newspapers. Periods and commas are placed inside closing quotation marks.	"Whatever you are, be a good one," said Abraham Lincoln. Abraham Lincoln said, "Whatever you are, be a good one." My brother just read <u>Lord of the Rings</u>. "How Healthy Is Your Ocean?" is an interesting article.
Rule 10: Use a colon to introduce a list. The colon sometimes follows summary words like *the following*.	Our part of the city has been invaded by the following: raccoons, coyotes, and deer.

Following Proper Mechanics

The rules of mechanics deal with capitalization, plurals, abbreviations, and spelling. Here are 10 important mechanics rules.

Rule 1: Capitalize proper nouns and words used as names. A proper noun names a specific person, place, thing, or idea.

Jimmy Donal Wales helped start **Wikipedia**, the free online encyclopedia.

Rule 2: In titles, capitalize the first word, last word, and words in between except for articles (*a, an, the*), short prepositions (*of, in, with*), and connecting words (*and, but, or, nor, for, so, yet*).

The movie *The Chronicles of Narnia* was distributed by **Walt Disney Pictures**.

Rule 3: Capitalize the names of races, languages, nationalities, and religions, whether the words are used as nouns or adjectives.

Islam is the dominant religion in **Turkey**. About 96 percent of the **Turkish** people are **Muslim**.

Rule 4: Capitalize geographic place-names. This includes continents, countries, states, counties, cities, bodies of water, landforms, and public areas.

The **Mississippi River** is a major river flowing in the **United States**. It stretches from **Minnesota** to the **Gulf of Mexico**.

Rule 5: To form plurals of most singular nouns, add *s*. If the noun ends in *ch, s, sh, x,* or *z,* add *es*. If the noun ends in a consonant and a final *y,* change the *y* to *i* and add *es*.

The **ladies** who manage our cafeteria serve two **meals** a day. For each meal, we can choose from at least two main **dishes**.

Rule 6: Use words for numbers *one* through *nine*, and use numerals for numbers 10 and above.	There are **eight** major planets in the solar system. The diameter of earth (along the equator) is **12,756** kilometers.
Rule 7: Use a combination of numerals and words for very large numbers.	The Milky Way contains about **300 billion** stars.
Rule 8: In school-related writing assignments, spell out words except for titles and abbreviations such as these: *Mr., Mrs., Ms., Dr., Jr., a.m., p.m.*	Our meeting with **Dr.** Nelson is scheduled for 6:00 **p.m.**
Rule 9: Use the *i* before *e* spelling rule except when the two vowels come after *c* or when they sound like *a*, as in *weight* or *freight*.	We **received** orders to **relieve** the flight attendants after they'd served **eight** hours.
Rule 10: Use the silent *e* spelling rule. If a word ends with a silent *e*, drop the *e* before adding a suffix that begins with a vowel: *bike—biking; type—typing.*	We are **hiking** up an **unbelievably** beautiful mountain trail.

Understanding Commonly Confused Words

You may not be sure when to use *your* or *you're*, or *its* or *it's*. The next two pages will help you make the right choice concerning a number of commonly confused words.

Rule 1: bring, take
Bring refers to movement toward the speaker or writer; *take* refers to movement away from the speaker or writer.

Please **bring** me an empty bowl; then **take** this bowl of hickory nuts to your grandmother.

Rule 2: their, there, they're
Their is a possessive pronoun, *there* is an adverb that tells where, and *they're* is the contraction of "they are."

The two teams over **there** are practicing **their** plays. **They're** getting ready for the big game.

Rule 3: to, too, two
To (preposition) shows movement toward a place and also forms an infinitive verb *(to read)*. *Too* (adverb) means "also," "very," or "excessively." *Two* is the number 2.

We needed **two** boats for the trip **to** the island because there were **too** many of us **to crowd** into one.

Rule 4: than, then
Than is used in a comparison; *then* refers to time.

I like the new edition of the game more **than** the old one. Study the directions; **then** you'll understand the changes.

Rule 5: it's, its
It's is the contraction of "it is" or "it has." *Its* is a possessive pronoun.

It's sad that the town lost **its** funding for the public pool.

Rule 6: fewer, less *Fewer* refers to countable units *(fewer pies)*; *less* refers to value, degree, or bulk quantity *(less energy, less water)*.	If we have **less** money, we will buy **fewer** gifts.
Rule 7: affect, effect The verb *affect* means "to influence." The noun *effect* means "the result."	The flu **affected** everyone in my family; the **effect** was a week of misery.
Rule 8: capital, capitol The noun *capital* refers to a city or money. *Capitol* always refers to a building.	Madison is the **capital** of Wisconsin. Visit its **capitol** to see some stunning architecture.
Rule 9: good, well *Good* is always an adjective *(a good idea)*. *Well* is almost always an adverb; but as an adjective, *well* indicates a state of health *(I am well)*.	The rehearsal for our concert went **well**; let's hope for a **good** performance tomorrow.
Rule 10: past, passed *Passed* is the past tense of the verb "pass" and means "went by." *Past* is a noun or an adjective referring to a time gone by.	The sprinter easily **passed** all of her opponents and gave a stronger performance than in any of her **past** races.

Using Complete Sentences

Sentences share your ideas, so they need to be correct. The next three pages will help you write complete, correct sentences.

Sentence Basics

- A **sentence** is one or more words that state a complete thought.

> I want to learn about old buildings in my town.

- A sentence must have a **subject** and a predicate.

The **subject** is the part of the sentence that is doing something or about which something is being said.	**The oldest house** was built in 1840.
The predicate is the part of the sentence that says something about the subject.	The oldest house **was built in 1840**.

- The **subject** and predicate (the verb) must agree in number.

If you use a **singular subject**, you must use a singular verb.	**Jessie** lives in a cobblestone house.
If you use a **plural subject**, you must use a plural verb.	My **grandparents** own the oldest gas station in town.
If the **subject** is a word such as *everything, somebody,* or *anyone,* use a singular verb.	**Everybody** learns about science and math in school.
With the subjects *all, any, half, most, some,* or *none,* check the noun in the prepositional phrase that comes between the subject and the verb. If the noun is plural, use a plural verb. If it is singular, use a singular verb.	**Most** of the old buildings look very small. **Half** of my research comes from old books.

Common Sentence Errors

Fragments

A **sentence fragment** is a group of words that is missing a subject, a verb, or both. A fragment does not express a complete thought.

Incorrect: Sleep a lot. *(missing subject)*

Correct: Dogs sleep a lot.

Incorrect: Our dog food three times a day. *(missing verb)*

Correct: Our dog **gobbles** food three times a day.

Comma Splices

A **comma splice** occurs when two simple sentences are connected with only a *comma* and no connecting word.

Incorrect: Mr. Cosford worked for a tractor company, he operated a huge crane. *(comma splice)*

A comma splice can be corrected by forming two sentences, by using a semicolon, or by adding a coordinating conjunction.

Correct: Mr. Cosford worked for a tractor company. He operated a huge crane.

Correct: Mr. Cosford worked for a tractor company; he operated a huge crane.

Correct: Mr. Cosford worked for a tractor company, **and** he operated a huge crane.

Run-Ons

A **run-on sentence** occurs when two or more simple sentences are connected without punctuation or a connecting word.

Incorrect: Fishing season starts tomorrow my casting rod is all set.

Correct: Fishing season starts tomorrow. My casting rod is all set.

Correct: Fishing season starts tomorrow, **and** my casting rod is all set.

Rambling Sentences

A **rambling sentence** goes on and on, connecting many short ideas with "ands" and "buts." To correct this, rearrange the ideas contained in the sentence, making shorter sentences that use only the necessary "ands" and "buts."

Rambling: Walter Deer grew up on a farm in the early 1900s and he had it hard because he had to do chores every morning before going to school and at night after returning home and during the harvest he had to stay home from school the entire day and help in the fields and during his junior year in high school his dad made him quit school to work permanently on the farm.

Improved: Life was not easy for Walter Deer. He grew up on a farm in the early 1900s and had to do chores every morning before going to school and every night after returning home. During the harvest, he had to stay home from school the entire day to help in the fields. Sadly, when Walter was a junior in high school, his dad made him quit school to work permanently on the farm.

Double Subjects

A **double subject** occurs when a noun subject is followed immediately by a pronoun. To correct the error, drop either the pronoun or the noun, but not both.

Incorrect: Jakira she always reads fantasy novels.

Correct: Jakira always reads fantasy novels.

Double Negatives

A **double negative** occurs when two negative words are used in the same clause.

Incorrect: We **don't** have **no** tall boys in our school.

Correct: We **don't** have **any** tall boys in our school.

Conventions Activities

Use these activities to review the basic rules for punctuation, capitalization, word use, and sentences.

Traffic Signals

Writer Patricia T. O'Conner compares punctuation marks to traffic signals. For example, she compares periods to red lights because they signal a full stop, and commas to yellow lights because they signal only a pause. Ms. O'Conner does this to help people remember how and when to use different punctuation marks.

Our best advice: Use punctuation marks to guide your reader through your writing.

Write your own sentences to show how to use the punctuation marks discussed in rules **1–7** on pages **162–163**. Then have a classmate check your sentences. Correct any errors.

Showing Ownership

Apostrophes are used in contractions like *don't, isn't,* and *haven't.* They are also used to show possession. Rule **8** on page **163** discusses how to form both singular and plural possessives.

Our best advice: Carefully study rule **8** for a basic understanding of how to use an apostrophe to show possession. Also pay attention to words with apostrophes as you read books and articles.

Write a sentence for each of the following nouns, using it in its possessive form. Afterward, have a classmate check your sentences. Then correct any errors.

mother	coaches	laptop
friends	bus	bikes
teammate	cats	

Using Titles

When you write a book review or a research report, you must give credit to the sources of the information you use in your writing. As a result, you need to know how to punctuate and capitalize titles. (See pages **163** and **164**.)

Our best advice: Pay special attention to the capitalization and punctuation of titles in newspapers, magazines, and online articles.

 Follow the directions below to write four sentences. Afterward, ask a classmate to check your capitalization and punctuation. Then correct any errors.

Write a sentence including the title or name of . . .
- your favorite movie.
- a book you've recently read.
- a favorite song.
- an online article.

Fixing Run-On Sentences

Readers may stop reading if they cannot understand your writing. That is why it is so important to write complete, correct, easy-to-follow sentences.

Our best advice: Before turning in your writing, check it for run-on sentences, comma splices, and sentence fragments. (See page **169**.)

Write four run-on sentences, each one describing a vacation you have taken or would like to take. (For example: My mom drove us to the Grand Canyon we rode mules down the winding path to the bottom.) Exchange your work with a partner and correct each other's sentences.

Do you know what you're looking at?

Chapter 13
Improving Viewing Skills

From shooting stars to your own backyard and beyond, there is much to see in this world. Visual images bombard us constantly—in charts and graphs, photographs and posters, artwork and advertisements. Because these images are everywhere, it's important to understand what they mean. This chapter can guide you as you develop your visual literacy.

You will learn . . .

- An Introduction to Visual Literacy
- Active Viewing
- The Basics of Visual Design
- Understanding Symbols
- Interpreting Visuals

An Introduction to Visual Literacy

You probably know that *visual* means "able to be seen by the eye," and *literacy* can mean "the quality of becoming knowledgeable." So visual literacy is becoming knowledgeable about things you see.

Digital tools and technology make it very easy to express ideas visually. So you need to be able to "read" visual images just as easily as you read words on the page. This is what visual literacy is all about.

A First "Reading"

Here are four images for you to view:

1.

2.

3.

4.

Neftali / Shutterstock.com

Your Turn Number your paper from 1 to 4, leaving three or four lines between numbers. Then explain each image above—what it shows, what it means to you, and/or what questions, if any, you have about it. Afterward, share your thoughts with your classmates.

Active Viewing

Active viewing is the process of identifying the meaning and/or value of a visual. The following steps will help you become an active viewer. These steps are especially helpful when an image has many parts.

1. **Observe** the image as a whole. What do you see and how does it make you feel?

2. **Notice** the individual parts—the words, colors, symbols, etc. Is there one part that gets your attention? Are there any moving parts?

3. **Describe** what you see without worrying about its meaning or value.

4. **Ask** questions about it. Who made it? Where did it come from? What don't you understand about it?

5. **Connect** the image, if possible, to what you already know or have experienced.

6. **Explain** the visual's meaning or message. What does it do, say, or show? What is its purpose or value? (Also see page 180.)

 Your Turn Use the first five steps to actively view the image on this page. Then explain on paper what it means to you.

The Basics of Visual Design

In art class, you learn about the common elements of visual images such as line and shape. These elements will help you "read" and discuss visuals, which means they will improve your visual literacy.

- **Lines** form boundaries, outline shapes, and add to the overall effect of a visual. Soft lines obviously soften the effect of an image, while hard lines add boldness to an image.

- **Forms** (shapes) may be geometrical—built with straight lines, circles, and squares, for example. Or they can be free flowing or irregular—like a bolt of lightning or a cloud.

- **Value** relates to the lightness and darkness of a visual. The contrast between light and dark can help define an image, even make it more dramatic.

- **Colors** add to the appearance and meaning of an image. For example, red is considered a hot, energy-packed color, while blue is considered a cool, calming color. (See page 178.)

- **Space** considers the front, middle, and back parts of an image. It also considers the balance of all of the parts and the use of white space (empty space).

- **Texture** refers to the quality of the surface and appeals to the sense of touch. Texture may be real or implied.

Your Turn Find a photograph or painting that you like in your science or social studies book. Then discuss it as a class for each of the elements above.

A Closer Look at Design

The basic elements such as shape and color serve as the core of visual design. In order for those elements to work well, they must be used in just the right way. To look more closely at the elements in a visual, you need to consider the following points of design.

- **Unity** refers to the relationship between the elements. When a visual is unified, all of the parts seem to work well together.

- **Balance** measures how effectively the parts of a visual fit on the page or screen. A dark object can be balanced by a light object. On the other hand, a large object may not be balanced by many little objects scattered all about.

- **Direction** refers to the flow of the design—how the viewer's eyes follow the visual.

- **Emphasis** refers to the area or element that first attracts the viewer's attention.

- **Contrast** refers to the effect of opposites such as black and white, shadow and light, soft lines and hard lines, and so on.

- **Scale** refers to the actual size of something, while **proportion** refers to something's size in relation to other things around it.

Design in Action

This photograph appears to meet the guidelines for effective design. The top and bottom part seem to be in balance, the use of contrast (light and dark) works well, and the scale of two main parts seem effective, as does the proportion of the plane and runway.

Your Turn Using the design guidelines explained above, make two additional comments about the photograph from the activity on page 176.

A Closer Look at Color

Color often contributes to a visual's main message or the feeling it suggests, so you need to understand how colors relate and work together. The information on this page can serve as your color guide, starting with the color wheel that shows the spectrum of colors.

- **Primary colors** are red, blue, and yellow. They are not made up of other colors.

- **Secondary colors** are orange, green, and violet (purple). They are the product of mixing two primary colors together (red and blue combine to make violet).

- **Tertiary colors** are red-orange, yellow-orange, yellow-green, blue-green, blue-violet, and red-violet. They are created by combining a primary color with a secondary one.

- **Complementary colors** appear opposite each other on the color wheel, such as blue and orange. These colors, when placed next to each other, serve to brighten each other.

- **Related colors** appear close to each other on the color wheel, such as red and violet. They tend to blend with each other.

- **Hot colors** are red, orange, yellow, and the colors connected to them. They are bright and eye-catching.

- **Cool colors** are green, blue, and violet. They are calming and soothing.

Your Turn Using the information above as a guide, make one or two observations about the use of color on the visual that you selected for the activity on page 176.

Understanding Symbols

In a very general sense, a symbol is one thing that represents something else. More specifically, a symbol is an object, mark, or shape that represents something bigger or more complex. For example, an olive branch usually represents peace. A sign with a white capital H on a light blue background represents a hospital.

A Symbol Sampler

Symbols are used in many different areas, such as mathematics, chemistry, and biology. In fact, there are few areas of life in which symbols are not used. Here is a sampler of common symbols.

Mathematics:		**Astronomy:**
Chemistry:		**Traffic:**
Biology:		**Service signs:**
Meteorology:		**Editing symbols:**

Why do we have symbols?

Some symbols help you do things. Others tell you where something is. Still others identify things or stand for a group or business. Some symbols have more than a literal or surface meaning. For example, the American flag identifies the United States, but on a deeper level, it can make a person feel patriotic or proud.

Your Turn Identify three symbols, each one from a different area, to share with your classmates.

Interpreting Visuals

Interpret means "to explain the meaning and value of something." A visual is a form of communication, so when you interpret a photograph, poster, painting, or graphic art, you can use the following elements of communication (plus "design") as a guide.

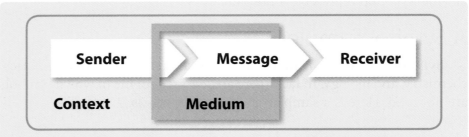

Sender   Message   Receiver

Context   Medium

- **Sender:** Who created the visual?
- **Receiver:** Who is the intended viewer or audience?
- **Medium:** What type of visual is it (painting, photograph, poster, sculpture, monument, advertisement, etc.)?
- **Context:** What is the purpose of the visual? How is the image viewed? In person? In a magazine? On a Web site?
- **Message:** What is the visual attempting to communicate? To what extent does it succeed or fail?
- **Design:** How is the visual put together or designed? Consider the elements that you learned about on pages 176–177.

Your Turn   Interpret the magazine visual on this page. To get started, list the elements (sender, receiver, etc.) on a piece of paper, leaving two or three lines after each one. Then answer the questions following the elements as best you can. (There may be a question or two that you won't be able to answer.)

Viewing-Skills Activities

Use these activities to practice your viewing skills. Once you try these exercises, think of others for practicing viewing skills.

Design Practice

Page through your textbooks, check out a Web site, or just look around your classroom, and you will see all sorts of visuals, many of which contain valuable information. Because you are exposed to so many visuals, you must develop your viewing skills.

Our best advice: Get into the habit of viewing images with care to improve your visual literacy. Follow the guidelines in this chapter to help you "read" each one.

Your Turn Review a poster displayed in one of your classrooms for its design elements, using page 176 as a guide. Consider referring to pages 178 and 179 as well. Record your ideas on paper.

A Colorful Reminder

You may or may not think a lot about colors, unless you're in art class or you're deciding what to wear. Artists and designers, on the other hand, pay careful attention to colors when they are at work. They know all about the color wheel.

Our best advice: Whenever you are reviewing or interpreting a visual, be sure to consider its use of color.

Your Turn Analyze the colors used in the logo for (1) a sports team, (2) a food product or chain, and (3) another business. In your analysis, explain how and why the particular colors are used. (See page 178 for help.)

Symbols, Symbols, Everywhere

You may not be fully aware of all of the symbols that you come across on a daily basis. They are on billboards, in books and newspapers, on the Web, and so on. Why should you care? Many of them provide valuable information. Just think what mathematics would be like without symbols.

Our best advice: Pay more attention to the symbols that you come across in school and in daily life. Consider their effectiveness and value (or lack of it).

Your Turn For one morning, afternoon, or evening, list some of the symbols that you encounter. (See page 179.) Share your list with your classmates, and discuss the purpose and value of the symbols you've identified.

Here's what I see.

It's one thing to say you like or dislike a photograph or that you find a diagram interesting. It's quite another thing to interpret it, because you must consider its sender, message, medium, and so on. (See page 180.)

Our best advice: Interpreting a visual is much the same as analyzing it, so be prepared to examine it carefully to help you determine its meaning and value.

Your Turn Interpret a photograph from a magazine or a Web site, using page 180 as a guide. First, list the elements (sender, receiver, and so on) on a piece of paper, leaving two or three lines after each one. Then answer the questions following the elements as best you can. (There may be a question or two that you won't be able to answer.)

A phonograph?
What does it do?

Chapter 14
Using Information and Media

Talking out loud lets you share information with a few people, but in 1877, the phonograph made it possible to record and play back information to many people. Today, media like audio recordings, radio, film, the Internet, and books allow us to share information with the whole world.

You will learn . . .
- The Purpose of Media
- Evaluating Messages
- Appreciating Print Media
- Understanding Graphics
- Using Radio and Television
- Evaluating Advertisements
- Watching Movies
- Understanding the Internet
- Evaluating Online Sources

Understanding the Purpose of Media

What is the purpose of the texts you read, the images you view, the video you watch, and the audio you hear? Media are used to educate, to entertain, and to persuade. Recognizing the purpose of each media message you encounter will help you become a more informed media consumer.

■ To Educate

A book, a movie, a podcast, and other media can teach you knowledge or show you how to do something. Examples include your textbooks, historical documentaries, or foreign-language audio programs.

■ To Entertain

Having fun is an important part of daily life. Novels, TV shows, music, and games all offer entertainment. They also represent a snapshot of popular culture.

■ To Persuade

Many media messages are intended to persuade you—to accept a certain way of thinking, to buy a certain product, or to support a certain politician. Being aware of persuasive methods can help you make wise decisions about the information presented to you.

Your Turn

1. Think of something you learned from a movie. List two questions you still have about that subject. Where will you go for answers?
2. Describe your favorite advertisement. Explain why you like it. Do you use the product advertised? Why or why not?

Evaluating Messages

Every media message has five features: sender, receiver, content, medium, and context. You can use a message evaluation sheet like the one below to evaluate the features of any media message.

Message Evaluation Sheet

Sender: Who created this message? Why did they make it? What do they hope to gain from it?

_____

_____

Receiver: What audience is the message designed for? How does the message relate to me?

_____

_____

Content: What does the message say? What questions does it answer? What questions does it leave unanswered? How fair and accurate does it seem?

_____

_____

Medium: What form is the message presented in (newspaper article, TV show, etc.)? How does that medium affect its impact?

_____

_____

Context: What is the purpose of the message? How recent is the information?

_____

_____

Your Turn Complete a message evaluation sheet about a message on your favorite Web site.

Appreciating Print Media

Print media have been around for a very long time. The ancient Egyptians printed information on papyrus 5,000 years ago. Paper itself was invented nearly 2,000 years ago. Even so, printed material remains popular today for recording and presenting information.

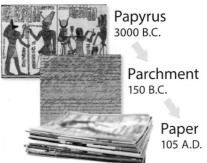

Papyrus
3000 B.C.

Parchment
150 B.C.

Paper
105 A.D.

Types of Print Media

Different types of print media have slightly different purposes. This affects their form.

- **Books** are sturdy, so they can preserve information for years. This makes them great for stories, law, history, and math.

- **Magazines** provide more up-to-date information than books. They are also more cheaply printed and less durable. They may be published weekly, monthly, or on some other schedule. Scholarly magazines are called "journals."

- **Newspapers** are even more up-to-date and cheaply printed than magazines. Many are published daily. Some local papers are published weekly. Old newspapers can be an interesting source of history. Nearly all newspaper publishers keep an archive of past issues. These may be in print, on microfilm, or on computer.

- **Booklets** include pamphlets, brochures, and fliers. Your doctor's office probably has lots of pamphlets and brochures about medical topics. Each explains a particular subject.

- **Ground Mail** is used for letters, greeting cards, and business advertisements.

Evaluating Print Media

Not all printed messages are reliable. Some important parts of a topic may be missing because of limited space, author bias, or other factors. You can use the message evaluation chart on page 185 to judge the trustworthiness of a print-media story.

Features of Print Media

Print media use many features to make a text easier to read and understand.

- **Headings** tell you at a glance what the text is about. Chapter titles and newspaper headlines are examples of major headings. Subheadings inside a chapter or a story indicate main points. You can use headings to get an overview before reading a text.

- **Columns** keep lines of text short so that you can read quickly. Textbooks often use two columns. Newspapers and magazines may use three or more.

- **Lists** make a set of items memorable. Bulleted lists (like this one) mean the items have equal importance. Numbered lists mean the items follow a certain order.

- **Graphics** include drawings, photos, charts, and tables. These help to present information quickly.

- **White space** refers to blank parts of a page. This includes page margins, space above and below headings, text indentations, and space around graphics. White space helps make a page interesting and easy to read.

- **Pop quotes** draw attention to a statement on the page or to a famous quotation.

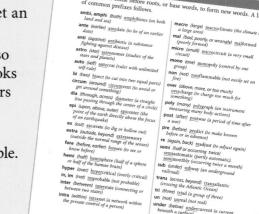

> **Pop quotes** (like this one) draw attention to a statement on the page or to a famous quotation.

Your Turn Search your *Inquire* handbook for an example of each element listed above. (For more help reading print media, see pages 132–133.)

Understanding Graphics

Have you heard the saying "A picture is worth a thousand words"? That's because a graphic can present lots of information at once.

By Lareel123 via Wikimedia Commons

Photos

A photograph can show great details about a setting or an event. Remember, though, a photographer can affect your reaction in many ways. Lighting, camera angle, setting, and exact moment chosen help determine what you see.

Illustrations

Like a photo, a drawing or painting shows a picture. But that picture can be of anything at all—real or not. An artist's style also affects an illustration's look and appeal.

Diagrams

Diagrams are a special sort of drawing. Some diagrams show the parts of a thing. Others show comparisons. This diagram shows field positions for a game of cricket. (Cricket is a British sport similar to American baseball.)

sightscreen
long stop
fine leg
third man   infield
slips   wicket keeper
gully   square leg
point
pitch   close infield
cover   mid-wicket
bowler
mid-off   mid-on
long on
long off
straight hit
sightscreen

Your Turn

1. What does the photograph reveal about the gymnast? What emotion does she display?
2. In this drawing, what do you think the octopus's mood is? Why do you think that?
3. Draw and label a diagram for your favorite sport.

Graphs

Graphs are illustrations that show facts and figures. Different graphs are useful for different types of information.

Pie Graph

A pie graph shows how something is divided up. Each color on the graph represents one part and shows its proportion to the whole.

Water in Earth's Oceans

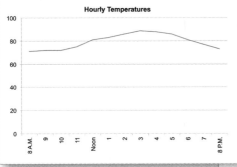

- Pacific Ocean
- Atlantic Ocean
- Indian Ocean
- Arctic Ocean
- Southern Ocean

Hourly Temperatures

Line Graph

A line graph shows how things change. The track on the left shows amount. The track across the bottom shows time. The moving line shows the amount at each point in time.

Bar Graph

A bar graph uses columns to compare things.

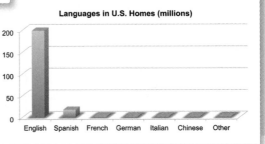

Languages in U.S. Homes (millions)

English Spanish French German Italian Chinese Other

Your Turn Choose a graph to show what you do on your weekends. Draw the graph and label each part. Share your graph in class. (See pages 307–318 for more on graphing.)

Evaluating Graphics

Remember that graphics may not always "show the whole picture." Use the message evaluation sheet on page 185 to judge their worth to you.

Listening to the Radio

The first radio stations in North America were licensed around 1920 and were owned by stores selling radios or by newspaper publishers. Today radio is supported by advertising or by public funds and private donations. Many types of programs are broadcast.

- **Music radio** usually targets a specific audience. One station might play country music, while another plays pop. Advertisers choose a station that reaches their customers.
- **News radio** focuses on news reports. Programs may include special-interest topics like science, news, or poetry.
- **Sports radio** broadcasts sports events and sports news programs.
- **Talk radio** features many different topics. One show may be about cars, another about gardening or politics. Listeners may call in to ask questions or share their opinions.
- **Public radio** was originally created to reach regions where no commercial stations existed. Many public radio stations are affiliated with a university and have an educational purpose.

Evaluating Radio Messages

Most radio is funded by advertising. This affects what the station broadcasts. The audience a station serves will also affect its programming. When listening to radio, keep in mind the questions from the message evaluation sheet on page 185.

In Focus FM radio is a newer technology than AM radio. FM can broadcast in stereo, so it is great for music. AM is now used mostly for news, sports, and talk radio.

Viewing Television

By 1928, the first television broadcasts became public. Within 30 years, TV spread to most of the world. Like radio, TV offers a variety of programs.

- **Dramas** are fictional stories with a serious tone.
- **Sitcoms** (situation comedies) are fictional stories designed to make you laugh.
- **Reality shows** show real people in real settings. However, some events are rehearsed, and other events are left out. Also, the camera affects how people behave.
- **Sports events** are popular TV programs.
- **News programs** are usually scheduled early in the morning, at noon, at dinner, and at bedtime. Many people find these times most convenient to catch up on news.
- **Documentaries** are programs investigating a specific subject. You may see a documentary about a historical event, a science discovery, or an animal's native habitat.
- **Infomercials** (information commercials) are programs that discuss and promote a specific product. The point is to convince you to buy.
- **Game shows** give people problems to solve or questions to answer. Contestants must pass an audition before being chosen for the show.
- **Variety shows** may include a mix of music, dance, short comedy sketches, and celebrity interviews.
- **Music TV** presents popular songs, often as short music videos.
- **Public TV**, like public radio, was created to reach areas where no commercial stations existed. Many public TV stations are affiliated with a university and have an educational purpose.

Evaluating TV Programs

Like radio, most TV is funded by advertising. Use the message evaluation sheet on page 185 to help judge the value of what you watch.

Evaluating Advertisements

Advertisements such as TV commercials can be very entertaining. But remember that advertisers want you to buy something or to believe something. Here are five common advertising techniques.

■ **Cult of Celebrity**

Companies may hire a celebrity to recommend their product. They know the celebrity's fans want to be like that person. But the celebrity is paid and may not actually use the product.

■ **Problem-Solution**

In some commercials, a person has a problem, and a friend recommends a product to solve it. The manufacturer hopes that the next time you face that problem, you'll buy their product. Often the problem is exaggerated, or another solution may be better.

■ **Ask an Expert**

Sometimes a doctor or other expert talks about why a company's product is so good. Often these "experts" are just actors. They may leave out important information, giving you just one side of the story.

■ **Part of the Gang**

We all need to feel like we belong. Advertisers use this to sell you brand-name clothing, food, and entertainment. Brand-name products usually cost more than similar products.

■ **Funny Bone**

Funny commercials make you feel good about a product so that you will buy it. However, they may tell you little about the product's real worth.

Your Turn The next time you see or hear an advertisement, ask yourself if it uses one of these five methods. You can also ask the questions from your media evaluation sheet on page 185.

Watching Movies

The next time you watch a movie, stay through the credits. Most movies involve dozens or even hundreds of people. Each has some influence on what you see. Most movies also cost millions of dollars to produce. Movie studios count on sales to make back the cost of making the film. Here are some other ways movie studios make money.

- **Theaters** rent movies from movie studios. Theater owners want films that are popular and will sell lots of tickets, popcorn, and drinks.
- **Video sales and rentals** are another source of income for studios. Fans love to feel they own a favorite film. Just remember that when you buy a video, you own only a copy of the original.
- **TV networks** may rent movies to broadcast. Often these films are a few years old, and the networks cut them to insert commercial breaks. Networks may even delete parts of a film for length or to make it more family friendly.
- **Product placements** in a film help to pay its production cost. Manufacturers may pay to have a character use a particular product during the story.
- **Public figures or organizations** sometimes spend their own money to produce a movie. These films often promote a certain cause.

Your Turn   Journaling is a great way to evaluate movies. After every film, review the message evaluation sheet on page 185. Then take 10 minutes to freewrite your thoughts about the movie. Save your journal, and read the entry again a year from now.

Understanding the Internet

People often confuse the words "Internet" and "World Wide Web." The two are not the same. The following list defines each term along with other notable Internet terms.

- The **Internet** is a worldwide network of computers. The network is connected by cables, radio waves, and satellite communication.

- The **World Wide Web** is a collection of interconnected "pages" on the Internet, viewed with a Web browser.

- **Email** and **instant messaging** are both ways of sending electronic messages by Internet.

- A **modem** is a device for connecting to the Internet.

- A **router** lets several devices—computers, printers, game consoles, televisions, and so on—share one modem. It can also let them communicate to each other.

- **Ethernet cables** are wires for connecting a router to a modem and other devices to the router.

- **Wi-fi** uses radio waves instead of a cable to connect a device to a router. ("Wi-fi" is short for "wireless fidelity.")

- **3g**, **4g**, and so on are wireless telephone networks. (The "g" stands for "generation.") They are not part of the Internet but can connect to it.

- **Desktop computers** usually network by Ethernet cables for best connection speed. Laptop and tablet computers use wi-fi for convenience. Smartphones may use wi-fi when near a router and a telephone network the rest of the time.

Your Turn What devices do you see at school, at home, and in public? How are they commonly used? Discuss your observations in class.

Browsing the Web

The World Wide Web is full of fun and useful information. You just have to know how to use it and how to stay safe online.

Using a Web Browser

A Web browser displays Web pages. Unlike a book page, a Web page can include more than just text and images.

The address bar shows the current page's Web address.

The Web search box lets you find pages about a topic.

Navigation buttons let you revisit pages you have seen.

Tabs hold additional pages.

The refresh button reloads the current page.

The status bar shows the Web address of links your mouse points to.

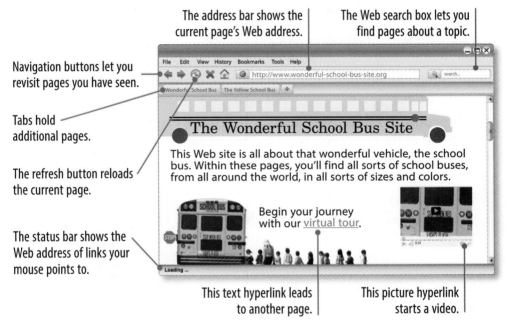

This text hyperlink leads to another page.

This picture hyperlink starts a video.

Staying Safe Online

Not everyone online is honest. Here are some ways to stay safe online.

- **Use trusted sites.** Sites that have a worldwide or national reputation are generally trustworthy. Avoid unknown sites.

- **Protect your identity.** Don't reveal your age, home address, or telephone number online.

- **Look before you click.** Not all links are what they seem. If you aren't sure, don't click.

- **Don't download anything without an adult's permission.** Many viruses are disguised as music, games, and such. Always ask an adult before downloading anything.

Using Search Engines

Search engines are sites that help you to find information on the Web. If you type "llama wool" into your browser's search box, the search engine will give you a list of Web pages about that topic.

Tips for Searching

- **Use the best search terms.** Before you search, think of the best words to describe what you want to know. The more exact your search terms, the better your results will be.

- **Look beyond the first page.** A search may result in many pages of suggestions. Sometimes what you want is on a later page of listings. Later pages may also help you decide on better search terms.

- **Recognize advertisers' links.** Advertisers pay to have their links listed at the top of the page and in the right sidebar. Often these links are together in a colored box. Other links on the page may be more helpful.

- **Try different search engines.** Ask an adult for help finding a different search site. Your search terms may bring different results there.

Saving What You Find

When you find a page with helpful information, you should make a record of it so you can use it later. Here are some ways to keep a record of useful Web pages.

- Take good notes of helpful information.
- Use your printer to make a copy of pages with important graphics or quotable sentences.
- Save helpful pages on a flash drive or other electronic storage.
- Ask an adult how to bookmark useful sites.

Evaluating Search Results

Each page on the Web has its own unique address, like a street address for a building. A Web address is made up of a unique set of letters and numbers.

Example Web Address

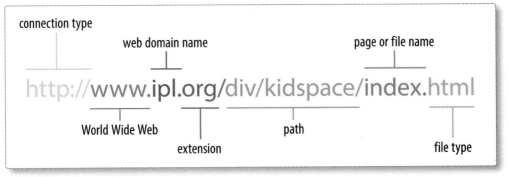

Common Domain Extensions

A domain extension indicates the type of organization in charge of the Web page. Here are the most common domain extensions.

.com a business site (commerce)
.gov a U.S. or state government site
.edu a school site
.org an organization, often nonprofit
.net a network
.mil a military site
.biz a business site
.info an information site

Other Domain Extensions

Many countries outside the U.S. have their own domain extensions. For example, Canadian sites have **.ca** on the end. New domain extensions are made sometimes to expand the Web.

Visit a favorite Web page. Try to identify each part of the Web address by using the information on this page. What did you learn about the page that you didn't know before?

Evaluating Online Sources

Not all Web sources are equally valuable. Think about the following when you view a source.

■ Author

Who made the site? What is that person or organization's authority? How well respected is the author? Information from a well-respected expert is valuable.

■ Balance or Bias

Does the site show all sides of a topic? Or does it present only one viewpoint and ignore others? Sites that ignore opposing viewpoints are less trustworthy.

■ Accuracy

Is the information up to date and correct? Sites with old information are less valuable.

■ Quality

Polished, professional-looking sites are often more valuable than amateur ones. Sites with broken links and misspelled words probably have other errors, too.

■ Copyright and Plagiarism

Many Web resources have a copyright statement telling who owns the material. (It is usually near the bottom of the page.) Even if there is no copyright stated, or a source says you can use it freely, be sure to give credit in your work. Not giving credit is called plagiarism, and it is stealing. (See page 255.)

Your Turn Find a Web resource about a topic you are studying. Evaluate it using the guidelines above and on page 185. Write a paragraph explaining what you learned. Be sure to include where you found the information.

Media Activities

Try the following activities to practice your media knowledge.

Multi-Spectrum News

Different media have different strengths and weaknesses. Compare sources to get a bigger picture of a topic.

Our best advice: Media messages that are delivered quickly, such as text messages and radio reports, sometimes sacrifice accuracy for speed of delivery. Media like books and journals take much longer to create but include many more details.

Your Turn Choose a current event you are studying in class. Find a print newspaper or magazine article about it. Also find a Web page—with a video, if possible. Finally, find a book related to the subject. What did you learn from each? How are the sources alike and different?

Truth-o-Meter

Advertisements can be entertaining, but their main goal is to persuade you to buy something or believe something.

Our best advice: Professional advertisement companies are hired to make you want specific products. Always consider if a product truly satisfies your personal values and needs before purchasing it.

Your Turn Draw a thermometer down the right side of a piece of poster paper, with "True" at the top and "Suspicious" at the bottom. Clip ads from newspapers and magazines, and print ads from Web sites. Investigate the truth of each ad and paste it on the poster paper in the appropriate spot.

Our Neighborhood

Online map sites use satellite photos to make their maps. You can discover a lot about the world on these maps.

Our best advice: Online map sites allow you to take a virtual tour of a location from different perspectives. A satellite view will let you know what a location looks like from above. A street view lets you see an address as if you were looking at it out a window of a parked car. Use both settings to get the most accurate view.

 Look up your home address on a map site. Zoom in and out to see what you discover about your neighborhood. Compare the map view to the photo view.

Waiting Room Wonders

Print media are diverse and share a lot of information. When you research a topic, it is helpful to use a variety of print sources.

Our best advice: Your local library is like a treasure trove of print media. Go there to find books, magazines, old newspapers, and more. What's more, the librarians and media specialists can help you with your search.

 Ask your doctor's or dentist's office for a pamphlet on a subject of your choice. Then visit the library and find one book, one magazine article, and one newspaper story on that subject. Share what you learned with your class.

Tweet, tweet?

Chapter 15
Using Social Media

Connecting with your friends has never been easier. You can phone them, email them, text them, and more. Online, you can post short messages on microblogging sites, video-chat, and discuss ideas on message boards. Social media open up a world of communication possibilities.

You will learn . . .
- Chatting and Texting
- Using Voice and Video Chat
- Emailing
- Using Blogs and Wikis
- Other Types of Social Media

Chatting and Texting

Two of the most commonly used social media are texting and chatting.

Chatting

"Chatting" is a short word for "Internet chat" or "instant messaging." It means having a conversation online by typing instead of speaking. Some Web sites have a chat function built into them. A company's Web site might have a chat box for talking with customer service. Many online games include a chat function.

 LILDAVE: Hi, Grandpa! I can't wait to come visit you next week!
October 26 at 2:23 pm

 DOUGJAMES: Hi, Davey! We're looking forward to it. Grandma's baking a cake.
October 26 at 2:29 pm

Texting

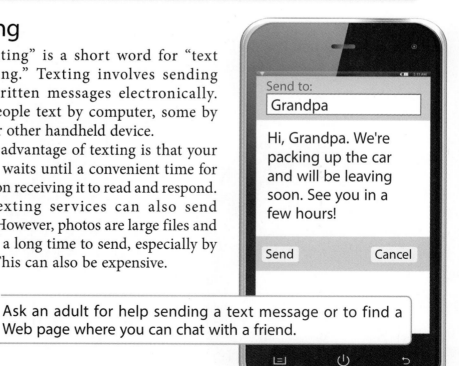

"Texting" is a short word for "text messaging." Texting involves sending short written messages electronically. Some people text by computer, some by phone or other handheld device.

One advantage of texting is that your message waits until a convenient time for the person receiving it to read and respond. Some texting services can also send photos. However, photos are large files and can take a long time to send, especially by phone. This can also be expensive.

Send to:
Grandpa

Hi, Grandpa. We're packing up the car and will be leaving soon. See you in a few hours!

Send   Cancel

Your Turn Ask an adult for help sending a text message or to find a Web page where you can chat with a friend.

Using Voice and Video Chat

You can use an Internet-connected computer with a speaker and a microphone for voice chat. Many online games support voice chat so that you can talk with other players. With the right software, voice chat can act like a telephone. If your computer has a video camera, you can even talk face-to-face online. Some handheld devices like smartphones support voice chat and video chat.

Benefits of Voice Chat

- **Long distance doesn't cost extra.** You can talk to someone on the other side of the world as cheaply as next door.
- **You can tell if someone is online before you call.** If they are using the same software, your voice-chat program will alert you when they come online.
- **You can click to call telephone numbers.** If your account can call regular phones, you don't need to dial. Just click the phone number on your screen.

Benefits of Video Chat

- **It's almost like speaking in person.** Seeing the person you're talking to makes communication much easier.
- **You can share the camera with other people.** Your whole family can gather around the computer and join in the conversation.

Problems with Voice and Video Chat

- **The voice quality may be poor.** The person on the other end may hear an echo. Or there may be a delay in the conversation.
- **The video quality may be poor.** The picture may freeze, or the color may be wrong.

Your Turn Ask an adult to help you make a voice or video chat with a friend or relative.

Emailing

Email (short for "electronic mail") is like a super-powered text message. Here are some things email does especially well.

- **Email can look like a Web page.** You can use different fonts and colors, bullet points, indents, and so on to format an email message.

- **Email can carry attachments.** Some text messages can include photos. But email messages can have many types of files and can carry more than one at once. You might send an email with photos, music, or documents attached to it.

- **Email lasts longer.** If you use an email program instead of an online service, downloaded email remains on your computer until you decide to delete it.

- **Email can be forwarded.** With one click, you can send a message you've already received to another person.

- **Email can target one person or several.** You can address many people with the same email.

○ ○ ○   Guitar Recital   [Send]

Helvetica ⟂ | 12 ⟂ | ■ | B *I* U | ☰ ☰ ☰ | ☰▾ | ➡▾

To: Vincent Guirand

Subject: Guitar Recital

Attachment: 001.jpg; 002.jpg; song.mp3

From: Josephine Guirand ⟂

Dear Uncle Vincent,

Thank you so *much* for lending me your guitar while you are overseas. I have taken good care of it. See photo 1 as proof.

You said not to let it get lonely, so I'm taking guitar lessons. See photo 2 of me at a guitar recital. Also attached is a recording of the song I played.

Missing you,

Joey

 Your Turn Send some personal news in an email to friends or family members. Ask them to write you back.

Using Blogs

The word "blog" is short for "Web log." Many people use blogs for journaling. Schools can use blogs for posting public announcements. Some teachers or classrooms use a private blog to discuss school-related subjects.

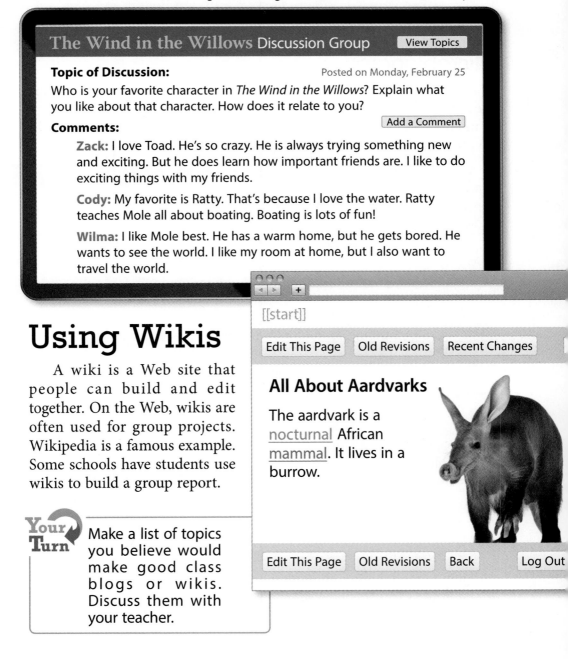

The Wind in the Willows Discussion Group   `View Topics`

Topic of Discussion: Posted on Monday, February 25

Who is your favorite character in *The Wind in the Willows*? Explain what you like about that character. How does it relate to you?

Comments: `Add a Comment`

Zack: I love Toad. He's so crazy. He is always trying something new and exciting. But he does learn how important friends are. I like to do exciting things with my friends.

Cody: My favorite is Ratty. That's because I love the water. Ratty teaches Mole all about boating. Boating is lots of fun!

Wilma: I like Mole best. He has a warm home, but he gets bored. He wants to see the world. I like my room at home, but I also want to travel the world.

`[[start]]`

`Edit This Page`   `Old Revisions`   `Recent Changes`

All About Aardvarks

The aardvark is a nocturnal African mammal. It lives in a burrow.

`Edit This Page`   `Old Revisions`   `Back`   `Log Out`

Using Wikis

A wiki is a Web site that people can build and edit together. On the Web, wikis are often used for group projects. Wikipedia is a famous example. Some schools have students use wikis to build a group report.

Your Turn Make a list of topics you believe would make good class blogs or wikis. Discuss them with your teacher.

Other Types of Social Media

Your parents or older siblings may have an account on a service like Facebook, MySpace, Google+, LinkedIn, or Twitter. Because of the Children's Internet Protection Act, you must be at least 13 years old to have your own. But you can view posts on a family member's account, so it's important to know how the services work.

Microblogging

Microblogging is a lot like texting. The difference is that a text message goes to just one person, but a microblog goes on a Web page. A microblog page can be public, or it can be limited to specific people. Twitter is a famous microblogging service.

1. The latest message is at the top.

2. Older messages get pushed down the page by newer ones.

3. The user name identifies the writer.

4. The time stamp shows when the post was written.

5. This message starts a conversation.

Profile   Settings   Sign Out

What's Happening?

Marion
10:37 a.m. via Seesmic
I'm always in the mood for Thai food. How does that sound?

Teresa
10:23 a.m. via TweetDeck
That sounds great! Where should we eat?

Neil
10:14 a.m. via Twitter
Let's have our families meet for lunch on Saturday.

Your Turn Ask a parent or older sibling to show you his or her social media page. How does he or she use that site?

Using Social Sites

Social sites like Facebook and MySpace allow "status updates" that are like microblog messages. These sites also support photos, videos, and social games.

Using Media-Sharing Sites

Some sites like Flickr and Wikimedia Commons host photos uploaded by users. You can search these photos and use some of them in your schoolwork. Remember to give credit for whatever you borrow. (See page 255.)

Besides photos, sharing sites may also have other helpful media such as videos or audio files. YouTube is a popular video-sharing site.

Using Message Boards

When searching the Web for information, you may find answers on a message board. Message boards are sites where people post questions and answers or discuss a topic.

Visiting Virtual Worlds

Many online games involve multiple users. So do sites such as Whyville.net. You can explore these worlds and meet other people online.

Using Social Media Safely

1. **Always ask a parent before starting an account.** Your parents need to know where you are—even online.
2. **Don't reveal any personal details online.** Don't even tell your first name. It's best to use a nickname instead.
3. **Report any suspicious activity to an adult.** If something makes you even a little uncomfortable, tell an adult. Better to be safe than sorry.
4. **Never meet someone face-to-face without a parent.** Online friends are for online chat only.

Social-Media Activities

Use these activities to improve your social media skills.

Safety First

The world of social media is full of great people and helpful information. But not everyone online is a "good guy." You have to protect your privacy, and your family's, whenever you are online.

 Discuss in class the possible dangers of giving personal information online. As a class, create a "Cyberspace Safety" checklist for each student to check and sign.

Email Mastery

Email can be a great way to communicate, especially when messages are well prepared. Use the guidelines for effective writing to create your messages. (See pages 290–291.) And always include a helpful subject line.

 Make a list of people who would appreciate an email message from you. Choose one of those people, write a message, and send it. Remember to use the guidelines for effective writing. (See page 290.) Be certain to include a helpful subject line.

Wiki Wise

A wiki can be a wonderful class project. You can build a wiki about any topic. And when it is finished, you can make it public so that other people can learn from it.

Your Turn As a class, choose a topic that you are studying. Break it down into subtopics, and assign teams to research each one and prepare a report. Share those reports in class. Then work together to build a wiki from the reports. Make the site public when it is done.

Chapter 16
Learning About Money

Sadly, empty piggy banks do not magically fill up. You may sometimes get money as a gift or earn it by doing chores. In the future, you will earn money in the workplace. But in order to have "money in the bank," you must spend it wisely and save. This chapter covers important information about earning and handling money.

You will learn . . .

- Taking Financial Responsibility
- Understanding Incomes, Jobs, and Careers
- Understanding Risk and Insurance
- Controlling Personal Information

Taking Financial Responsibility

We live in a capitalist society. That means people can own their own businesses and property. We are also consumers, buying products from stores that compete with each other.

In this kind of society, people are responsible for taking care of themselves. They earn money and decide how to spend it. That includes saving it for the future.

Understanding Consumer Protection Laws

Our government protects consumers from businesses that may do unfair things.

- **Monopolies:** A monopoly happens when one company controls and sells a certain product. Because the company has no competition, it can raise prices as much as it likes. Monopolies are illegal.

- **Safety:** Food, medicines, automobiles, toys, and other products must be safe to use. The government has passed laws about this.

- **Truth in advertising:** Another law says that businesses cannot lie about their products. Some may exaggerate about how good their products are, however. So consumers must be careful and even do some research before buying big items.

Many businesses do care about the people who buy their products, and they have their own policies to protect consumers.

Your Turn Choose two or three stores where you shop. In each store, ask what its policy is for returning merchandise. How do these policies compare? Discuss the information with your classmates.

Making Smart Financial Decisions

Take a look around your room. Do you see anything you once just had to have but doesn't seem so important now? Perhaps it's a toy, brand-name jeans, or a video game. Sometimes we all wish we had saved our money instead of buying a thing.

Being a smart consumer means making good decisions. That may mean finding the best deal, deciding not to buy, or even saving up to buy something later. It is wise to avoid "impulse buying."

> 1. Make a list of things you need and things you want. Number the items in order of importance.
> 2. Choose one item and make a plan for buying it.
> 3. Online, research different stores that have the item and how much it will cost.

Saving and Investing

The purpose of saving and investing is to have money for the future.

Saving

Saving means putting your money in a safe place like a bank.

Imagine that on your eighth birthday you deposit $10 in a savings account. Then you deposit another $10 every month for 10 years. On your 18th birthday, your account would hold $1,721.80! Besides the $1,210 you saved, the bank has given you $511.80 in interest. Interest is money a bank pays you for using the money you put into an account.

Investing

Investing means buying something you hope will become more valuable so you can sell it for the higher price.

People invest in businesses, art, land, collectibles, and many other things.

One difference between saving and investing is that you can withdraw savings more easily when you need money. Selling an investment can take time, and you may lose the money you hoped to make.

Understanding Incomes, Jobs, and Careers

The words *job* and *career* are related, although they do not mean exactly the same thing. The same is true of the words *salary* and *wages*. The following definitions will explain these and other words.

- **Wages** are money paid for time spent working. Part-time jobs usually pay wages. The more hours worked, the more wages paid.

- **Salary** is money paid for work, regardless of the time spent working. Most teachers receive a salary. Often, they work more than eight hours a day, five days a week.

- **Income** is money received on a regular basis. It may come from wages, a salary, an allowance, or payments from investments.

- **Taxes** are money paid to the government for services like roads, schools, firefighters, and police. Income tax is taken from wages and salary. Property tax is based on the houses, land, and businesses people own, and sales tax is charged on purchases.

- **Jobs** are specific types of work, like delivering newspapers or stocking store shelves.

- **Careers** are fields of work. A singing career, for example, may begin with musical training and then various jobs in the field, like working backstage, before becoming a paid singer.

Knowing the Law

U.S. child labor laws say you must be 14 or older to work. However, before that age, you may deliver newspapers, babysit occasionally, act, or work in your parents' nonhazardous business. Your limit is three hours of work per school day unless you are working for your parents.

Your Turn

1. Make a list of the ways you receive or earn money. Talk with a parent or a guardian about other possibilities.
2. Choose a career you may be interested in pursuing. Make a list of the education you'll need and the kinds of jobs available in that particular field.

Making Payments

People pay for things in different ways. These are the most common.

- **Cash** (coins and paper bills)
- **Check** (paper slip printed with bank account information) On a check, you write the name of the person being paid and the amount. Only the named person can cash that check.

> ### U.S. Coins
> **Penny** ➝ 1 cent (1/100 dollar)
> **Nickel** ➝ 5 cents (1/20 dollar)
> **Dime** ➝ 10 cents (1/10 dollar)
> **Quarter** ➝ 25 cents (1/4 dollar)
> **Half dollar** ➝ 50 cents (1/2 dollar)
> **Dollar** ➝ 100 cents

- **Credit card** (a card that allows you to borrow from an account) If you make a purchase with a credit card, you must pay back the amount borrowed plus interest.
- **Debit card** (a card that allows you to withdraw money from your checking or savings account) If you make a purchase with a debit card, you do not pay interest on the amount.
- **Automatic deduction** (an amount regularly taken from your bank account) For example, you may pay a monthly phone bill using automatic deduction.
- **Barter** (exchanging items or time) Examples are trading used games with a friend or agreeing to do your sister's chores for a week in exchange for a favor.

See pages **210–211** for information about smart ways to shop, save, and invest for the future.

Your Turn How do you usually pay for things? Talk with your parents/guardians about how they pay for things. Which payment options explained above do they prefer and why?

Understanding Risk and Insurance

How would your parents or guardians replace all the things in your house after a fire or a bad storm? Where would the money come from? Or what would they do if they lost their jobs or got sick and couldn't work? Who would pay the bills and buy groceries?

Insurance

Buying insurance can help with these problems. For a monthly fee called a premium, which the insurance company saves and invests, the company pays for things when tragedies happen.

Property insurance replaces things that have been damaged or destroyed. Fire insurance pays for fire damage, flood insurance for water damage, earthquake insurance for earthquake damage, and so on.

Vehicle insurance is a special type of property insurance. Its main purpose is to pay for damage done by or to a vehicle.

Health insurance pays for medical treatment. Dental insurance pays the dentist to care for your teeth. Optical insurance pays for glasses and eye care.

Unemployment insurance gives you money to pay bills for a while if you lose your job. The government takes the premium out of your paychecks (while you are employed) to pay for this insurance.

Social Security helps older, retired people to pay their bills. The government takes the premium to pay for this insurance out of workers' paychecks.

Your Turn Do you know someone who was helped by insurance? How was the person helped? (Ask your parents for an example if necessary.)

Wills

A will is a legal document prepared by a person before he or she dies. It tells how personal belongings will be divided between relatives, friends, and organizations according to the person's wishes. Without a will, a person's property is divided according to inheritance laws.

Your Turn Do you know people who inherited something from a relative? What was it? What does that inheritance mean to them?

Controlling Personal Information

You may have heard of identity theft. It is using someone else's name, Social Security number, bank account, or other personal information. Identity thieves use Web sites, email, or even the phone to "phish" for personal information. Protect yourself with these guidelines:

- **Don't give personal information over the phone.** You can't be sure who the other person really is.

- **Don't follow links in emails.** Scammers make their emails look official and disguise links to look safe. Don't click on links you receive from people you don't know.

- **Don't reveal personal details online.** Protect your privacy by keeping your last name, school, home address, phone number, and other personal details secret.

- **Don't download files without an adult's permission.** Identity thieves and hackers may tempt you with free files that will infect your computer with viruses.

Your Turn Find a news story about personal information being hacked. Discuss the details with your classmates. Who were the victims? How were they affected? What should they do now to protect their information?

Financial-Literacy Activities

Making a Budget

According to an old proverb, "Failing to plan is planning to fail." The surest way to achieve a goal, then, is to make a plan. A budget is a plan to achieve your goals for earning, spending, and saving money.

 Divide a piece of paper down the middle. On one side, list the amounts of money you will receive next month. On the other side, list the items, along with their cost, that you plan to buy. Then add up each side to see whether your income can support your spending. Is there anything left over to save? Make a plan to improve your budget.

Visiting a Bank or Credit Union

Regular banks are businesses that make a profit. They offer their customers loans, pay interest on accounts, cash checks, and provide other services. Credit unions are not-for-profit organizations owned by their customers, or members. They offer similar banking services.

 Ask your teacher about arranging a class field trip to a bank, or ask to interview a banker for a school report. If possible, also visit a credit union or interview a credit-union manager. Discuss the two institutions in class.

Choosing a Career

You hear it all the time. "What do you want to be when you grow up?" Here is a follow-up question: "What will it take to achieve that goal?" Knowing what education you'll need and what jobs are available in a particular field can help you plan.

 Choose a career that interests you. Then research the career and someone who works in that field—an actor, a firefighter, a doctor, and so on. If possible, interview that person. How has what you learned affected your plans?

Part II:
Using
the
Inquiry
Process
→

Part II:
Using the
Inquiry Process

This section leads you through the steps in the inquiry process, from questioning to creating to presenting. As you learn about this process, you will apply many of the skills that you learned in Part I. You will also use the inquiry process to complete the great projects in Part III.

Chapters in This Section

Hey, where are you going?

Chapter 17
Learning About the Inquiry Process

With the inquiry process, you might not always know where you're going, but you'll probably enjoy the trip!

The inquiry process can launch an adventure. Beginning with a question, the process takes you through planning, searching, and discovery. Eventually, you might even create something surprising. In the next pages, you will learn about Kim, her classmates, and the question that started their journey. This chapter shows you how the inquiry process really works.

You will learn . . .
- Understanding Inquiry
- Question
- Plan
- Research
- Create
- Improve
- Present

Understanding Inquiry

A process, like baking cookies or getting ready for school in the morning, has several steps. Inquiry is a process, too. You can't complete an inquiry all at once. Here are the steps:

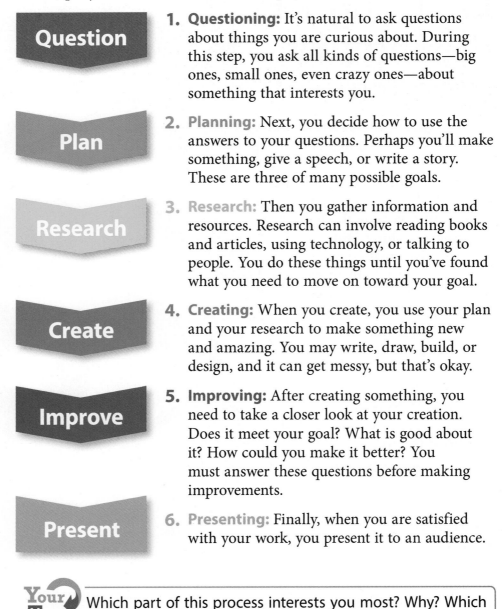

Question

1. **Questioning:** It's natural to ask questions about things you are curious about. During this step, you ask all kinds of questions—big ones, small ones, even crazy ones—about something that interests you.

Plan

2. **Planning:** Next, you decide how to use the answers to your questions. Perhaps you'll make something, give a speech, or write a story. These are three of many possible goals.

Research

3. **Research:** Then you gather information and resources. Research can involve reading books and articles, using technology, or talking to people. You do these things until you've found what you need to move on toward your goal.

Create

4. **Creating:** When you create, you use your plan and your research to make something new and amazing. You may write, draw, build, or design, and it can get messy, but that's okay.

Improve

5. **Improving:** After creating something, you need to take a closer look at your creation. Does it meet your goal? What is good about it? How could you make it better? You must answer these questions before making improvements.

Present

6. **Presenting:** Finally, when you are satisfied with your work, you present it to an audience.

Your Turn Which part of this process interests you most? Why? Which part sounds the hardest for you? Why?

1. Question

Inquiry begins by asking questions about the situation. The situation may be a topic you are curious about, a school assignment, or an idea you have for a project. In any case, the basic questions you ask yourself are the same (see page **229**).

---

5 W's and H

(*Example:* Kim and her classmates have some tadpoles to care for.)

Who is involved?	My science classmates and I
What is our topic?	Amphibians, especially our classroom tadpoles
Where is this happening?	In Mrs. Hartford's classroom
When will we work together?	Over the next two weeks
Why are we doing this?	Need to know how to take care of our tadpoles
How can we do this?	Read about tadpoles—what they eat, where they live

---

Brainstorm

Next, it's time to think big by brainstorming about the topic. One way to do this is to create a cluster: Write your topic in the middle of a piece of paper. Then add facts and ideas all around it. (See also page **231**.)

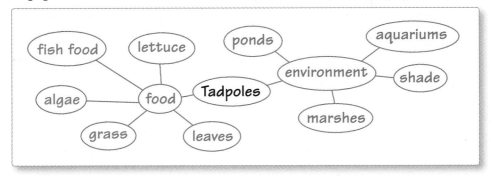

Your Turn Learn about a topic, an assignment, or a project you are doing by answering the 5W's and H about it. Then create a cluster like the one above.

2. Plan

After you've come up with lots of information and ideas, it's time to plan. Planning means deciding what to do—setting a goal and creating objectives to accomplish it. A planning sheet can help.

Planning Sheet

Goal: We will build an aquarium for tadpoles to become frogs.

Objectives:

- Who? My classmates and myself
- What? Design a living space for our classroom tadpoles
- Where In Mrs. Hartford's science classroom
- When? Over the next two weeks
- Why? To provide a safe habitat for our tadpoles to grow
- How? Build a special aquarium

Tasks: **Time:**

Start . . . .

1. Learn about tadpoles' habitats and diet.   March 1
2. Visit a local pond.   March 4
3. Brainstorm design ideas.   March 8
4. Draw a model.   March 8–10
5. Gather supplies and materials.   March 10–12
6. Construct the aquarium.   March 15–17
7. Place tadpoles in the aquarium.   March 18
8. Monitor growth, diet, and habitat.   March 18–??
9. Release frogs into the wild!   Not sure when

Finish . . . .

Team: Mrs. Hartford's fifth-grade students

Tools: We'll use the Internet and the library to do research. We'll also visit the pond at the park. Maybe a park ranger can help. We'll choose materials after we know more.

Your Turn Go to **thoughtfullearning.com/e222** to download a planning sheet. Complete a plan for the idea you chose on page 221.

3. Research

The next step is to do your research. You need to find as much information as you can about your topic. Always take notes on the important information you find. Kim wrote her notes on note cards.

1

What do tadpoles eat? How do they get their food?
- Tadpoles are herbivores, so they only eat plants.

Some things they can eat:
- Algae
- Plants
- Lettuce (!)

"How to Raise Tadpoles" Allaboutfrogs.org

2

What habitat do tadpoles prefer?
- Fresh pond water
- No chlorine or pollution
- Shady areas
- Fallen leaves and sticks in water

"Backyard Habitat," Animal Planet

3

What should our aquarium include?
- Fresh water from the local pond
- One big rock and lots of small rocks
- Green leaves and sticks and twigs
- Electronic filter

Your Turn

Research the project you have started. Use note cards to collect the information.

4. Create

After you do your research and gather all the materials you need, it's time to make your creation. This part is fun but also challenging. If an idea doesn't work, you may have to try something else, and that's okay. The following notes are about Kim's aquarium project:

These are pictures of materials we used: bucket, strainer, rocks, pond water, lettuce, sticks, leaves, tall potted plant.

Tadpole Aquarium

plant

rock

sticks   leaves

Here's a drawing of our plan for the aquarium.

The electronic filter was too expensive, so we tried out different plants instead.

5. Improve

When you finish your project, it's time to evaluate it and make improvements. Start by looking at your plan again. Did you meet your objectives and reach your goal?

Rubric Sheet

Name: Kim   Project: Frog Life Cycle

Goal:	Evaluation:	Rating			Score
We will build an aquarium for tadpoles to become frogs.	We built an aquarium, and many of our tadpoles are growing.	**Beat** 60	**Met** (40)	**Didn't** 20	40
Objectives:					
1. My classmates and I will work together.	Mrs. Hartford advised us.	**Beat** 10	**Met** (6)	**Didn't** 2	6
2. We will design a living space for our classroom tadpoles.	We built an aquarium!	**Beat** 10	**Met** (6)	**Didn't** 2	6
3. We will work in Mrs. Hartford's science classroom.	We also visited a local pond.	**Beat** (10)	**Met** 6	**Didn't** 2	10
4. We have two weeks.	We built it. Now we wait for the tadpoles to grow.	**Beat** 10	**Met** (6)	**Didn't** 2	6
5. We want a safe habitat for our tadpoles to grow in.	We need to find a safe alternative filter.	**Beat** 10	**Met** 6	**Didn't** (2)	2
6. We will build a special aquarium.	That's what we did.	**Beat** (10)	**Met** 6	**Didn't** 2	10
				Total:	80

6. **Present**

When you are satisfied with your work, it's time to present it. Here's how Kim's science class concluded the aquarium project:

> Kim and her classmates fed their tadpoles, watched them grow, and kept the aquarium fresh by adding pond water. When the tadpoles finally grew into frogs, the class hosted a release party at the pond. They invited friends, family, and park rangers to watch the frogs return to the wild.

Inquiry Process in Review

So what did Kim and her classmates accomplish? You are correct if you say they built a safe and suitable tadpole aquarium. But that's only half the story. They also used the inquiry process and practiced 21st century skills. The same process and skills can work for other projects, even finishing your chores or improving your soccer skills.

The Inquiry Process	21st Century Skills
▪ question	▪ creative thinking
▪ plan	▪ critical thinking
▪ research	▪ communicating
▪ create	▪ collaborating
▪ improve	▪ reading/studying
▪ present	▪ using technology

Your Turn Think of something you need to do or want to accomplish. Review the steps of the inquiry process and write down three things you could do to work toward your goal.

Why is questioning
like opening a can
of worms?

Chapter 18
Questioning

Learning always begins with a question. And that question leads to another, and another, and so on. Finding answers for all those questions will give you the information you need to understand any topic that interests you. This chapter will help you practice your questioning skills so you can discover exactly what you want to know.

You will learn . . .

- Basic Types of Questions
- Asking the 5 W's and H
- Asking Sensory Questions
- Asking Thought Questions
- Asking About Your World
- Asking About Things Around You
- Asking Creative and Deep Questions
- Asking Driving Questions
- Using the SCAMPER Method

Basic Types of Questions

Different types of questions call for different types of answers.

Closed-Ended Questions

A closed-ended question seeks a simple answer—*yes, no,* or a simple fact. Closed-ended questions often start with *is, does, who, what, where,* or *when.*

Strength: Gains a precise answer

Weakness: Does not call for deep thinking

Examples: Is the sun on fire? What is the sun's energy process called?

Open-Ended Questions

An open-ended question seeks many possible ideas. Open-ended questions often start with *how* or *why.*

Strength: Encourages deep thinking, new ideas, and discussion

Weakness: May result in complex answers that are difficult to judge

Examples: How could my home use solar energy? Why does Europe have so many trains?

Theoretical Questions

A theoretical question seeks a hypothesis based on broad knowledge. Theoretical questions often start with *will, would, should, could* or *might.*

Strength: Encourages deep thinking and new understanding

Weakness: Generates uncertain answers that are difficult to judge

Examples: Will homes in the future generate their own energy? Would that be effective? Would it be safe?

Your Turn Write one example of each type of question about a topic you are researching for school.

Asking the 5 W's and H

The 5W's and H—*Who? What? When? Where? Why?* and *How?*—are the most important questions you can ask about any situation. These questions are also known as journalistic questions because newspaper writers (and police officers) use them to investigate what is happening around them. Once you find answers to the 5W's and H, you can begin to ask deeper questions about any topic or situation.

5 W's and H	Observing an Event or Situation	Planning a Project
Who?	Who is involved?	Who is on the team for this project?
What?	What happened?	What goal do we have? What do we need to get done?
Where?	Where did it happen?	Where will we work? Where will we present?
When?	When did it happen?	When is the project due? When is each task due?
Why?	Why did it happen?	Why are we doing this project?
How?	How did it happen?	How will we complete the work?

Your Turn Ask the 5W's and H about one of your favorite memories. Write your answers down or share them with a classmate.

Asking Sensory Questions

You learn the most from experiences when all five of your senses are involved.

What am I sensing?

Filling out a sensory chart like the one below can help you heighten each of your senses and gain the most from what you are experiencing. Sensory charts work best when you fill them with descriptive words. Here is a sensory chart by a student who visited her grandfather's home.

What do I . . .

see?	blue eyes, wrinkled smile, white hair, flowery chair, simple furniture, family pictures, framed war medals, gray corduroy pants, candy with gold wrappers, baby-blue carpet
hear?	wind chimes, deep laughter, soft voice, baseball announcer on the television
smell?	grandma's flowery perfume
taste?	caramel candy, Dr. Pepper, cashews
touch?	leathery skin, strong hands, soft hugs, warm air, chilled mugs, spongy carpet

From Flickr by Daveybot

Your Turn Make a sensory chart about visiting one of your family members. (Download a template of a sensory chart at **thoughtfullearning. com/e230**.)

Asking Thought Questions

To brainstorm for thought questions, you can use a mind map (sometimes called a "cluster") or freewriting.

Mind Map

To create a mind map, write a word or an idea and circle it. Then write other ideas around it and connect them to the first circle or to each other. Keep going until you have written everything you can think of.

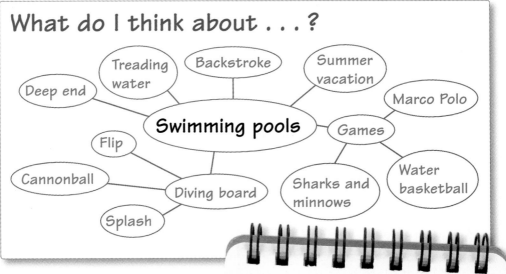

Freewriting

Freewriting means writing for five to ten minutes without stopping, letting your thoughts flow freely. While freewriting, don't stop to make corrections or craft the perfect sentence. Just keep writing.

What do I think about swimming pools?

Swimming pools remind me of happy times. Summers and vacation are the first things that come to mind. When my family goes on vacation, I don't really care where, as long as there's a swimming pool. That reminds me of my favorite vacation ever. . . .

 Your Turn Make a mind map or freewrite about a topic that interests you. Let your thoughts run freely, and write everything down.

Asking About Your World

Our world is filled with amazing places and amazing people. There's so much to see and so much to do. Scan the map on the next page, and then ask yourself questions about our world.

Name: Felix Mendoza

1. Where do you live? San Antonio, TX

2. Where did your parents grow up?
   Guadalajara, Mexico

3. Where have you been?
   Mexico, Dallas, and Albuquerque

4. Where is your favorite place to be?
   The zoo in my hometown.

5. What place do you wish you could go?
   Costa Rica

   Why? It has awesome beaches and a huge rain forest.

6. What place scares you?
   Antarctica

   Why? It's freezing there! And I'd get lost.

7. What place have you never heard of?
   Turkmenistan

   What continent is it on? It's in Asia.

8. What place do you wish you knew more about?
   Thailand

   Why? Because my dad goes to a Thai restaurant, and
   the owner is really interesting.

Your Turn Answer the questions above about our world. Discuss your answers with your friends. Listen to their responses. Are they the same or different? What answer surprises you the most?

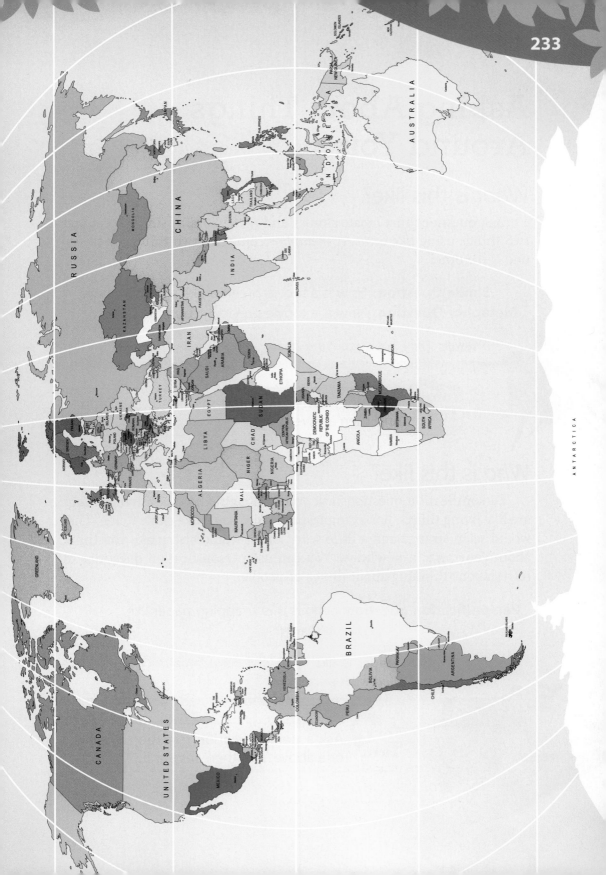

Asking About Things Around You

What is this like?

Ask questions that create similes and metaphors. A simile compares two things using *like* or *as*. A *metaphor* compares two things by saying one *is* the other.

Simile Question: How is a movie preview like a bumble bee?
Metaphor Question: How is a movie preview a bumble bee?

Answer: They both create a buzz.

 Pose your own simile and metaphor questions. And then answer them.

Who is this like?

Personification questions ask you to imagine how nonliving things are like living things. For example, imagine if your bike came to life. That would seem strange and a little scary, but it would also make you think about your bike in new ways. You can use personification questions to refresh your thinking about things or people.

Personification question: Who is this wrapping paper like, and why?

This wrapping paper is like my friend Sara because it is colorful and filled with surprises.

 Ask a personification question like the one above, and then answer it.

Asking Creative Questions

Questioning is the product of curious minds. Have you ever thought of a strange question you were too afraid to ask? The questions that seem the oddest are often the ones that lead to the most interesting answers. Never be afraid to ask creative questions.

Creative Questions

- How long can someone live under water?

- What qualities make a president great?

- How did pink and purple come to represent "girl" colors?

- What is the strongest rock on earth?

- How did the Hawaiian Islands become a state?

- What makes some people more talkative than others?

- Has there ever been world peace?

- Why do kids get chickenpox?

- Why does laughter make you feel good?

- How do accents develop?

- Why does sneezing force you to close your eyes?

- What does courage look like?

Your Turn Spend 5 minutes writing down creative questions of your own.

Asking Deep Questions

Some questions reveal deeper answers than others. Benjamin Bloom created a scale to show different kinds of questions. The farther you go down the scale, the deeper the questions become.

Levels of Thinking	One Student's Questions
To remember, ask about facts. ■ **What** happened? ■ **Who** was involved? ■ **Where** did it take place? ■ **When** did it happen?	The Louisiana Purchase • What land was part of the Louisiana Purchase? • Who was involved? • Where and when did the Louisiana Purchase take place?
To understand, ask about meaning. ■ **Why** did happen? ■ **How** did it happen?	The Louisiana Purchase • Why did Napoleon agree to sell the land? • How did the sale affect America?
To apply, ask how to use ideas. ■ **What** can I do with this idea? ■ **How** could I use it?	Bargaining • What bargaining tips can I learn from the Louisiana Purchase? • How can I apply that knowledge in my own life?
To analyze, ask about the parts. ■ **What** are the parts? ■ **How** do they fit together?	Lewis and Clark's Expedition • Who were Lewis and Clark? • How did they avoid getting lost?
To evaluate, ask about quality. ■ **What** is important about this? ■ **Does** it fulfill its purpose? ■ **How** could it be better?	Lewis and Clark's Expedition • Why was Lewis and Clark's trip important? • Did the trip achieve its goals? • What would've improve the trip?
To create, ask about making something. ■ **Could** I create something? ■ **Should** I combine things?	Mapping • What new map could I make? • What images/technology could I use to make it easier to read?

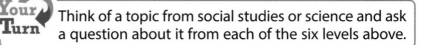

Your Turn Think of a topic from social studies or science and ask a question about it from each of the six levels above.

Asking Driving Questions

A driving question is a question that cannot be answered with "yes" or "no." Instead, the answer requires careful thought and research. You can ask driving questions as a starting point for a project or investigation.

Qualities

A good driving question is . . .

- **Challenging,** meaning it is not easily answered.
- **Relevant,** meaning it relates to something you are interested in, or a topic you are studying in school.
- **Interesting,** meaning someone else would be curious about it.

Examples

Here are some examples of driving questions.

- *Social Studies:* How was democracy created?
- *Science:* What characteristics make a planet suitable for life?
- *English:* How did the question mark develop?
- *Math:* How was math used in the ancient Aztec civilization?

Getting Unstuck

You can ask driving questions to guide your own projects and investigations. If you are having trouble coming up with a good question, consider . . .

- **Causes and effects.** What caused America's westward expansion? What were the effects?
- **Problems and solutions**. Are we running out of fresh water? How can people conserve it?
- **Different perspectives.** How would your life be different if you grew up during the American Revolution?

Your Turn Create two or three driving questions and share them with a partner. Choose your favorite one and decide if you can make a project out of it.

Using the SCAMPER Method

The SCAMPER questions are a set of questions that you can ask to think critically about any topic. A researcher named Bob Eberle came up with the list, taking the first letter from each type of question to form **SCAMPER**. Here are some sample SCAMPER questions:

Question Type	Questions to Ask
Substitute	■ What else can I use instead? ■ Who else can be involved instead? ■ What other materials can I use? ■ Where else could I do this?
Combine	■ How could I put two or more things together?
Adapt	■ What changes would improve this?
Magnify	■ How can I make this bigger or more powerful? ■ How can I slow this down or speed it up?
Put to Other Uses	■ What else could I do with this? ■ Who else would be interested in this?
Eliminate	■ How can I make this smaller or more specific? ■ How can I streamline this?
Rearrange	■ How can I look at this from a completely different perspective? ■ How can I solve a different part of the problem?

Your Turn Think of a project you are working on at school or home. Answer one question for each letter in SCAMPER. What new possibilities come to mind? (Download a SCAMPER sheet from **thoughtfullearning.com/e238**.)

Do I really need all
this stuff?

Chapter 19
Planning

A plan always helps. This chapter shows you
how to manage the who, what, where, when, why,
how, and even "how much" of any project you take
on. You'll be setting goals and objectives, gathering
tools and materials, and much more. Having a plan
is a good plan.

You will learn . . .

- Setting Goals, Objectives,
  and Tasks
- Scheduling Time
- Building Your Team
- Gathering Your Tools
- Creating a
  Planning Sheet
- Planning Throughout
  the Process

Setting Goals, Objectives, and Tasks

A good plan begins with a goal and objectives. After those are in place, focus on the tasks—and the people, tools, and materials needed to complete them.

Setting Your Goal

When you set a goal, you consider all of the questions and topics you thought of in the previous chapter and pick out an idea that really interests you.

Ideas	**+**	**Opportunity**	**=**	**Goal**
Something you want or need to do		A time, place, or purpose for your idea to happen		An idea in focus

Create a digital poster.

Mr. Adams wants us to know about waves.

I will **create** a **digital poster** about wave properties.

Defining Objectives

Objectives tell what you intend to do in a project in order to achieve your goal. Find your objectives by asking the 5 W's and H about the project (see page **229**).

Objectives

Who?	I'll work with a partner to create the poster.
What?	We'll create a digital poster about wave properties.
Where?	We'll create it in the computer lab at school but do our research at home.
When?	It needs to be done by Wednesday of next week.
Why?	We are doing a poster presentation in science class.
How?	We'll show examples of waves and their properties.

Listing Tasks

After you define your goal and objectives, think about the tasks you will need to accomplish to complete your project.

What do I need to do?	What do I need to learn?
1. Research waves with my partner. 2. Make a sketch of the poster. 3. Find a free digital poster service on the Web. 4. Create the digital poster. 5. Improve the poster. 6. Present it to my class.	We learned about the crest and trough of waves in science class. Now I think we should focus on how to measure a wave's speed.

Your Turn List your goal, objectives, and tasks for a project you are doing or for one you would like to do.

Scheduling Time

Your schedule starts at the moment you get an assignment and ends on the due date. To do your best work, do not wait until the last minute to get things done. Using a calendar will help you visualize what needs to get done and when.

Sunday	Monday	Tuesday	Wednesday	Thursday	Friday	Saturday
27	28 Assignment: Create a digital poster about waves.	1 Begin research.	2 Discuss research with Raul.	3 Make sketch.	4 Review sketch with Mr. Adams.	5
6 Find pictures, video, etc., for digital poster.	7 Finish first version of the poster.	8 Improve poster.	9 Project due: Present poster to my class.	10	11	12

Making Adjustments

Check the schedule as you work on your project. Speed up or slow down as needed.

- **If you are falling behind,** either work faster or devote more hours to the project.
- **If you still can't catch up,** find out if the due date can be moved.
- **If you are ahead of schedule,** check your work to make sure it is as good as you want it to be. Either slow down to make improvements, or use the extra time at the end.

Your Turn Find either an online or a print version of a calendar (or visit thoughtfullearning.com/e242 for a blank one). Record your start date and end date. Then schedule the tasks for your project in between.

Building Your Team

Some projects require teamwork. Anytime you work with others, it is important to understand your role within the group. The list of possible roles below is followed by one student's ideas about roles for his team.

Common Roles

Actor	Explorer	Promoter
Announcer	Host	Presenter
Artist	Interviewer	Reporter
Builder	Leader	Researcher
Business person	Listener	Salesperson
Chef	Manager	Scientist
Debater	Marketer	Speaker
Designer	Musician	Tailor
Director	Playwright	Teacher
Editor	Poet	Writer
Entrepreneur	Politician	

My Role: I will research and design the digital poster. Once it is finished, I will present it.

Other Roles: Raul will help with research and design, and since he is a good artist, he can sketch the poster. I'd like his help with presenting, too.

Possible Team: Raul is my partner for this project.

Note: Some projects will involve bigger teams than the one described above.

 Your Turn Write down the role or roles that you and others will fill in your project. Then list your possible team members.

Gathering Your Tools

Every project needs specific tools, materials, information, and resources. Here is a list of tools needed to create a digital poster.

What **equipment** do I need?
- Computer
- Online poster program, like Glogster
- Projector

Notes:
We can use our school's computer lab. Mr. Adams is going to set up the projector on presentation day.

What **materials** do I need?
- Sketching paper
- Pencils

Notes:
Raul will sketch the poster.

What **information** do I need to discover?
- What is the difference between the crest and the trough?
- What is amplitude?
- What is wavelength?

Notes:
Crest is the highest point; trough is the lowest point. Amplitude is the distance between the middle of the wave and its crest and trough; wavelength measures crest to crest or trough to trough.

What **resources** are available?
- Internet
- Science book
- Library books
- Mr. Adams

Notes:
We are going to create our poster based on our research and Raul's sketch.

Creating a Planning Sheet

This is the planning sheet for completing the digital poster.

Planning Sheet

Goal: I will create a digital poster about wave properties.

Objectives:

Who? I'll work with a partner to create the poster.
What? We'll create a digital poster about wave properties.
Where We'll create it in the computer lab at our school.
When? It needs to be done by Wednesday of next week.
Why? We are doing a poster presentation in science class.
How? We'll show examples of waves and their properties.

Tasks: **Time:**

Start . . . .

1. Research wave properties.   March 1
2. Create sketch of poster.   March 3
3. Review sketch.   March 4
4. Find pictures and video for poster.   March 6
5. Create digital poster.   March 7
6. Improve poster.   March 8
7. Present poster to our class.   March 9

Finish . . . .

Team: Raul and Martina

Tools: Equipment: computer, online poster program, projector
Materials: sketching paper, pencils
Information: crest and trough, wavelength and amplitude
Resources: Internet, science book, library books,
Mr. Adams

Note: Keep your planning sheet in a safe place. You will refer to it during the entire inquiry process (see page 246).

Your Turn Complete a planning sheet for your project. (Go to thoughtfullearning.com/e245.)

Planning Throughout the Process

For all projects, you can refer to your planning sheet at any point during the inquiry process. The following ideas explain ways to use your plan.

Organizing

Your plan tells you who is involved, what needs to get done, and when.

Gathering

Your plan guides you as you do research. It lists the tools and materials you need to gather.

Developing

Your plan lays out the tasks you must do to complete your project.

Evaluating

Your plan will tell you whether you met your goals and objectives.

Do I have to be a
scientist to do
research?

Chapter 20
Researching

You don't have to be a scientist to do research, but you can learn a lot from scientists. They are curious about many things. Are you? When a topic fascinates you and you start digging for information about it, you are doing research. It's all about asking questions and looking for answers. In this chapter, you will learn how to explore a variety of sources as you search for the answers you need.

You will learn . . .

- Asking Questions
- Finding Information
- Using the Library
- Using Primary and Secondary Sources
- Using the Internet
- Avoiding Plagiarism
- Taking Notes
- Organizing Your information
- Using an Outline

Asking Questions

Research begins with your own questions and curiosity. What do you need to know? Research will help you find answers.

Using Triggering Questions

On pages 227–238, you asked many interesting questions. One of them might give you a starting point for your research. Also consider questions like those below, which can trigger your curiosity.

People

- What person interests me?
- Which Native American tribe is most amazing?
- Whom do I wish I could meet?
- What scientist do I admire?
- Who has made the biggest difference in the world?

Things

- What would it be like to have a dog's sense of smell?
- How do rainbows happen?
- What is the strangest invention ever patented?
- Why does music so strongly affect our emotions?
- How does the Internet work? Where is it?

Places

- What would my perfect place look like?
- What is life like in China?
- Where have big asteroids left craters on Earth?
- Why are so many cities near large bodies of water?
- What public park is most beautiful?

Ideas

- How would I describe my culture to a stranger?
- What is compassion? Why is it important?
- What does patriotism involve?
- What makes someone a genius?

Your Turn Review the questions above and those that you wrote in the questioning chapter. Choose four or more questions that you would like to explore. Share your list with your classmates.

Listing Pointed Questions

Once you decide on a main question to explore, you can begin to ask more questions about the topic. Pointed questions are specific questions that help you plan and organize your research. You can write pointed questions by answering the five W's and H. Here are some pointed questions that a student might ask about Cherokee Indians.

Triggering Question:	Who are the Cherokee Indians?
Pointed Questions:	
Who?	Who leads the Cherokee now? Who are their great leaders of the past?
What?	What language do the Cherokee speak? What is Cherokee culture like?
Where?	Where did the Cherokee originate? Where do the Cherokee live now?
When?	When did the Cherokee first meet settlers?
Why?	Why did the Trail of Tears happen?
How?	How do the Cherokee live now?

Note: Think of your first list of pointed questions as a starting point for your research. You can continue to ask questions throughout the research process.

Your Turn Choose a triggering question that you asked in the "Your Turn" on the previous page. Then use the 5 W's and H to create at least six pointed questions that could help you explore your main question.

Finding Information

You have many options for finding answers to your research questions—from searching the Internet to conducting face-to-face conversations. Here's a basic review of where to look for information.

- The **Internet** can get your research started. Go to a search site and enter keywords related to your topic (see page 254).

- **Social media** can help you talk to people who are involved in your topic. With your parent or guardian's supervision, you can email questions to experts or talk with knowledgeable people on forums, message boards, wikis, and other sites.

- **Reference books,** such as encyclopedias, almanacs, and atlases, can also serve as good starting points.

- **Magazines** and **newspapers** provide up-to-date information on just about any topic, and most come in print and online versions.

- **Other people** can serve as rich sources of information. Consider your teachers, librarians, media specialists, parents, and community members.

- **Direct observations** or **experiences** allow you to see for yourself how something works or how something happens. Your observations are primary research (see page 252).

Your Turn Do some early searching about your topic to see what types of information are available. Identify at least four resources that you can use.

Using the Library

Your school and city libraries contain many helpful resources for research. Beyond the many stacks of books, libraries include computers, magazines, movies, and journals.

Using a Computer Catalog

You can use your library's computer catalog to find specific books and materials related to your question or topic. Information is listed on this catalog according to titles, authors, and subjects.

1. **Title** If you know the title of the book, search for it by name to determine if your library has the book in its collection.
2. **Author** If you are interested in a specific author, enter his or her name. The catalog will show the author's works that are available in the library or system.
3. **Subject** Key in the subject or a related phrase to see what materials your library has to offer.

Computer Card Entry

Author:	Conley, Robert J.
Title:	The Cherokee
Published:	Chelsea House, 2011 111pp.
Subjects:	Cherokee, Indians, Native Americans, Indians of North America
STATUS:	Not checked out
CALL NUMBER:	J970.0049
LOCATION:	General collection

Note: If you have any trouble finding the information or resources you need, ask a librarian or media specialist for assistance.

Your Turn What types of information can you search for in the computer catalog? List searches you could make for the topic that you have chosen to research.

Using Primary and Secondary Resources

Whenever you begin a research project, your instructor may ask that you use a mix of primary and secondary resources. A primary source is information that you collect firsthand. A secondary source is information that you get from other people.

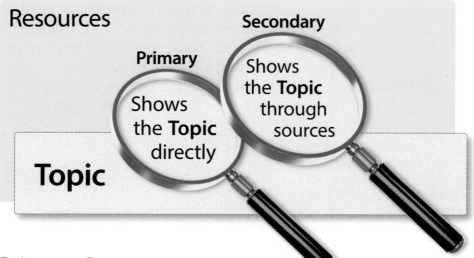

Resources

Secondary

Primary

Shows the **Topic** through sources

Shows the **Topic** directly

Topic

Primary Sources

A primary source puts you in direct contact with the topic. Here are examples of primary sources:

- Observing something firsthand
- Experiencing an event yourself
- Interviewing someone
- Conducting a survey
- Reading original letters, diaries, or documents
- Visiting a place
- Making something
- Conducting an experiment

What is the value of primary sources?

Primary sources let you deal with the topic directly and discover things for yourself. These sources prevent you from being influenced by others. However, the information is sometimes hard to gather and understand.

Secondary Sources

A secondary source provides secondhand information. Instead of giving you direct access to the topic, a secondary source tells what someone else thought or felt about it. Here are common types of secondary sources.

- Nonfiction books
- Encyclopedias, atlases, and almanacs
- Textbooks
- Informational brochures and pamphlets
- Magazine and journal articles (in print or online)
- Television specials and news shows

What is the value of secondary sources?

Secondary sources help you understand subjects by getting expert explanations about them. These sources let you know if your own thinking is in line with others' thinking. However, these sources do not give you direct access to the topic.

Focusing on the Topic

To decide if a source is primary or secondary, think about whether you are in direct contact with the topic. See the examples below:

Topic: The Hunger Games
↳ **Primary source:** Reading the novel
   ↳ **Secondary source:** Reading a review of the novel

Topic: Cherokee Ceremonies
↳ **Primary source:** Attending a Cherokee powwow
   ↳ **Secondary source:** Reading about a powwow

Topic: Decomposition
↳ **Primary source:** Running a decomposition lab
   ↳ **Secondary source:** Watching a video about decomposition

 Identify one primary and one secondary source that you could use to learn about your research topic.

Using the Internet

The Internet gives you access to all sorts of information, including both primary and secondary sources. (See also pages 252–253.)

Navigating Tips

Keep these points in mind as you use the Internet for research.

Work smart.	Know the basics of Internet searching, including how to use keywords. (See below.)
Be creative.	If one route or keyword doesn't lead you in the right direction, choose a different one.
Check many choices.	For most searches, you will have many options to review.
Stay on task.	Avoid the temptation to take side trips.
Take notes.	Write down or print out key information.

A Basic Keyword Guide

The success of your Internet search will depend on the quality of the keywords you use. Simple changes to a keyword can provide you with completely different results.

1. Type in the topic of your research: **horses, soccer, cookies**.
2. Add a more specific word before or after it, and you will call up pages that contain any of the words: **Clydesdale horses, soccer moves, cookie recipes**.
3. Enclose the phrase in quotation marks, and you will receive just the pages containing that phrase: **"soccer moves."**
4. Use words such as **and** (+) or **not** (-) to narrow or focus your search: **soccer and dribbling, soccer not scores**, and so on.

 Your Turn Follow the tips above to conduct a keyword search about a topic that you are studying.

Avoiding Plagiarism

Imagine you want to surprise your mom by cleaning the kitchen while she is out of the house. You do a really good job, but when she comes home, your brother or sister takes credit for all your work. That wouldn't be fair!

Plagiarism is taking credit for someone else's work, just as the brother or sister did in the story above. Plagiarism occurs if you use the words or ideas of others as if they were your own. You should always do your best to avoid plagiarism by doing the following.

Ways to Avoid Plagiarism

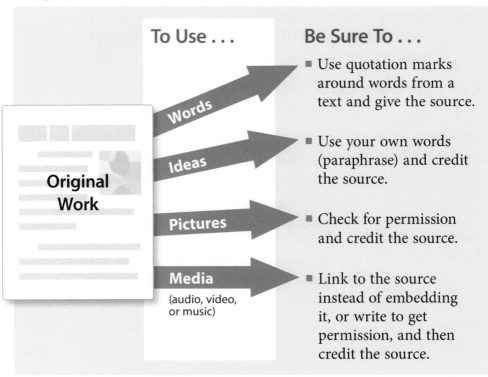

Original Work

To Use . . .

Words

Ideas

Pictures

Media
(audio, video, or music)

Be Sure To . . .

- Use quotation marks around words from a text and give the source.

- Use your own words (paraphrase) and credit the source.

- Check for permission and credit the source.

- Link to the source instead of embedding it, or write to get permission, and then credit the source.

Your Turn With the help of a partner, go to the Internet to find one or two facts about plagiarism. Create a list of all the facts you and your classmates find. List your sources.

Taking Notes

Taking good notes is one of the most important responsibilities of a researcher. Notes help you gather important information and avoid plagiarism.

Using Note Cards

One way to record your notes is on note cards. Here are some tips for using note cards.

1. **Write a specific question** at the top of each card.
2. Underneath the question, **record important facts and details** that answer the question. Try using your own words instead of copying the source word for word.
3. **Identify the source of information** at the bottom of the card.
4. **Number the cards** so you know what order they go in.

Example Note Card

Card number — ③

Topic question — What language do the Cherokee speak?

Research findings —
- The Cherokee of colonial America spoke a Cherokee Indian language.
- Today they speak English but also use their native language.
- The language is made up of many soft sounds.
- Their writing system was invented by Sequoyah.

Source — "Cherokee Indian Fact Sheet"

In Focus You can also use your notebook to take notes. In fact, notebooks give you more room to write. You can set up each page like a note card. Or you can use a two-column system and add your own comments (see pages 118–119).

Using Electronic Notes

Another option for taking notes is to use a laptop or other electronic device. If you can use a keyboard and type faster than you can write, this might be a good option for you. Here are some pros and cons of taking electronic notes.

Pros	Cons
Your electronic notes are . . .	Your electronic notes . . .
■ neat and easy to read.	■ require a computer or laptop.
■ stored safely, as long as you save your work.	■ may tempt you to copy text and images that you don't have the right to copy.
■ easy to change and delete.	
■ good for clickable links to source material.	

In Focus Your school might have special note-taking programs that you can use. Otherwise, use your device's basic writing program.

Electronic Note Page

Cherokee Indians Notes

Fonts

Where did the Cherokee come from?

- Once part of the Iroquois tribe near the Great Lakes
- Moved to the Southeast
- Mostly in Georgia, North Carolina, South Carolina
- Appalachian Mountains
- Forced to move into Oklahoma following Trail of Tears

Facts for Kids

Map of Tribes of the Indian Nation

Your Turn Take notes on a note card, in a notebook, or on a laptop for one of the pointed questions you listed on page 249. Use the strategies you learned on the last two pages.

Organizing Your Information

Once you choose a topic and research information about it, the next step is to organize your research so that it's easy to use. First, you should decide on a main idea or focus for your work. For example, a project on the Cherokee Indians might focus on the tribe's relationship with early American settlers.

Then you should arrange your notes in a logical order, keeping your focus in mind. A graphic organizer or outline can help you put your ideas in the right order. Common graphic organizers are shown on the next two pages, and a guide to outlining appears on page 260.

Graphic Organizers

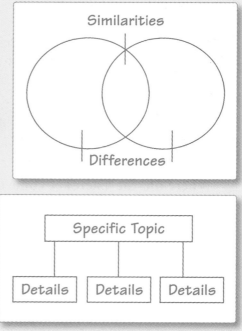

■ Venn Diagram

A Venn diagram helps you take notes on the similarities and differences between two subjects. Draw two circles that overlap. In the space that overlaps, write similarities. In the spaces that don't, write differences.

■ Line Diagram

A line diagram helps support a main idea. The top box includes the topic or focus. The bottom boxes include details about the topic. A separate line is used to connect each detail with the topic.

■ Before-After Chart

A before-after chart explains what came before and after an event. The top half explains what happened before. The bottom half explains what happened after.

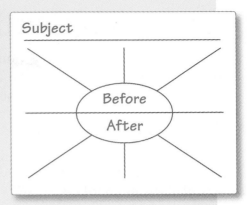

■ Cycle Diagram

A cycle diagram shows how something works. Each arrow represents a step in the process.

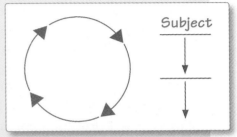

■ 5 W's and H Chart

A 5W's and H chart identifies the key details of a situation. **Who? what? when? where? why?** and **how?** appear on one side of the chart, and answers go on the other side.

Who?	
What?	
Where?	
When?	
Why?	
How?	

■ Time Line

A time line explains the order in which something happens.

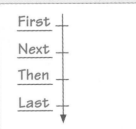

Your Turn Which of these graphic organizers would be most useful for your own project? Why? Discuss your answers with a partner.

Using an Outline

Another way to organize your information is to create an outline. An outline puts your details into an organized list. You can follow your outline to create a project or report.

Sentence Outline

Here is how you can create a sentence outline.

- Turn the questions at the top of your note cards into statements.

> **Question:** Where did the Cherokee Indians live?
>
> **Statement:** The Cherokee Indians lived in the Southeastern United States.

- List these statements in the order that you want to include them. Use Roman numerals (I., II., III.) to number them.
- Leave space below each statement to include main supporting points. Start each point with a capital letter (A., B., C.).

Outline *(first part)*

I. The Cherokee Indians lived in the Southeastern United States.
   A. The Cherokee were once the largest nation in eastern North America.
   B. They settled in the Carolinas and Virginia.
   C. They defended their land against European settlers.
II. Later, the U.S. government forced the Cherokee to move to Oklahoma.
   A. In the early 1800s, the U.S. government set up Indian Territories in Oklahoma and sent the Cherokee there.
   B. The Cherokee called their move to Oklahoma the Trail of Tears because of the terrible hardships they endured.

Your Turn Create a sentence outline for your own research. Turn the questions on your note cards into statements. List statements in order, starting each with a Roman numeral. Under each statement, list details, starting each with a letter.

Where did I get this?
I made it!

Chapter 21
Creating

Taking your ideas and turning them into
something real is an exciting part of any project.
This chapter will help you get started and keep
moving as you work on your own creations.

You will learn . . .

- A Guide to Creating
- Creating Basic Structure
- Using Informational Structures
- Creating Narrative Structure
- Creating Visual Structure
- Tips for Getting Unstuck

A Guide to Creating

Creating can be the most exciting part of the inquiry process. You've questioned, planned, and researched to prepare. Now it's time to make something of your own.

Creating can also be a nervous part of the process, especially if you aren't fully ready. To see if you are ready to create, study "Checking for Readiness" below. Then use the "Getting Started" tips to begin creating and to keep things moving smoothly.

Checking for Readiness

You're ready to create after you have . . .

- ☑ asked the right questions about your topic,
- ☑ filled out a planning sheet (see page 245), and
- ☑ gathered lots of information about your topic.

Getting Started

These tips will help you move through the work of creating.

- **Follow your schedule.** Check your plan to see when each task needs to be completed.
- **Be prepared.** Gather all of the tools and materials you will need.
- **Find a good place to work.** Consider how much space you'll need and whether you'll be able to concentrate in the place you choose.
- **Expect changes.** Adjust your schedule if necessary. Accept new ideas as they occur to you.
- **Finish it.** Make a complete version of your creation before trying to improve it.

Q In Focus You can do very good work when you truly care about your topic and creation. If you begin to lose interest, try something different or look for a new approach.

Creating Basic Structure

Think of your favorite story. Whether it's a book, a movie, or even a tall tale, it is likely to have three parts: a beginning, a middle, and an ending. Without each part, a story is not complete.

Many of your projects—writing assignments, speeches, presentations, and so on—also need three parts. Each part has a special purpose.

Beginning

The beginning gets the attention of your audience and provides background information. It tells *what* the project is about and *who* is involved. It also identifies the main point.

Middle

The middle, or main part, presents the important information. It gives key details and may include images. It must be organized and easy to follow (see pages 264–265).

Ending

The ending ties everything together and may repeat the main idea. It gives final details to help the audience understand your message.

Using Informational Structures

The next two pages explain several ways to organize information. These strategies work well for projects that share a lot of information—writing assignments, debates, videos, speeches, and oral presentations.

Importance

Use order of importance to rank your ideas from least important to most or from most important to least. When you want your audience to agree with you or take some action, save your most important point for last.

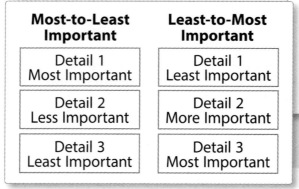

Most-to-Least Important	Least-to-Most Important
Detail 1 Most Important	Detail 1 Least Important
Detail 2 Less Important	Detail 2 More Important
Detail 3 Least Important	Detail 3 Most Important

How to Approach a Horse

Horses scare easily, so always approach them in a way that makes them feel safe. First of all, never walk right up to a horse. Instead, move toward the side of the horse's face in a relaxed manner. Let the horse know you are coming by whistling or speaking softly. Keep walking unless the horse flinches or acts nervous. Whatever you do, never sneak up from behind. Horses don't like surprises!

Location

When you want to describe a person, thing, or place, arrange your details by location. You could describe the topic in ways like these:

↓ top to bottom → left to right ↻ front to back

Your Turn Describe the photograph on this page from the foreground (front) to the horizon (back).

Time

Use time order to show the order in which events happen. Time order works well for telling a story, explaining how to do something, or talking about a historical event.

Lincoln and the Civil War

Nov. 6, 1860	Abraham Lincoln elected President of the United States
April 12, 1861	Confederate soldiers attack Ft. Sumter
July 21, 1861	First major battle
Jan. 1, 1863	Emancipation Proclamation
Nov. 19, 1963	Gettysburg Address
April 9, 1865	War ends

Comparison-Contrast

Use comparison-contrast organization to explain how two things are alike and different. You can describe one thing entirely and then the other, or explain first how the things are similar and then how they are different. (See the Venn diagram on page 258.) The example below uses the similarities/differences pattern.

Ecosystems: Biotic vs. Abiotic Factors

Similarities	Differences
• Make up an ecosystem • Affect survival of animal and plant life • Affect each other	***Biotic*** • Living factors—plants, animals, fungi, bacteria • Can be dead • Cannot survive without abiotic factors ***Abiotic*** • Nonliving factors—air, wind, light, temperature, soil • Are not dead • Can function without biotic factors

Creating Narrative Structure

A narrative is a story. It follows a special three-part structure (see page 263) that includes extra details to make the story exciting. You can use this structure, which is called a plot line, when you write stories, create cartoons, make videos, or share favorite memories.

1. **Exposition (beginning):** The characters and setting are introduced. Then the main character faces an obstacle, or problem.

2. **Rising action (middle):** The main character faces more challenges as he or she tries to solve the problem. Each challenge adds drama.

3. **Climax (middle):** The character finally faces the problem head-on and either overcomes it or learns something. This is the most exciting point in the story.

4. **Resolution (ending):** The story wraps up in a satisfying way.

As the details of a narrative get more exciting, the audience's interest level rises. Check out the chart below to see how different parts of a narrative affect the viewer.

Your Turn Think back to some of the best days of your life. Choose your most favorite, and place each part of that special day on a plot chart.

Creating Visual Structure

Visual projects are usually not neatly divided into three parts. Instead, they are experienced all at once, and this gives them a unique structure.

Visual Elements

Every visual project contains the six elements defined below. Use these elements to create the best effects in your artwork, posters, and comics. (See also pages 176–178.)

- **Line** creates shapes and textures. It leads the viewer's eye.
- **Color** adds emotion and sets a mood.
- **Value** is the lightness or darkness of a color.
- **Form** refers to the shapes in a visual work.
- **Texture** is the character of a surface—smooth, rough, patterned.
- **Space** is the area within or between the parts of a visual work.

Your Turn Look carefully at the painting above to find the six visual elements it contains. With a partner, discuss how each element is used in the painting.

Tips for Getting Unstuck

Sometimes you will run into problems and not be able to move ahead with a project. If this happens, consider the following tips for getting unstuck.

- **Review your planning sheet.** After reading your goal and objectives, decide if there is some other way to achieve them.

- **Ask for help.** Ask someone you trust to look at your work. Explain the problem and listen for suggestions.

- **Do more research.** Perhaps more information about the topic will help you. Also look for others who may have encountered similar problems with their projects. What did they do?

- **Work on other parts.** Move on to a different part of the project. Then go back to the part that was giving you problems.

- **Take small steps.** Don't try to complete the project all at once. Break the problem into parts and solve it bit by bit.

- **Take a break.** Step away from the project for a while. Do something completely different.

- **Come back.** Return to the project with a fresh mind and keep working.

ROAD CLOSED

 Your Turn Think of other ways you have used to get unstuck while doing school work. Share your ideas with a partner.

Is there really room for improvement?

Chapter 22
Improving

Yes, there is almost always "room for improvement." Rarely will you create a perfect project in one try. That is why this step in the inquiry process is so important. It offers you the chance to evaluate your work and make it the best it can be. This chapter focuses on improving your creation so you can honestly say, "I love it."

You will learn . . .

- Evaluating
- Getting a Second Opinion
- Making Improvements
- Perfecting Your Work

Evaluating

When you evaluate your creation, you decide on its quality or worth—both what is good about it and what could be better. This is the first step toward improving a project. The best way to evaluate your work is to see if it meets your goal and objectives. You can check this by making a rubric sheet like the one on the next page. Use your planning sheet to get started (see page 245).

How can I create a rubric sheet?

1. **Copy the goal and objectives** from your plan onto a rubric form.

2. **Evaluate your project.** Write a sentence that describes how well you met your goal. Then write the same kind of sentence for each objective.

3. **Rate your project.** Decide whether you beat, met, or didn't meet your goal and each objective. Circle the best answer and write the assigned number of points in the "Score" column.

	Goal	Objectives
■ **Beat:** You did better than you had planned.	60	10
■ **Met:** You did what you had planned.	40	6
■ **Didn't:** You fell short of what you had planned.	20	2

4. **Total your score:** Add the points you recorded for your goal and each objective. The following scale tells what different total scores mean.

120	100	90	80	70	60	40
Amazing!	Great	Strong	Good	Okay	Poor	Incomplete

Your Turn Refer to the planning sheet for your project. Then download a rubric sheet from thoughtfullearning.com/e270 and fill in your goal and objectives. Make enough copies so that you, your teacher, and classmates can evaluate your project.

Rubric Sheet

Name: _Martina Searcy_   Project: _Wave Wonders (Digital Poster)_

Goal:	Evaluation:	Rating			Score
Create a digital poster about wave properties.	We show good information, but is it clear?	**Beat** 60	**Met** (40)	**Didn't** 20	40
Objectives:					
1. Who? I'll work with a partner to create the poster.	I worked with Raul but could have used him more.	**Beat** 10	**Met** (6)	**Didn't** 2	6
2. What? We'll create a digital poster about wave properties.	We made the poster, but we could improve its design.	**Beat** 10	**Met** (6)	**Didn't** 2	6
3. Where? We'll make it in the school's computer lab but research at home.		**Beat** 10	**Met** (6)	**Didn't** 2	6
4. When? It needs to be done by Wednesday of next week.	We got done early, with lots of time to practice presenting.	**Beat** (10)	**Met** 6	**Didn't** 2	10
5. Why? We are doing a poster presentation in science class.	We still need more practice; poster should look better.	**Beat** 10	**Met** 6	**Didn't** (2)	2
6. How? We'll show sample waves and their properties.	We included a video in our digital poster!	**Beat** (10)	**Met** 6	**Didn't** 2	10
				Total:	80

Fill in a rubric sheet like the one above about your project.

Getting a Second Opinion

After you do your own evaluation, it helps to get another opinion. Ask a classmate or teacher to evaluate your project, because a fresh set of eyes can identify trouble spots that you missed.

How to Ask for Help

Remember that you know a lot about the project and the work you've done so far. A reviewer can offer suggestions and encouragement, but you will make the final decision about what to do or not do with your creation. Use these tips when asking for another opinion.

- **Introduce the project.** Explain what you have made.

- **Discuss your goal and objectives.** Show the reviewer your plan for the project. Explain the goal and the *who? what? where? when? why?* and *how?* objectives you set for the project.

- **Ask for feedback.** Tell the reviewer what you need to know. For example, you might ask:
    Does the project meet the goal?
    Does it share necessary information about the topic?
    Does it leave any important questions unanswered?
    Is the project clear?
    What changes would improve it?

- **Present your project.** Hand over your project and a rubric sheet with the goal and objectives filled in (see page 271).

- **Give the reviewer space.** Let the person fill out the evaluation sheet privately, and give him or her enough time. Then discuss the results together.

Tip: It can sometimes be hard to have someone else point out flaws in your work. But remember that the reviewer is trying to help, and that he or she is showing how your final audience may respond.

Your Turn Present your project to a reviewer. Follow the tips above to receive helpful feedback. Be sure to thank your reviewer for taking the time and effort to help.

The Reviewer's Role

You will likely be asked to review your classmates' projects at some point. It's important to be encouraging and helpful. Follow these tips:

- **Be friendly and show respect.** Let the person or group know that you want to help.

- **Learn about the project.** Look over the goal and objectives. Ask questions if you don't understand something.

- **Be positive.** Start with a compliment about a part of the project that is special or working well.

- **Talk about any problems in positive terms.** Mention the trouble spot, but then suggest how to correct and improve it to match the rest of the project.

- **Brainstorm solutions with the project leader.** When it comes to solving the biggest problems with a project, ask for the leader's input. He or she understands the project best.

- **Step back.** After you have finished making comments, let the project leader make the final decision on any changes.

 Your Turn Help another person with his or her project. Learn about it, review the goal and objectives, and then consider solutions to any problems you see. Use the tips on this page to help.

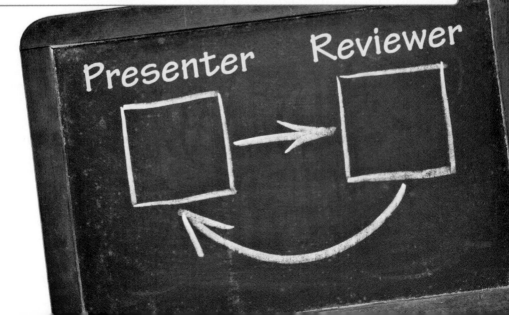

Making Improvements

Now that you have evaluated your project and asked for a second opinion, you can begin making improvements. Improving your work will require both critical and creative thinking.

Critical Improvements

Cutting

Ask yourself the following question to decide what to cut.

> Which parts give information that doesn't fit the topic?

Rearranging

Ask yourself the following question to decide what to rearrange.

> Are any parts or details out of order?

Creative Improvements

Reworking

Ask yourself the following question to decide what needs to be redone.

> Which parts are confusing or poorly done?

Adding

Ask yourself the following question to decide what to add.

> Which parts are missing important information?

 Your Turn Answer the questions above about your own project in an improvement plan like the one on the next page.

Using an Improvement Plan

Here is an improvement plan created by Martina, the student who made a digital poster on wave properties. (Go to **thoughtfullearning. com/e275** to download a blank improvement plan for your own work.)

Name: <u>Martina Searcy</u>   Project: <u>Wave Wonders (Digital Poster)</u>

Critical Improvements

Cutting: Which parts give information that doesn't fit the topic?
<u>The picture of the ocean doesn't really show off individual waves.</u>

Plan: <u>I'll find another picture with bigger waves, so I can point out the trough and crest better.</u>

Rearranging: Are any parts or details out of order?
<u>The bottom half of the poster is cluttered.</u>

Plan: <u>I'll move the ideas about radio waves to the top and rearrange the bottom half.</u>

Creative Improvements

Reworking: Which parts are confusing or poorly done?
<u>The design needs help to look more professional.</u>

Plan: <u>I'll experiment with different fonts and sizes.</u>

Adding: Which parts are missing important information?
<u>The part about wavelength is still hard to understand.</u>

Plan: <u>I'll add a visual aid to go with my written description of wavelength.</u>

Perfecting Your Work

After making the big improvements, it is time to put the finishing touches on your project.

For writing projects . . .

- ☑ Correct any errors in spelling, capitalization, punctuation, and grammar.
- ☑ Check that all information is correct.
- ☑ Perfect the design so that it is easy to read.

For speaking projects . . .

- ☑ Practice your presentation until you are comfortable with it.
- ☑ Check that your visual aids are clear and easy to see.

For visual projects . . .

- ☑ Create a clean, correct finished piece.
- ☑ Add color for energy.
- ☑ Darken lines so they can be seen from a distance.

For digital projects . . .

- ☑ Be certain the technology and equipment are working.
- ☑ Correct any errors in spelling, capitalization, punctuation, and grammar.
- ☑ Make final design changes to give a professional appearance.

Your Turn Put the finishing touches on your project by following the tips above.

Chapter 23
Presenting

To present well takes a lot of practice. How much exactly? You must practice enough to be confident when you walk in front of the classroom or take the stage. You must practice enough to give your audience clear information, an inspiring monologue, or a beautiful solo. You have developed your project through each step of the inquiry process. This chapter will help you step up to present your work well to others.

You will learn . . .
- Understanding the Situation
- Presenting in Person
- Presenting on the Web
- Promoting Your Project

Understanding the Situation

To prepare the best possible presentation, analyze the situation by asking the 5 W's and H about it.

Situation Analysis

Name: _Martina Searcy_   Project: _Wave Wonders (Digital Poster)_

1. **Who** is your audience?
   My classmates and family members are my audience.

2. **What** do you want the audience to experience?
   I want them to see a cool-looking poster and learn a lot
   about waves.

3. **Where** will you present your work?
   Raul and I will present the poster in class and on our
   classroom blog.

4. **When** will you present your work?
   The poster presentation is on Wednesday.

5. **Why** are you presenting this work?
   It's an assignment for our science unit this month.

6. **How** will you present your work?
   Raul and I will present the poster on a big projector screen.
   Afterward, I'll post it on the classroom blog.

Your Turn Answer the questions above about your own presentation situation.

Presenting in Person

At some point, you will be asked to make a presentation in front of your class or some other group. Even if this makes you nervous, being prepared can calm your nerves. Practicing until you feel comfortable with your presentation is very important. Here are two ways to prepare:

Note Cards

Use note cards to remind you of what to say during your presentation. Follow these steps:

1. **Write out your introduction and conclusion** word for word on separate cards.
2. **Write only the main points on the other cards.** (Use words and phrases instead of complete sentences.)
3. **Put your cards in the right order and number them.**
4. **Glance at your cards during your presentation to stay on track,** but look at your audience for the most part.

Outline

Build an outline that uses sentences or phrases to organize the key points about your project. Then use it as a reminder while you present the information.

Sample Outline

1. Explain why waves are cool.
2. Describe the parts of the poster.
   A. Crest
   B. Trough
   C. Amplitude
   D. Wavelength
3. Invite the audience to ask questions.

 Create note cards or an outline for your presentation.

Presenting on the Web

The Web offers opportunities for you to show your work to many people. Here are some ways to publish your work online.

Classroom Wiki	A classroom wiki is a Web site that you, your classmates, and your teacher build and edit together. Posting your work on a wiki makes it available to many friends, family, and classmates.
Classroom Blog	A classroom blog is an online journal for your classroom. Posting your work on a blog allows your classmates to view and respond to it.
Personal Web Site	You can also post your project on a personal Web site created by you, a family member, or a trusted friend. On a personal Web site, you can change or improve your work at any time.
Social Media	Social media sites and networks can be the best way to broadcast your work to a large number of people. Email is especially useful for directing your work to a particular group.

Promoting Your Project

Here are some ways you can promote a project.

1. **Create a poster or handout.** You can create a poster to hang in your school hallways, or create a handout such as a brochure or flier to pass out to classmates. Make sure your promotional material includes a catchy heading or attractive graphics.
2. **Engage your community.** Consider submitting a promotion to a community calender or writing to your local newspaper about your project. You could also ask local businesses to display your promotional material.

Part III:

Developing Projects

$\rightarrow$

Part III:
Developing Projects

This section is overflowing with project ideas using the inquiry process. There are writing projects, graphing projects, Web projects, design projects, and much more. Each specific project includes guidelines, visuals, and examples. Listed below are the types of projects covered in Part III. Remember that these are just starting points. Let inquiry lead you to make these projects your own.

Chapters in This Section

> **What am I doing? I'm listing the steps of cat care.**

Chapter 24
Writing Projects

Listing your own thoughts and ideas is one way to collect details for a writing project—anything from a paragraph to a poem to an essay. Doing experiments and reading articles, books, and Web sites are other ways to collect facts and ideas. Finally, putting all of the information into writing lets you share it with others. This chapter takes you through the steps for completing several kinds of writing projects.

You will learn . . .

- Writing Paragraphs
- Writing Summaries
- Writing Email
- Writing Narratives
- Writing Literature Responses
- Writing Poems
- Writing Lab Reports
- Building Paragraphs and Essays
- Writing an Expository Essay
- Writing a Persuasive Essay

Project Overview

Here is an overview of the writing projects in this chapter.

Paragraph

A paragraph introduces a topic or an idea and supports it with details and reasoning. (See pages 286–287.)

Summary

A summary identifies the main ideas and the details of another reading selection. (See pages 288–289.)

Email

An email is an electronic message you can send to friends, family, classmates, or teachers. (See pages 290–291.)

Narrative

A narrative is a real or imagined story. Most narratives include characters, dialogue, and specific details. (See pages 292–293.)

Not So Badlands

Badlands National Park in South Dakota is like being on a different planet. Miles and miles of twisting canyons and spiraling rock formations cover one part of its grounds. Red stripes line many of the rock walls. If you squint, it almost looks like the canyons are rolling like ocean waves. The terrain on the other side of the park is much different. It is filled with green and golden prairie grass waving in the wind. Many

---

Shake It Out

"Wet-Dog Wiggle" by Erica Brown explains why dogs need to shake to dry off. Water sticks to a dog's hair because of surface tension. Shaking is necessary to break the tension. The water flies off as dogs oscillate. To oscillate means to shake back and forth. Scientists at Georgia Tech observed the oscillation of 40 animals, and they discovered smaller animals need to oscillate much faster than bigger animals do to dry off. Shaking is important because it helps animals stay warm. Scientists say that without this ability, wet animals could point just t

---

Classroom Guest

To: ehoffman@drewparkschool.edu
Subject: Classroom Guest

Hi Mrs. Hoffman,

Last night, I talked to my uncle, Ezra, about visiting our classroom. He is an architect, and he designs cool apartment buildings and other living spaces.

He told me he uses a lot of math on the job. Since we are doing a unit on geometry and angles, he would make a helpful classroom speaker.

Batter Up

My first year in Little League started rough. It was a lot different than Rookie League. In Rookie League, I was among the oldest players. Coaches pitched to us, and I was pretty good. Little League was different.

I made a team called the Hardware Mariners. I was nervous during the first practices. I hustled but didn't get to play much in games. Batting was difficult. The pitchers threw fast. Some could even throw curve balls.

I started coming to practice early so Coach Harvey could give me hitting tips. I learned to "choke up" on the bat against fast pitchers. That meant moving my hands higher on the handle so that I could swing more quickly.

During our next game, I got a chance to bat with the score tied in the last inning. There was one out, with a runner on third base. A hit would win the game.

The first pitch was too high, but I swung anyway and missed. The next pitch I let go by. Strike two. I stepped out of the batter's box and remembered coach's advice. I choked up on my bat and stepped back up to the plate.

Literature Response

A literature response reflects on the contents of a book, a poem, or another form of literature. Additionally, it may share the writer's feelings toward the work. (See pages 294–295.)

Poem

A poem is a writing form with a special shape and sound. It uses creative language to express an idea in an interesting way. (See pages 296–297.)

Lab Report

A lab report records the entire process of a scientific experiment. (See pages 298–299.)

Expository Essay

Essays provide space to explore a topic in greater detail than paragraphs. You will learn the parts of an essay (see pages 300–301). Then you will learn how to write an expository essay. Expository essays explain something. (See pages 302–303.)

Persuasive Essay

A persuasive essay shares your opinion about something. It uses strong reasons to support the opinion. (See pages 304–306.)

Hatchet

Hatchet by Gary Paulsen is a story about overcoming adversity. Brian is flying on a plane through the Canadian wilderness when the pilot has a heart attack. The plane crashes into a small lake, but Brian is able to swim to shore. He is stranded by himself in the middle of a forest. All he has with him is a windbreaker and a hatchet. There are no cell phones,

---

Ellis Island

On the ferry to Ellis island,
we passed Lady Liberty,
standing tall, proud, and confident,
like Washington crossing the Delaware.

Lab Report: Neighborhood Plants

Question: What plant life is in my neighborhood?

Hypothesis: I live near a path with many kinds of trees, so there will be diverse plant life.

Materials: Poster board, sandwich bags, marker, ruler, botany books, computer with Internet

Procedure:

1. Explored the trail in our neighborhood.

Tundra Life

Life at the top is not always easy. Both the top of the world and the top of mountains are part of the tundra biome. A biome is a place that has a unique climate and special plant and animal life. The tundra biome seems like it is too harsh to support life, but that's not the case.

The tundra climate is cold. Of the world's five biomes, the tundra is the coldest. During winter, arctic tundra temperatures get as low as –25 degrees. In the summer, temperatures reach 40 degrees. There's also little rain fall, and the land is frosty for most of the

---

Time to Learn a Foreign Language

My friend Tony speaks Spanish at home but uses English at school. He doesn't think knowing two languages is anything special, but it is. Being bilingual has many advantages. More young people should learn a foreign language.

To begin with, learning a foreign language opens the door to new cultures. Today's technology makes it possible to reach out to people in different countries. Knowing a second language helps you communicate with a whole new group of people. In the process, you can better understand and appreciate their culture. Remember that English is only the fourth most

Inquire to...

Write a Paragraph

1. **Question** the situation for the paragraph.
   - **Subject:** What topic will you write about?
   - **Purpose:** Why are you writing? To explain? To share? To persuade? To entertain?
   - **Audience:** Who will read this paragraph?

2. **Plan** your paragraph.
   - **Identify your topic.** Is it specific enough to cover in one paragraph?

3. **Research** your topic.
   - **Searching:** Study primary and secondary sources as needed to learn about your topic. (See pages **252–253**.)
   - **Focusing:** Decide on a part of the topic to focus on.

     Topic: *The zoo*   **Focus:** *is a location for learning*

     State the focus in a topic sentence.

     Topic sentence: *The zoo is a good location for a field trip.*
   - **Shaping:** List details that support the topic.

4. **Create** the first draft of your paragraph.
   - **Start** with your topic sentence.
   - **Follow** with your supporting details.
   - **End** with a sentence that ties everything together.

5. **Improve** your first draft.
   - **Evaluate** your first draft.
     - ▶ **Purpose:** Did you achieve your reason for writing?
     - ▶ **Audience:** Is the paragraph easy to read and understand?
   - **Revise** your writing.
     - ▶ **Rewrite** sentences that are confusing.
     - ▶ **Add** details to explain the topic more fully.
   - **Edit** your revised writing.
     - ▶ **Check** your writing for accuracy.

6. **Present** the final copy of your paragraph to your class or family.

Paragraph

Here is a sample paragraph created by a student for her social studies class. The paragraph includes a clear topic sentence, detailed supporting sentences, and a creative closing sentence.

The topic sentence (underlined) tells the reader what the paragraph is about.

The body sentences give details about the topic sentence.

The closing sentence provides a final thought about the topic.

Not So Badlands

Badlands National Park in South Dakota is like being on a different planet. Miles and miles of twisting canyons and spiraling rock formations cover one part of its grounds. Red stripes line many of the rock walls. If you squint, it almost looks like the canyons are rolling like ocean waves. The terrain on the other side of the park is much different. It is filled with green and golden prairie grass waving in the wind. Many rare animals live in the national park, like bison and bighorn sheep. Fossils from prehistoric ancestors of the rhinoceros were discovered there, too. The Badlands got its name because the terrain was too difficult to cross. To me, "Badlands" is an inaccurate name because there's nothing "bad" about it.

Inquire to...

Write a Summary

1. **Question** the situation for your summary.
   - **Subject:** What specific topic is the reading selection about?
   - **Purpose:** Why is it important that you sum up the material? What are the most important parts of the reading?
   - **Audience:** Who will read your summary?

2. **Plan** your summary.
   - **Identify** the main point of the reading selection.

3. **Research** the reading selection.
   - **Searching:** Reread the selection, writing down any key points as you read.
   - **Focusing:** Pick out the reading's main idea. State the focus in a topic sentence.

     Topic sentence: *Watching too much TV is bad for your health, says Alice Park in "Turn off Your TV."*

   - **Shaping:** List the important details in your own words.

4. **Create** the first draft.
   - **Start** with your topic sentence. Include the title and author of the selection as well as the selection's main point (see above).
   - **Follow** with supporting details. Tell about the selection's most important parts in your own words.
   - **End** with a closing sentence that restates the selection's main point.

5. **Improve** your first draft.
   - **Evaluate** your first draft.
     - ▶ **Purpose:** Does the paragraph sum up the reading selection?
     - ▶ **Audience:** Would an audience member understand what the selection is about by reading the summary?
   - **Revise** your writing.
     - ▶ **Add** any clarifying details, and **cut** any unnecessary parts.
   - **Edit** your revised writing.
     - ▶ **Check** your writing for accuracy.

6. **Present** the final copy of your summary.

Article and Summary

A summary paragraph explains the main point of a reading selection. Here is the first part of a science article followed by a student's summary. The student is careful to use her own words to describe the article.

Article

Wet-Dog Wiggle
By Erica Brown

Spot's shake zone is well known. This chocolate lab loves to swim. When he's ready to dry off, he braces himself and shakes crazily. Water beads fly everywhere, so watch out!

Spot's shaking instinct is not uncommon. Dogs and other animals such as mice, tigers, and panda bears dry off by shaking. And, as researchers at the Georgia Institute of Technology found out, there's a science to the "wet-dog wiggle."

When a dog gets wet, surface tension between the water and a dog's hair causes water to stick to the animal. A great force is needed to overcome the tension. Shaking does the trick. . . .

Student Summary

Shake It Out

The **topic sentence** introduces the title, author, and main point.

The **body sentences** give key details in the student's own words.

The **closing sentence** refers back to the main point.

"Wet-Dog Wiggle" by Erica Brown explains why dogs need to shake to dry off. Water sticks to a dog's hair because of surface tension. Shaking is necessary to break the tension. The water flies off as dogs oscillate. To oscillate means to shake back and forth. Scientists at Georgia Tech observed the oscillation of 40 animals, and they discovered smaller animals need to oscillate much faster than bigger animals do to dry off. Shaking is important because it helps animals stay warm. Scientists say that without this ability, wet animals could get sick from being too cold. As the article points out, shaking is not some goofy thing dogs do just to annoy their owners. It is a survival instinct.

Inquire to...

Write an Email

1. **Question** the situation for the email.
   - **Subject:** What is the specific topic of your message?
   - **Purpose:** Why do you need to write an email?
   - **Audience:** Who will read your email—a teacher, a friend, a family member?

2. **Plan** your email.
   - **Be clear** about what you need to say and why.

3. **Research** your topic.
   - **Searching:** Confirm the correct email address of the receiver.
   - **Focusing:** Decide on your focus. The focus includes the topic and the reason for writing the email.

      Topic: *birthday party*   **Reason:** *to invite*

      Focus: *I want to invite you to my birthday party on May 5.*
   - **Shaping:** List any other important details you want to include.

4. **Create** the first draft of your email.
   - **Complete** the email header. Create a clear subject line that tells the reader what the email is about.
   - **Start** the message by greeting the reader and stating your focus.
   - **Follow** with any other important details.
   - **Politely** end the message. Explain any actions you would like the reader to take next.

5. **Improve** your first draft.
   - **Evaluate** your first draft.
      - ▶ **Purpose:** Did you fulfill your purpose?
      - ▶ **Audience:** Is the tone appropriate for your reader?
   - **Revise** your email.
      - ▶ **Break** any long passages into short, double-spaced paragraphs.
   - **Edit** your revised email.
      - ▶ **Check** your message for spelling and punctuation errors.

6. **Present** your email message by sending it.

Email

Here is an email from a student to her teacher. The message is clear and easy to read. It avoids spelling and punctuation errors.

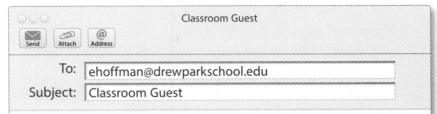

To: ehoffman@drewparkschool.edu

Subject: Classroom Guest

The beginning greets the reader and tells the main point of the message.	Hi Mrs. Hoffman,

Last night, I talked to my uncle, Ezra, about visiting our classroom. He is an architect, and he designs cool apartment buildings and other living spaces.

He told me he uses a lot of math on the job. Since we are doing a unit on geometry and angles, he would make a helpful classroom speaker. |
| **The middle** provides other details. | He gave me his email address in case you wanted to set up a time for him to visit. It is ezra@bradfordllc.com.

Thanks for listening to my idea. Please let me know if you have questions tomorrow at school. |
| **The ending** politely closes the message. | Thank you,

Tameka W. |

Inquire to...

Write a Narrative

1. **Question** the situation for writing.
   - **Subject:** Who is the main character? What will the story be about? Is the story real or made up?
   - **Purpose:** What conflict will the main character encounter? What is your reason for writing this narrative?
   - **Audience:** Who will want to read this story?

2. **Plan** your narrative. (Go to **thoughtfullearning.com/e292**.)
   - What are the key plot points? (See page **266**.)

3. **Research** your narrative.
   - **Searching:** Find primary and secondary sources as needed to learn more about the location, characters, and plot of your narrative.
   - **Shaping:** Decide on a climax for your narrative. The climax is the point where the main character faces her or his greatest challenge and either succeeds or fails.

4. **Create** the first draft of the narrative.
   - **Start** the narrative in a way that grabs the reader's attention.
   - **Follow** with rising action, adding suspense to your story.
   - **Lead** up to the climax, the most exciting point.
   - **End** with a resolution, showing the outcome of the character's struggle or conflict.

5. **Improve** your first draft.
   - **Evaluate** your first draft.
     - ▶ **Subject:** Is the main character interesting?
     - ▶ **Purpose:** Is the conflict in the story memorable?
   - **Revise** your writing.
     - ▶ **Rewrite** or **remove** any parts that do not fit in with the rest of the story.
     - ▶ **Add** any missing details.
   - **Edit** your revised writing.
     - ▶ **Check** your writing for accuracy.

6. **Present** the final copy to your class or share it online.

Narrative (Personal Experience)

The following personal narrative was created by a student for his English class. The narrative tells the story of "A time when I was proud."

Batter Up

The **beginning** sets the scene and introduces the conflict.

My first year in Little League started rough. It was a lot different than Rookie League. In Rookie League, I was among the oldest players. Coaches pitched to us, and I was pretty good. Little League was different.

I made a team called the Hardware Mariners. I was nervous during the first practices. I hustled but didn't get to play much in games. Batting was difficult. The pitchers threw fast. Some could even throw curve balls.

I started coming to practice early so Coach Harvey could give me hitting tips. I learned to "choke up" on the bat against fast pitchers. That meant moving my hands higher on the handle so that I could swing more quickly.

The **middle** provides specific details about the experience.

During our next game, I got a chance to bat with the score tied in the last inning. There was one out, with a runner on third base. A hit would win the game.

The first pitch was too high, but I swung anyway and missed. The next pitch I let go by. Strike two. I stepped out of the batter's box and remembered coach's advice. I choked up on my bat and stepped back up to the plate.

The story builds suspense as it nears the climax.

The pitcher wound up and released the ball. I swung.

"Ping!" The ball jumped off my bat and into the air in left field. It was the farthest I'd hit the ball all year. The outfielder ran backward, leapt, and caught the ball.

I was sad until I realized there were now only two outs in the inning. The runner on third base could tag up and score if he beat the outfielder's throw home.

The **ending** shows what the experience meant to the writer.

It wasn't close. By the time the ball reached home plate, our runner had scored. We won the game!

My teammates swarmed me near the dugout, greeting me with high fives. I was part of the team.

Inquire to...

Write a Literature Response

1. **Question** the situation.
   - **Subject:** What piece of literature will you respond to?
   - **Purpose:** What is your goal? Is it to summarize the plot and discuss its theme? To explain what you like or dislike about it?
   - **Audience:** What do readers need to know about the piece?

2. **Plan** your response.
   - **Review** the plot.

3. **Research** your topic.
   - **Searching:** Carefully study the selection. Reread any parts you are unsure of.
   - **Focusing:** Identify the theme and list the key plot points in order.

4. **Create** the first draft of your response paragraph.
   - **Begin** by naming the work's title, author, and theme.
   - **Follow** with the key plot points in your own words.
   - **End** with a sentence or two that ties everything together.

5. **Improve** your first draft.
   - **Evaluate** your first draft.
     - ▶ **Purpose:** Does the response fulfill your purpose?
     - ▶ **Audience:** Does the response tell readers what they need to know about the piece of literature?
   - **Revise** your writing.
     - ▶ **Rewrite** parts that are confusing or unclear.
     - ▶ **Add** details to explain or make your points more convincing.
     - ▶ **Cut** parts that don't support your analysis.
   - **Edit** your writing.
     - ▶ **Check** your writing for accuracy using pages 161–172 as a guide.

6. **Present** your analysis to your class or a book club, or post it to a literature blog or wiki.

Literature Response Paragraph

In this literature response, a student reviews one of his favorite books.

Hatchet

The topic sentence includes the title and author and a key theme in the story.

Hatchet by Gary Paulsen is a story about overcoming adversity. Brian is flying on a plane through the Canadian wilderness when the pilot has a heart attack. The plane crashes into a small lake, but Brian is able to swim to shore. He is stranded by himself in the middle of a forest. All he has with him is a windbreaker and a hatchet. There are no cell phones, so he can't call for help. Brian is distraught. But instead of giving up, he builds a shelter and teaches himself to hunt and fish for food. He encounters some wildlife, too. A porcupine attacks him in his shelter. Later, he's sprayed by a skunk. Then a moose goes after him. Things worsen when a tornado destroys his shelter. The tornado causes the tail of the crashed plane to stick out of the water. He swims to it and nearly loses his hatchet. In the process, he finds a surprise that changes everything. If you like adventure like me, you'll love this book. Many bad things happen to Brian, but he learns to never give up hope.

The middle explains the plot.

The ending gives the writer's opinion about the book.

Inquire to...

Write a Poem

1. **Question** the situation and your goal for writing the poem.
   - **Subject:** What topic will the poem be about?
   - **Purpose:** What feeling do you wish to express?
   - **Audience:** Who will read the poem?

2. **Plan** your poem, using a free verse or traditional form.
   - Free-verse poems do not have to rhyme.
   - Traditional poetry, like ballads and sonnets, has specific rhythm and rhyme patterns.

3. **Research** your topic.
   - **Gathering:** Use a cluster to brainstorm ideas about your topic. (See page **37**.)
   - **Listing:** List details about the topic that relate to the five senses— sights, smells, tastes, sounds, and touch.
   - **Research:** Study different poetic forms and techniques.

4. **Create** the first draft of your poem.
   - **Focus** on ideas and imagery relating to the five senses.
   - **Experiment** with sounds and organization.
   - **Shape** your ideas into a form—free verse or a traditional.

5. **Improve** the first draft.
   - **Evaluate** your first draft.
     - ▶ Does the poem accomplish your goal and connect with the audience in some way?
   - **Revise** your poem.
     - ▶ **Add** sensory details to make your topic clearer.
     - ▶ **Cut** any parts that are not needed.
     - ▶ **Rearrange** parts that are not in the best order.
     - ▶ **Rewrite** any unclear lines.
   - **Edit** your poem for spelling accuracy.

6. **Present** your poem during a classroom poetry reading or post it online.

Poem

A free-verse poem does not need rhyme or rhythm, but it should express a strong idea or feeling. The student writer below tells about Ellis Island in a unique way. Thousands of immigrants passed through the island's processing station in the 1920s.

The poem includes three different stanzas.

The writer broke each line where she heard pauses.

The poem ends in a creative way, evoking a feeling of what Ellis Island meant to immigrants.

Ellis Island

On the ferry to Ellis island,
we passed Lady Liberty,
standing tall, proud, and confident,
like Washington crossing the Delaware.

Floating farther on,
as our ancestors did before us,
we approached the island.

And when we reached it,
the gates were open for all of us
to enter.

Inquire to...

Write a Lab Report

1. **Question** the situation for your report.
   - **Subject:** What is the topic of your report?
   - **Purpose:** Why are you writing the report—to explain or to describe?
   - **Audience:** Who is the report for? What will they need to know?

2. **Plan** the basics for your report.
   - **Identify** your topic. Your topic will be the scientific question that you have explored or tested.
   - **Learn** the parts of the lab report, either ones provided by your teacher or the one on the facing page.

3. **Research** your report.
   - **Testing:** Carry out your experiment by following the scientific method (see pages **49–51**).
   - **Recording:** Take careful notes.
   - **Focusing:** Draw conclusions from your experiment results.

4. **Create** the first draft of your report.
   - **Start** your report with your scientific question and hypothesis.
   - **Follow** with the materials, step-by-step procedure, and observations.
   - **End** with the conclusion based on your findings.

5. **Improve** your first draft.
   - **Evaluate** your first draft.
     - ▶ **Purpose:** Does your report effectively explain or describe the experiment?
     - ▶ **Audience:** Is the report easy to follow?
   - **Revise** your writing.
     - ▶ **Rewrite** any parts that are confusing.
     - ▶ **Add** any important details you missed.
   - **Edit** your revised writing.
     - ▶ **Check** your writing for accuracy.

6. **Present** the final copy of your lab in class or post it on a classroom blog.

Lab Report

The following lab report describes plant life near a student's home.

The **beginning** identifies the question and hypothesis.

The **middle** shows the procedure step by step.

The **middle** also records the observations in a table. (The example table shows only the first three observations.)

The **ending** explains the findings.

Lab Report: Neighborhood Plants

Question: What plant life is in my neighborhood?

Hypothesis: I live near a path with many kinds of trees, so there will be diverse plant life.

Materials: Poster board, sandwich bags, marker, ruler, botany books, computer with Internet

Procedure:

1. Explored the trail in our neighborhood.
2. Collected eight different samples of plant life.
3. Stored each sample in a separate sandwich bag.
4. Researched each specimen using the Internet.
5. Labeled each sample on a white poster board.
6. Recorded additional observations in a data table, including name, description, and habitat.

Observations:

Name	Description	Habitat
Bur oak leaves	Yellow and orange, with 12 rounded lobes	Wooded area, cool climate
Pine tree branch	Clusters of green needles on a small brown branch	Wooded area, drier soil
Blue spruce	Short and sharp bluish-gray needles attached to a twig	Wooded area, cool climate

Conclusion: The Midwest's cool climate, changing seasons, and healthy soil make it a great place for certain plant life to grow. The woods near my home are proof of that. But if the trees are cleared for more homes, my neighborhood will lose its great plant life.

Building Paragraphs and Essays

You might think writing essays is much more difficult than writing paragraphs. But if you can construct a paragraph, you can also build an essay. After all, an essay is just a series of paragraphs.

The construction of paragraphs and essays is very similar. Each is made up of three working parts. The chart below takes a closer look at these parts.

Construction of a Paragraph

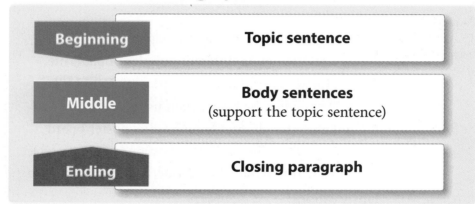

Beginning	**Topic sentence**
Middle	**Body sentences** (support the topic sentence)
Ending	**Closing paragraph**

Construction of an Essay

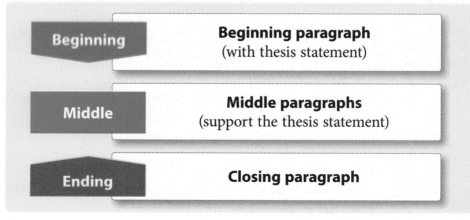

Beginning	**Beginning paragraph** (with thesis statement)
Middle	**Middle paragraphs** (support the thesis statement)
Ending	**Closing paragraph**

Tip: Just remember, the building blocks of paragraphs are sentences. And the building blocks of essays are paragraphs.

Controlling Sentences

Both paragraphs and essays include a statement early on that establishes the focus of the writing.

- **A topic sentence** controls each paragraph. It includes the topic and focus of the paragraph.
- **A thesis statement** controls an essay. It includes the topic and focus of the essay. Each paragraph that follows in an essay includes a topic sentence that supports the thesis statement.

Using Transitions

Transition words are connecting words. In paragraphs, they connect different sentences and ideas. In essays, they connect different sentences as well as one paragraph to the next. Notice how the bolded words connect ideas in following example:

> There are many reasons to exercise. **First of all**, exercise keeps you in shape and tones your muscles. It is the best way to stay fit. **Next**, exercise gives you energy and keeps you alert. Staying in shape contributes to a strong mind. **Finally**, exercise can be a whole lot of fun.

Here are some examples of transition words and phrases to use in your writing.

To show location	To show time	To show value	To show information
Above	Before	Least important	Additionally
Below	After	More important	Also
Between	During	Most important	Another
Inside	Later	Good	First of all
Outside	First	Better	Next
Around	Second	Best	Lastly
By	Next		For example
Near	Finally		
Under			
Over			

Inquire to...

Write an Expository Essay

1. **Question** the situation for the essay.
   - **Subject:** What specific topic will you write about?
   - **Purpose:** Are you to explain, inform, or describe?
   - **Audience:** Who will read this essay?

2. **Plan** your essay.
   - **Pick a topic** that interests you and that you can say a lot about.

3. **Research** your topic.
   - **Searching:** Use primary and secondary sources to find information about your topic. (See pages **252–253**.)
   - **Focusing:** Form a thesis statement, expressing a specific thought about your topic.

     Topic: *Jupiter*   **Thought:** *is different than Earth.*

     Thesis statement: *Jupiter is a much different planet than Earth.*
   - **Shaping:** Arrange important details about your topic in an outline or graphic organizer.

4. **Create** the first draft of your essay.
   - **Start with an opening paragraph** that introduces your topic and includes a thesis statement.
   - **Follow with middle paragraphs** that support your thesis.
   - **End with a closing paragraph** that revisits your thesis.

5. **Improve** your first draft.
   - **Evaluate** your first draft.
     - ▶ **Purpose:** Did you meet your purpose?
     - ▶ **Audience:** Will the essay interest your audience?
   - **Revise** your writing.
     - ▶ **Rewrite** any confusing sentences.
     - ▶ **Add** helpful transitions or connecting words.
     - ▶ **Cut** any unnecessary parts.
   - **Edit** your revised writing.
     - ▶ **Check** your writing for accuracy.

6. **Present** the final copy of your essay to your class.

Expository Essay

An expository essay explains or describes someone or something. In this essay, Shanise describes a special biome for her science class.

Tundra Life

The beginning presents the topic and focus in a thesis statement (underlined).

Life at the top is not always easy. Both the top of the world and the top of mountains are part of the tundra biome. A biome is a place that has a unique climate and special plant and animal life. The tundra biome seems like it is too harsh to support life, but that's not the case.

The tundra climate is cold. Of the world's five biomes, the tundra is the coldest. During winter, arctic tundra temperatures get as low as −25 degrees. In the summer, temperatures reach 40 degrees. There's also little rain fall, and the land is frosty for most of the year.

Each **middle** paragraph explains a different aspect of the topic.

The dry and chilly climate makes it difficult for plant life to grow on the tundra. The biome is mostly barren. In fact, the word *tundra* comes from a Finnish word meaning "treeless plain." However, plant life does exist, including small shrubs, moss, and flowers.

There's just enough greenery to support animal life. In fact, the tundra is home to many interesting animals. There are plant eaters, such as caribou and arctic hares. There are meat eaters, such as foxes, wolves, and polar bears. There are birds, such as ravens, falcons, and gulls. There are even fish, such as salmon and trout, swimming in frigid rivers. The variety is amazing.

The **closing** paragraph revisits the thesis and leaves the reader with something to think about.

People mostly keep away from the tundra biome. It's too dark and cold. Yet humans make an impact on the tundra. Global warming is causing the arctic tundra to shrink. This threatens many of the animal species there. Survival in the tundra is already hard as it is; humans do not need to make it worse.

Inquire to...

Write a Persuasive Essay

1. **Question** the situation for your essay.
   - **Subject:** What specific topic will you write about? Do you have strong feelings about it?
   - **Purpose:** What message do you want to get across to your audience?
   - **Audience:** What action do you want your audience to take?

2. **Plan** the basics for your essay.
   - **Identify** a topic. Make sure it is something you care a lot about.

3. **Research** your topic.
   - **Research** primary or secondary sources about your topic.
   - **Focus:** Decide on a focus for your essay and state it in a thesis statement (see page 301).
   - **List** reasons to support your opinion.

4. **Create** the first draft of your essay.
   - **Start** by introducing your topic and stating your thesis.
   - **Follow with support.** Each middle paragraph should either support your thesis or deal with opposing viewpoints.
   - **End with a strong closing point.** Tell your readers how they should use the information.

5. **Improve** your first draft.
   - **Evaluate** your first draft.
     - ▶ **Purpose:** Does the essay achieve your goal?
     - ▶ **Audience:** Does your essay do enough to convince your audience to agree with your opinion?
   - **Revise** your writing.
     - ▶ **Rewrite** parts that are confusing or unclear.
     - ▶ **Add** details to better support your ideas.
     - ▶ **Cut** parts that don't advance your thesis.
   - **Edit** your writing.
     - ▶ **Check** your writing for accuracy.

6. **Present** the final copy of your essay in person or online.

Persuasive Essay

In the essay below, a student writer explains why it is important to learn a foreign language.

Time to Learn a Foreign Language

The **beginning** introduces the topic and states a thesis (underlined).

My friend Tony speaks Spanish at home but uses English at school. He doesn't think knowing two languages is anything special, but it is. Being bilingual has many advantages. <u>More young people should learn a foreign language.</u>

To begin with, learning a foreign language opens the door to new cultures. Today's technology makes it possible to reach out to people in different countries. Knowing a second language helps you communicate with a whole new group of people. In the process, you can better understand and appreciate their culture. Remember that English is only the fourth most common native language in the world.

Each **middle** paragraph focuses on a new reason to support the thesis.

Next, learning a second language helps you advance in school and prepare for a career. Most high schools and colleges require students to take foreign language classes. Learning a language now gives you a head start. Also, many jobs require fluency in a second language. Imagine how important it is to understand Spanish in a hospital that serves Hispanic patients!

The most important reason to start learning a second language now is that it becomes harder the older you get. That's right, studies show the best time to learn new languages is before middle school. Younger learners are more likely to develop better pronunciation skills than older learners. It also puts you on the right track to learn more languages when you get older.

The **last** paragraph ends with a call to action.

The world seems like it is shrinking. Foreign speakers, restaurants, and businesses are common in American cities, big and small. Computer programs let you talk face to face with people oceans away. Don't get left behind in this global society. If you are already in a foreign language class, practice hard. If you're not, start learning a new language on your own.

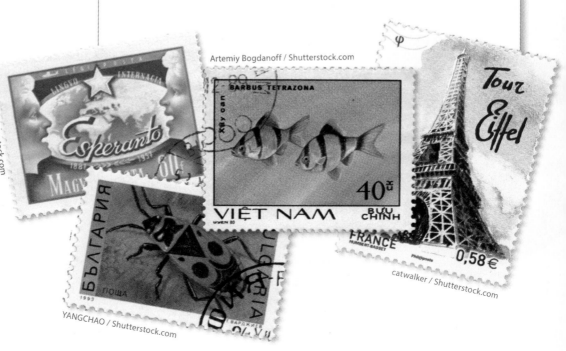

rook76 / Shutterstock.com

Artemiy Bogdanoff / Shutterstock.com

catwalker / Shutterstock.com

YANGCHAO / Shutterstock.com

Are we there yet?

Chapter 25
Graphing Projects

Just like words, graphics can communicate information. With a graph, you can see how far you've come and how far you must go to meet your goal. This chapter explains how to make bar graphs, tables, diagrams, and more.

You will learn . . .

- Creating Pie, Line, and Bar Graphs
- Creating Tables
- Creating Diagrams and Time Lines

Project Overview

These two pages give a quick overview of the graphics in this chapter.

Pie Graph

A pie graph shows how something whole is divided into parts. Each slice represents one part. (See page 311.)

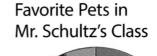

Favorite Pets in Mr. Schultz's Class

Crab 1
Turtle 2
Cat 5
Parakeet 2
Hamster 3
Dog 4

Total Pets: 17

Line Graph

A line graph shows changes over time. Quantity or amount is marked on the left side. Time is marked across the bottom. The line on the graph shows how things change. (See page 312.)

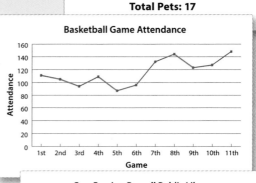

Basketball Game Attendance

Attendance (y-axis: 0, 20, 40, 60, 80, 100, 120, 140, 160)
Game (x-axis: 1st, 2nd, 3rd, 4th, 5th, 6th, 7th, 8th, 9th, 10th, 11th)

Bar Graph

A bar graph compares amounts. Bars are set side by side so their heights can be compared. (See page 313.)

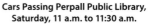
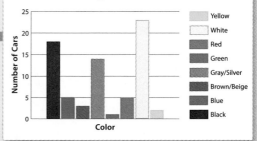

Cars Passing Perpall Public Library, Saturday, 11 a.m. to 11:30 a.m.

Number of Cars (y-axis: 0, 5, 10, 15, 20, 25)
Color (x-axis)

Legend:
Yellow
White
Red
Green
Gray/Silver
Brown/Beige
Blue
Black

Table

A table arranges information into a grid of rows and columns. Often, subjects are listed down the left, and traits are listed across the top. (See page 314.)

Moon Phase Facts

Phase	Visibility	Northern Hemisphere	Southern Hemisphere	Phase Midpoint
New	Thin crescent after sunset	Right crescent	Left crescent	Noon
Waxing Crescent	Afternoon and after dusk	Right 1–49%	Left 1–49%	3 p.m.
First Quarter	Afternoon and early night	Right 50%	Left 50%	6 p.m.
Waxing Gibbous	Late afternoon and most of night	Right 51–99%	Left 51–99%	9 p.m.
Full	Sunset to sunrise	100%	100%	Midnight
Waning Gibbous	Most of night and early morning	Left 51–99%	Right 51–99%	3 a.m.
Third Quarter	Late night and morning	Left 50%	Right 50%	6 a.m.
Waning Crescent	Pre-dawn and morning	Left 1–49%	Right 1–49%	9 a.m.
Dark	Thin crescent	Left crescent	Right	Noon

Diagram

A diagram is a picture with the parts labeled. The diagram may be a photo or a drawing. (See page 317.)

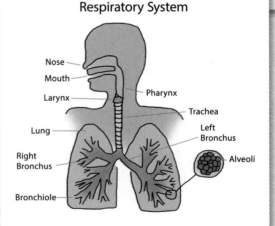

Respiratory System

Nose · Mouth · Larynx · Pharynx · Trachea · Lung · Right Bronchus · Left Bronchus · Alveoli · Bronchiole

Time Line

A time line lists events in the order they occurred. (See page 318.)

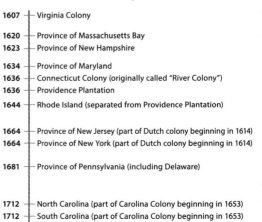

British Colonies Leading to the United States

1607	Virginia Colony
1620	Province of Massachusetts Bay
1623	Province of New Hampshire
1634	Province of Maryland
1636	Connecticut Colony (originally called "River Colony")
1636	Providence Plantation
1644	Rhode Island (separated from Providence Plantation)
1664	Province of New Jersey (part of Dutch colony beginning in 1614)
1664	Province of New York (part of Dutch colony beginning in 1614)
1681	Province of Pennsylvania (including Delaware)
1712	North Carolina (part of Carolina Colony beginning in 1653)
1712	South Carolina (part of Carolina Colony beginning in 1653)

Inquire to...

Create a Graph

1. **Question** the situation for the graph.
   - **Subject:** What information will the graph present?
   - **Purpose:** Will you use a pie graph to show the parts of a whole? Or a line graph to show changes over time? Or a bar graph to compare amounts?
   - **Audience:** Who will read the graph? What do they need to know?

2. **Plan** your graph. Study the type you will make. Gather supplies or learn the software you will use.

3. **Research** your topic.
   - **Gather** information to use in your graph.
   - **Organize** the information for your graph.

4. **Create** your graph.
   - **Pie graphs** show the parts of a whole. See page 311 for tips on creating pie graphs.
   - **Line graphs** show changes over time. See page 312 for tips on creating line graphs.
   - **Bar graphs** compare amounts. See page 313 for tips on creating bar graphs.

5. **Improve** your graph.
   - **Evaluate** your graph.
     - ▶ Is it accurate? Is it attractive? Does it include a title and labels?
   - **Revise** your graph.
     - ▶ **Remove** any unneeded details.
     - ▶ **Redo** parts that are unclear.
     - ▶ **Add** any missing information or labels.
   - **Perfect** your graph. Make it clean and correct.
     - ▶ **Ink** the drawn lines.
     - ▶ **Color** or shade parts to make the graph more readable.

6. **Present** your graph in a report or online.

Pie Graph

The following pie graph shows one classroom's favorite types of pets. Each student voted for one favorite. The whole pie represents the entire classroom.

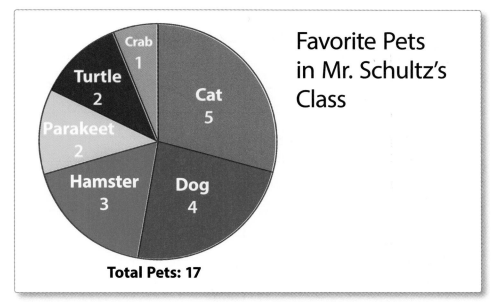

Favorite Pets in Mr. Schultz's Class

Crab 1
Turtle 2
Cat 5
Parakeet 2
Hamster 3
Dog 4

Total Pets: 17

Tips for Pie Graphs

Use a pie graph to divide something whole into its parts.

- **Include no more than six slices.** Combine small slivers into one slice called "Other."

- **Start at the twelve o'clock position** with the largest slice. Move clockwise from there.

- **Add the other slices in descending order,** from largest to smallest.

- **Label each slice** and provide amounts or percentages.

- **Use the equation to the right** to calculate the width (in degrees) for each slice.

1. Part ÷ whole amount × 100 = percentage
2. Percentage × 3.6 = number of degrees

Parts	Total: 17	100%	360°
Cat	5	29.4	105.8°
Dog	4	23.5	84.6°
Hamster	3	17.6	63.4°
Parakeet	2	11.8	42.5°
Turtle	2	11.8	42.5°
Crab	1	5.9	21.2°

Line Graph

In the following line graph, a class records the number of people attending school basketball games. Notice how the graph shows changes in attendance over time.

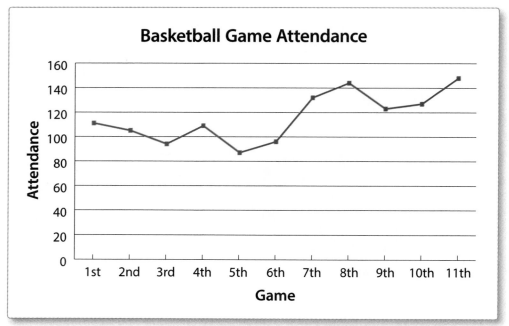

Basketball Game Attendance

Tips for Line Graphs

Use a line graph to compare changes in quantity over time.

- **Plot time horizontally (across the bottom).** Mark units of time on the *x* axis (horizontal).
- **Plot quantity vertically (along the side).** Mark units of quantity on the *y* axis (vertical).
- **Mark a dot** where quantity and time intersect.
- **Draw lines** to connect the dots.
- **Title the graph** clearly.

Bar Graph

For the bar graph below, a pair of students spent a half hour noting the colors of cars passing their public library one Saturday.

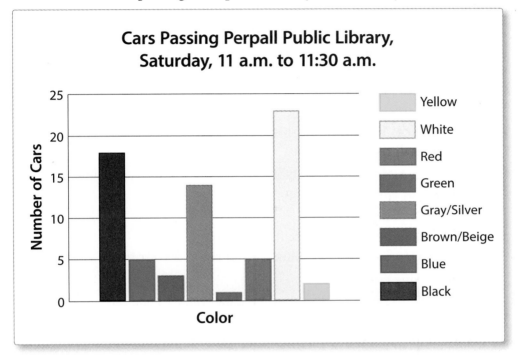

Tips for Bar Graphs

Use a bar graph to compare quantities.

- **Plot type or time horizontally (across the bottom).** Mark items to compare or units of time on the *x* axis (horizontal).
- **Plot quantity vertically (along the side).** Mark units of quantity or number on the *y* axis (vertical).
- **Create consistent bars.** All should be the same width.
- **Use different colors** for different items, and provide a key.
- **Give your graph a helpful title.**

Inquire to...

Create a Table

1. **Question** the situation for the table.
   - **Subject:** What topic does the table address? What features and amounts should it show?
   - **Purpose:** How will this table be used? What information is most important?
   - **Audience:** Who will use this table? What will they need from it? What will they expect?

2. **Plan** your table. Check the table-making features of your writing software or spreadsheet program.

3. **Research** your topic.
   - **Gather** information to use in your table.
   - **Decide** how to use the columns and rows in your table.

4. **Create** your table.
   - **Choose** the number of columns. Label them at the top.
   - **Create** the rows. Label them along the left side.
   - **Include** a title that clearly identifies the table's information.

5. **Improve** your table.
   - **Evaluate** your table.
     - ▶ Is each column and row labeled clearly? Is each cell accurate? Does the table include needed units of measure?
   - **Revise** your table.
     - ▶ **Remove** any columns or rows that don't include essential information.
     - ▶ **Rearrange** columns or rows for a better order.
     - ▶ **Redo** any parts of the table that are unclear.
     - ▶ **Add** columns and rows as needed.
   - **Perfect** your table. Make it clean and correct.

6. **Present** your table in a report or online.

Table

The following table presents information about the phases of the moon. It arranges facts in noticeable rows and columns with clear headings.

Moon Phase Facts

Phase	Visibility	Northern Hemisphere	Southern Hemisphere	Phase Midpoint
New	Thin crescent after sunset	Right crescent	Left crescent	Noon
Waxing Crescent	Afternoon and after dusk	Right 1–49%	Left 1–49%	3 p.m.
First Quarter	Afternoon and early night	Right 50%	Left 50%	6 p.m.
Waxing Gibbous	Late afternoon and most of night	Right 51–99%	Left 51–99%	9 p.m.
Full	Sunset to sunrise	100%	100%	Midnight
Waning Gibbous	Most of night and early morning	Left 51–99%	Right 51–99%	3 a.m.
Third Quarter	Late night and morning	Left 50%	Right 50%	6 a.m.
Waning Crescent	Pre-dawn and morning	Left 1–49%	Right 1–49%	9 a.m.
Dark	Thin crescent before sunrise	Left crescent	Right crescent	Noon

Tips for Tables

Use a table to compare lists of information.

- **Make rows and columns.** Label the rows with item names down the left side. Label the columns across the top with traits. (You can reverse this order if there are more traits than items.)
- **Fill in the boxes.** Place information in each box to match that column and row.
- **Provide units of measure** when numbers are given.
- **Provide a title.** Clearly identify the topic of the table.

Inquire to...

Create a Diagram or Time Line

1. **Question** the situation for the graphic.
   - **Subject:** What is the topic of the graphic?
   - **Purpose:** Will your graphic show the parts of something (diagram) or a sequence of events (time line)?
   - **Audience:** Who will read the graphic? What information do they need?

2. **Plan** your graphic. Gather materials you will need to draw it by hand. Or make sure you understand the software you will use to make it.

3. **Research** your topic.
   - **Gather** information to use in your graphic.
   - **List** the parts of the object or the events in the time line.

4. **Create** your graphic.
   - **Diagrams** show the parts of an object. Find or create a picture of your object and label the parts. Include a title. See page 317 for tips on creating diagrams.
   - **Time lines** show events in order. See page 318 for tips on creating time lines.

5. **Improve** your graphic.
   - **Evaluate** your graphic.
     - ▶ Does it make the topic clear? Is it accurate and attractive? Does it include a helpful title and labels? Do readers understand it?
   - **Revise** your graphic.
     - ▶ **Remove** any unnecessary parts.
     - ▶ **Rearrange** parts that are out of order.
     - ▶ **Add** any missing details.
   - **Perfect** your graphic. Make it clean and correct.

6. **Present** your graphic in a report or online.

Diagram

The following diagram identifies the parts of the human respiratory system.

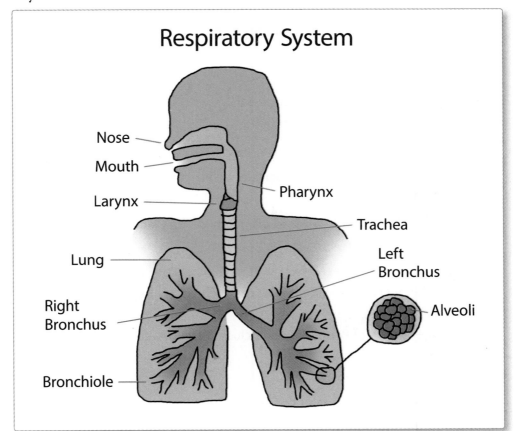

Tips for Diagrams

Use a diagram to show the parts of a complex thing.

- **Select a topic** that you need to show in a diagram.
- **Draw, photograph, or find the image** that you want to present.
- **Label the parts of the image** and draw lines to each.
- **Add a descriptive title** for the diagram.

Time Line

The following time line shows the British colonies in what later became the United States.

British Colonies Leading to the United States

1607	Virginia Colony
1620	Province of Massachusetts Bay
1623	Province of New Hampshire
1634	Province of Maryland
1636	Connecticut Colony (originally called "River Colony")
1636	Providence Plantation
1644	Rhode Island (separated from Providence Plantation)
1664	Province of New Jersey (part of Dutch colony beginning in 1614)
1664	Province of New York (part of Dutch colony beginning in 1614)
1681	Province of Pennsylvania (including Delaware)
1712	North Carolina (part of Carolina Colony beginning in 1653)
1712	South Carolina (part of Carolina Colony beginning in 1653)
1733	Province of Georgia

Tips for Time Lines

Use a time line to show a sequence of events.

- **Choose the right scale.** This may be by hour, day, month, year, decade, century, or something else.
- **Record your information.** Place each event in sequence.
- **Title the time line** to identify its contents.

Could this be my opening slide?

Chapter 26

Audio-Visual Projects

New technologies have made it easier than ever to record, photograph, video, and edit sounds and images for your audio-visual projects. With the latest tools, a good plan, and some hard work, you can turn an idea into a media masterpiece. This chapter will show you how.

You will learn . . .

- Creating Audio Podcasts
- Creating Slide Shows
- Making Videos
- Basic Types of Videos

Project Overview

These two pages give a quick overview of the audio-visual projects in this chapter.

Audio Podcast

An audio podcast is like a radio show. The difference is that a podcast is downloaded from the Internet instead of broadcast on the radio. (See page 323.)

Brewster Honor Choir

Tish: Hi, I'm Tish Cole, and this is the Brewster Rooster Podcast. Today we're featuring a song that the Brewster Honor Choir performed at the sectional competition last weekend. We'll also be speaking with Mr. Finseth, the choir director. But first, let's hear them sing!

Recording of choir performing.

Tish: That was inspiring! Tell us, Mr. Finseth, how did Honor Choir do at the competition?

Mr. Finseth: Well, there were lots of great choirs there. More than 30 schools were represented. I'm happy to say we took second place overall. And one of our members, Andrew Smith, took first place for his solo.

Tish: Congratulations! That's great news!

Mr. Finseth: Thank you. We are very excited.

Tish: So, how does someone join Honor Choir?

Mr. Finseth: Well, Honor Choir members are chosen from the Choir Club. We welcome anyone to try out for that club. Not only does it sponsor Honor Choir, it also hosts performances at malls, hospitals, and

---

Slide Show

A slide show is a presentation using a series of images and text to communicate. Slide shows often serve as background for a speech. PowerPoint slide shows are often used in business. PechaKucha are special slide shows with exactly 20 slides showing for 20 seconds each. (See page 325.)

The Theory of Pangaea
Brandy Litherland

Scientists believe our continents started as one prehistoric land mass.

Pangaea
200 million years ago

Pangaea

Video

Many people record short videos on smart phones or pocket cameras. Then they post their videos on sites like YouTube. For more professional results, you may need to use a digital video recorder, camera tripod, and editing software. Planning ahead can help a recording even more. (See pages 327–328.)

Shelby's Tricks

Audio	Screen Shot
My dog Shelby likes to do tricks.	
When I say, "Sit," he sits and waits.	
When I say "Shake," he lifts his paw.	
By teaching Shelby tricks, I know him better. We have a stronger bond.	

Starring: Shelby
Narration: Zack Long
Recording: Rashad Lewis
Editing & Posting: Mr. Huse

Inquire to...

Create an Audio Podcast

1. **Question** the situation for the podcast.
   - **Subject:** What topic will the podcast cover?
   - **Purpose:** Do you want to entertain, educate, or persuade?
   - **Audience:** Who will listen to the podcast? What will they expect?

2. **Plan** your podcast using a planning sheet. (See page 245.)

3. **Research** your topic and your equipment.
   - **Tools:** Learn to use your recording equipment and editing software. Find a place online where your recordings can be posted. (Visit thoughtfullearning.com/e322 for advice.)
   - **Team:** Divide scripting, recording, editing, publishing, and on-air speaking among your team members.
   - **Topic:** Gather information about your subject.

4. **Create** your podcast using one of these approaches.
   - **Scripted:** Have the on-air people read from a script with a beginning, middle, and end. Rerecord parts as needed.
   - **Improvised:** Allow the on-air people to make up conversations using their notes as starting points. Be prepared to edit a lot.
   - **Mixed:** Have the on-air people work from a script for the beginning, middle, and end. But let them improvise between scripted parts. Be prepared to cut some rough parts.

5. **Improve** your rough recording.
   - **Evaluate** your podcast with your goal and situation in mind.
     - ▶ **Goal:** Did you meet your goal?
     - ▶ **Situation:** Did you cover the subject? Did you achieve your purpose? Will your audience like your podcast?
   - **Revise** your podcast as necessary.
     - ▶ **Cut** material that does not help you achieve your goal.
     - ▶ **Redo** weak parts to make them stronger.
   - **Perfect** your podcast, making it sound great.

6. **Present** your podcast by posting it online.

Audio Podcast

This transcript is from a podcast featuring a recording by a school choir.

Brewster Honor Choir

The **beginning** identifies the podcast, the speaker, and the subject.

Tish: Hi, I'm Tish Cole, and this is the Brewster Rooster Podcast. Today we're featuring a song that the Brewster Honor Choir performed at the sectional competition last weekend. We'll also be speaking with Mr. Finseth, the choir director. But first, let's hear them sing!

Recording of choir performing.

The **middle** part includes a recording from the choir's performance. It also has a question-and-answer session about the choir.

Tish: That was inspiring! Tell us, Mr. Finseth, how did Honor Choir do at the competition?

Mr. Finseth: Well, there were lots of great choirs there. More than 30 schools were represented. I'm happy to say we took second place overall. And one of our members, Andrew Smith, took first place for his solo.

Tish: Congratulations! That's great news!

Mr. Finseth: Thank you. We are very excited.

Tish: So, how does someone join Honor Choir?

Mr. Finseth: Well, Honor Choir members are chosen from the Choir Club. We welcome anyone to try out for that club. Not only does it sponsor Honor Choir, it also hosts performances at malls, hospitals, and nursing homes. We have a lot of fun.

The **ending** thanks the guest for attending and the podcast audience for listening.

Tish: It sounds like it. Thank you for joining us today, Mr. Finseth.

Mr. Finseth: It was my pleasure.

Tish: And thank you, listeners. This has been the Brewster Rooster Podcast, episode one. We hope you will join us again soon.

Inquire to...

Create a Slide Show

1. **Question** the situation for your slide show.
   - **Subject:** What is your topic? How will you focus that topic?
   - **Purpose:** Are you trying to entertain, educate, or persuade?
   - **Audience:** Who will view the slide show?

2. **Plan** your slide show using a planning sheet. (See page 245.)

3. **Research** your topic and tools.
   - **Write** questions to guide your research.
   - **Read** about your topic. Take notes and track your sources. (See pages 136–137 and 255–260.)
   - **Gather** photos and graphics that demonstrate your ideas.
   - **Organize** your information in a clear way. (See pages 258–259.)

4. **Create** your slide show, using a software program such as PowerPoint.
   - **Beginning:** Start with the title of the presentation, your name, and an attention-grabbing image. Follow with a few slides that introduce your subject and your focus.
   - **Middle:** Create middle slides that support your focus. Use strong visuals. Keep the text short and use lists for details.
   - **Ending:** Sum up your main point and leave viewers with a final thought.

5. **Improve** your slide show.
   - **Evaluate** it against your goal and situation.
     - ▶ **Goal:** Did you meet your goal? How could you improve it?
     - ▶ **Situation:** Did you cover the subject? Did you achieve your purpose? Does your audience like it?
   - **Revise** your slide show.
     - ▶ **Cut** slides that don't help you meet your goal.
     - ▶ **Reorder** slides for better flow.
     - ▶ **Redo** slides that are overcrowded.
     - ▶ **Add** slides to improve support.
   - **Perfect** your slide show. Polish the wording and proofread.

6. **Present** your slide show in person or online.

Slide Show

These slides are from a presentation about the theory of Pangaea.

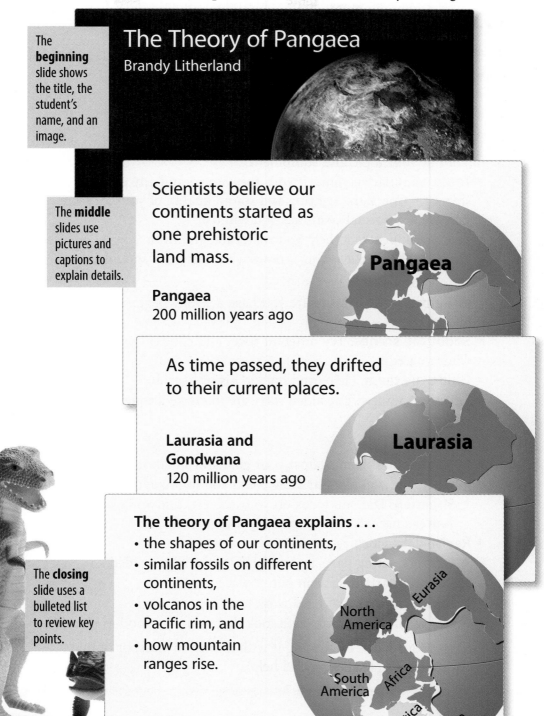

The **beginning** slide shows the title, the student's name, and an image.

The Theory of Pangaea
Brandy Litherland

The **middle** slides use pictures and captions to explain details.

Scientists believe our continents started as one prehistoric land mass.

Pangaea
200 million years ago

Pangaea

As time passed, they drifted to their current places.

Laurasia and Gondwana
120 million years ago

Laurasia

The **closing** slide uses a bulleted list to review key points.

The theory of Pangaea explains . . .
• the shapes of our continents,
• similar fossils on different continents,
• volcanos in the Pacific rim, and
• how mountain ranges rise.

Eurasia
North America
South America
Africa
Antarctica

Inquire to...

Create a Video

1. **Question** the situation.
   - **Subject:** What topic are you covering?
   - **Purpose:** Is your video intended to inform, persuade, or entertain?
   - **Audience:** Who will watch your video? What will they expect?

2. **Plan** your video using a planning sheet. (See page 245.)

3. **Research** your topic and equipment.
   - **Tools:** Familiarize yourself with the camera and any editing software. Check the lighting and sound quality of your location. Prepare any special costumes you will use.
   - **Team:** Ask people to help you write, act, and film.
   - **Topic:** Make sure everyone knows what the video should show.

4. **Create** your video.
   - **Write the script.** Make sure you have a strong beginning, middle, and ending.
   - **Shoot the scenes.** Try different takes and choose the best ones when you edit.
   - **Guide the team.** Help everyone do his or her job.
   - **Edit the footage.** Use video software to create a rough cut of your video.

5. **Improve** your video.
   - **Evaluate** your video against your goal and situation.
     - ▶ **Goal:** Did you meet it? How could you improve the video?
     - ▶ **Situation:** Did you focus on your subject? Did you meet the viewer's needs? Will people respond?
   - **Revise** your video as needed.
     - ▶ **Cut** distracting parts and **add** new material if needed.
     - ▶ **Reorder** parts that seem out of place.
     - ▶ **Rerecord** parts that need work.
   - **Perfect** your video to make it look and sound as good as possible.

6. **Present** your video by sharing it with family, in class, or online (with a parent's permission and help).

Video

In this part of a video transcript, a student demonstrates some of the tricks his dog can do. Although the video is fun, it also has a message.

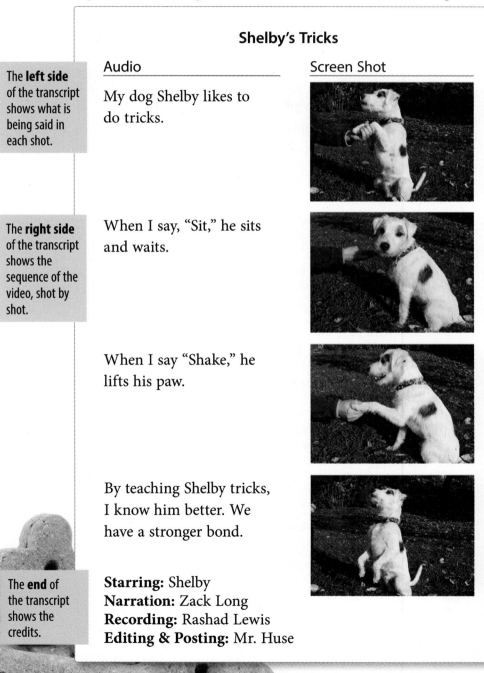

Shelby's Tricks

The **left side** of the transcript shows what is being said in each shot.

Audio

My dog Shelby likes to do tricks.

Screen Shot

The **right side** of the transcript shows the sequence of the video, shot by shot.

When I say, "Sit," he sits and waits.

When I say "Shake," he lifts his paw.

By teaching Shelby tricks, I know him better. We have a stronger bond.

The **end** of the transcript shows the credits.

Starring: Shelby
Narration: Zack Long
Recording: Rashad Lewis
Editing & Posting: Mr. Huse

Basic Types of Videos

You can create many types of videos. Here are a few ideas.

Fiction

A fiction video tells a made-up story.

- **Drama:** Dramas are serious stories. Some dramas are based on real events but add fictional details. A drama could be a detective story, a story about real life, a science-fiction story, and so on.
- **Comedy:** Comedies are funny stories. They may include zany characters, misunderstandings, goofy situations, and clever dialog.

Nonfiction

A nonfiction video presents a true situation. It may report on a topic, show an event, or make a persuasive argument.

- **News report:** A news report tells about an event. It may include interviews of witnesses and images from the event. News reports should present information without making judgments.
- **Documentary:** A documentary is a more in-depth report, usually after an event. Historical topics are often covered in documentaries.
- **Opinion:** In an opinion piece, the narrator offers his or her interpretation of a subject. An opinion piece is sometimes called an editorial or a personal commentary.
- **Music video:** A music video is a short film that features a song. The images may directly relate to the song or just add artistry.

Your Turn For more on making audio-visual projects, go to thoughtfullearning.com/e328.

What are you making?

Chapter 27
Design Projects

Some design projects are made just for the fun of it, like a mobile that highlights a favorite movie or a cartoon that tells a joke. Others share important information, like a poster or a T-shirt that promotes a good cause. Still others teach or explain a topic in a diorama or scale model. Whatever their purpose, design projects put your creative mind to work.

You will learn . . .
- Creating Cartoons
- Creating Posters
- Designing T-Shirts
- Designing Brochures
- Building Dioramas
- Building Scale Models
- Other Design Projects

Project Overview

Here is a quick overview of the design projects in this chapter.

Cartoon

You can create a cartoon to tell a story or to express an idea. (See pages **332–333**.)

Columbus Goes Sailing

Yes, India is east. But I know a western shortcut.

Okay. Here's some money. Buy some ships.

Are we here yet?

ell, I'm ure it n't rope!

Poster

A poster uses words and images to inform or persuade. (See pages **334–335**.)

Talent Show
Starring You!

T-Shirt

A T-shirt is like a poster that you wear. (See pages **336–337**.)

Be a Star!
(Ask me how.)

Brochure

Brochures provide a lot of information in a small space. They are intended to educate the audience about a specific topic. (See pages 338–339.)

Frequently Asked Questions

Q: Who started the club?

A: Students in Mr. Bendas's 2006 social studies class founded the club.

Q: Can I contribute cash to the club?

A: The club is not set up to take cash donations. But you can donate to the park at city hall.

Morledge Park Cleanup Club

Diorama

A diorama is a three-dimensional scene. Museums often use dioramas. (See pages 340–341.)

Scale Model

A scale model is a miniature version of something. The model is built "to scale." That means a small measure (inch or centimeter) on the model equals a much larger measure on the original. (See pages 342–343.)

Inquire to...

Create a Cartoon

1. **Question** yourself about the purpose of the cartoon.
   - **Subject:** What topic will your cartoon show?
   - **Purpose:** Is your cartoon intended to entertain, educate, or persuade?
   - **Audience:** Who will see the cartoon? Why will they be interested?

2. **Plan** your cartoon using a planning sheet. (See page **245**.)

3. **Research** the following:
   - **Topic:** Study your subject and come up with a starting idea.
   - **Tools:** Gather paper, pencils, and pens. Or learn to use a computer art program. (Visit **thoughtfullearning.com/e332** for advice.)
   - **Team:** Develop the cartoon by yourself or share the job with others. You might brainstorm as a group, then have one person write a script, another do pencil sketches, and another add color.

4. **Create** your cartoon.
   - **Finalize** your idea for the cartoon.
   - **Storyboard** the cartoon frame by frame. Sketch figures to show action. Then add narration boxes or thought bubbles.
   - **Draw** each frame in your cartoon.
   - **Letter** each caption or thought bubble neatly.

5. **Improve** your cartoon.
   - **Evaluate** your cartoon.
     - ▶ Does the cartoon meet your goal? Does it achieve your purpose?
   - **Revise** your cartoon.
     - ▶ **Remove** unneeded words and panels.
     - ▶ **Rearrange** panels for a clearer story.
     - ▶ **Redraw** parts that need work or **add** new panels as needed.
   - **Perfect** your cartoon. Make it clean and correct.
     - ▶ **Ink** the drawings.
     - ▶ **Color** the cartoon or leave it black and white.

6. **Present** your cartoon in a school newspaper or post it online.

Comic Strip

A comic strip uses a series of cartoon pictures to tell a fiction or nonfiction story.

The **beginning** introduces the situation.

The **middle** develops the story.

The **ending** finishes the story, often with a punch line.

Inquire to...

Create a Poster

1. **Question** the situation for your poster.
   - **Subject:** What is the topic of your poster? What is the specific focus?
   - **Purpose:** Is your poster intended to entertain, educate, or persuade?
   - **Audience:** Who will see your poster? Where will it be displayed? How far away will it be from viewers?

2. **Plan** your poster using a planning sheet. (See page 245.)

3. **Research** the following:
   - **Topic:** Gather all the information you need about your topic.
   - **Tools:** Gather paper, poster board, pencils, pens, and markers. Or design your poster on a computer, print it out, and mount it on poster board.
   - **Team:** Develop the poster yourself or share the work with a team.

4. **Create** your poster. Include a slogan, an image, and vital facts.
   - **Sketch** your idea on regular-sized paper.
   - **Copy** your drawing in light pencil onto a poster board.
   - **Ink** over the pencil lines and letters. Then add images and vital facts.

5. **Improve** your poster.
   - **Evaluate** the poster.
     - ▶ Does the poster meet or exceed your goals and objectives?
     - ▶ Does the poster focus on a clear topic? Does it fulfill its purpose?
   - **Revise** your poster.
     - ▶ **Remove** unneeded words and images.
     - ▶ **Rearrange** parts for clarity and attractiveness.
     - ▶ **Add** missing information or images.
   - **Perfect** your poster. Make it clean and correct.
     - ▶ Check to make sure all the information is correct.
     - ▶ Make sure your main information can be seen from a distance.

6. **Present** your poster by displaying it in a good place.

Poster

This poster advertises a student talent show. It was made with a computer drawing program. It uses clip art found on the Internet.

A colorful background image draws attention.

A catchy slogan gets the main point across.

The slogan is big enough to be seen at a distance.

Talent Show

Starring You!

Vital details are given in smaller text.

Tryouts Apr. 21, 3–5 p.m.
Brewster Elementary Gym
Performance May 9, 7:30 p.m.

Inquire to...

Design a T-Shirt

1. **Question** the goal for the T-shirt.
   - **Subject:** What will the T-shirt feature? Will it use text, images, or both?
   - **Purpose:** Is your T-shirt intended to inform, persuade, or entertain?
   - **Audience:** Who will see your T-shirt? What reaction do you want?

2. **Plan** your T-shirt using a planning sheet. (See page 245.)

3. **Research** the following:
   - **Topic:** Gather images and ideas that you want to use.
   - **Tools:** Learn how you can have a T-shirt made or learn how to hand-decorate one. For online printing, learn how to prepare your files and upload them. (Have an adult approve any purchases.)
   - **Team:** Do the project by yourself or work with friends.

4. **Create** your T-shirt design.
   - **Measure** the shirt space you will have to work with or use an online tool.
   - **Create** a design on paper or digitally.
   - **Use** the best images and words for your purpose.

5. **Improve** your T-shirt.
   - **Evaluate** your T-shirt's design.
     - ▶ Does the T-shirt meet or exceed your goals and objectives?
     - ▶ Does the T-shirt accomplish its purpose? Do people like it?
   - **Revise** your T-shirt design.
     - ▶ **Remove** unneeded words or images.
     - ▶ **Rearrange** parts to make it more attractive and effective.
     - ▶ **Redo** lettering or images that are unclear.
     - ▶ **Add** missing information or visual elements.
   - **Perfect** your T-shirt design to make it clean and correct.

6. **Present** your T-shirt.
   - **Print your design** on a T-shirt and wear it for others to see.

T-Shirt

This T-shirt was designed to help advertise the Brewster Elementary talent show. The designer kept things simple but dramatic.

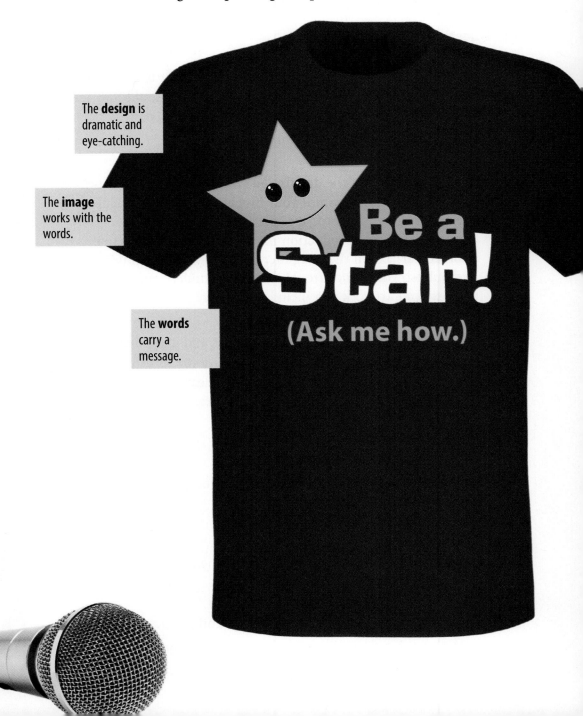

The **design** is dramatic and eye-catching.

The **image** works with the words.

The **words** carry a message.

Be a
Star!
(Ask me how.)

Inquire to...

Design a Brochure

1. **Question** the situation.
   - **Subject:** What is your brochure about?
   - **Purpose:** Is your brochure intended to inform or to persuade?
   - **Audience:** Who will read this brochure? What should they learn from it?

2. **Plan** your brochure using a planning sheet. (See page 245.)

3. **Research** the following:
   - **Topic:** Gather all of the details you will include in your brochure.
   - **Team:** Work with a team if your brochure represents a club or group. Or design the brochure on your own.
   - **Tools:** Decide on a production method: online? color printer? photocopier? Learn the computer application you will use to design and publish your brochure. Make sure to understand the rights to any text and artwork you include. (See page 255.)

4. **Create** your brochure.
   - **Write** the text that tells your main points and gives details.
   - **Add** images that attract the eye and clarify the information.
   - **Use** an attractive design and one or two clear type styles. Fold your brochure in half to make it four pages. Or fold it in thirds to make it six pages.

5. **Improve** your brochure.
   - **Evaluate** your brochure.
     - ▶ Does it meet your goal and purpose? Does it focus on a clear topic? Do people understand it?
   - **Revise** your brochure.
     - ▶ **Cut** unnecessary words and images.
     - ▶ **Reorder** parts for a smoother arrangement.
     - ▶ **Redo** parts that are unclear.
     - ▶ **Add** missing details or helpful graphics.
   - **Perfect** your brochure to make it clean and correct.

6. **Present** your brochure. Pass it out or post it online.

Brochure

This brochure is designed to build support for a park cleanup. Its purpose is both to inform and to persuade, but it also seeks to make the event fun and exciting.

Back Page

Front Page

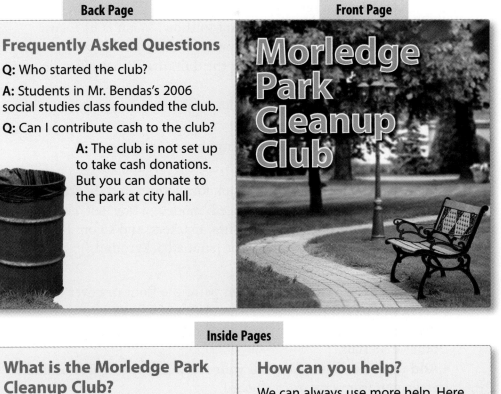

Frequently Asked Questions

Q: Who started the club?

A: Students in Mr. Bendas's 2006 social studies class founded the club.

Q: Can I contribute cash to the club?

A: The club is not set up to take cash donations. But you can donate to the park at city hall.

Morledge Park Cleanup Club

Inside Pages

What is the Morledge Park Cleanup Club?

Who? Brewster School students, parents, and anyone else who wants to volunteer

What? Pick up litter, plant flowers, trim bushes, paint benches

When? 9 a.m. on the second Saturday of each month

Where? Southeast corner of Morledge Park

Why? To have fun keeping our park beautiful

How? Working in teams

How can you help?

We can always use more help. Here are ways you can get involved:

- **Join the cleanup crew.** More hands are always welcome.

- **Donate supplies.** We can always use new work gloves, trash bags, and gardening supplies.

- **Help with lunch.** After every cleanup, we have a picnic lunch in the park. When weather is bad, we meet in the Brewster School gym for a potluck.

Contact Mr. Bendas at Brewster School for more information.

Inquire to...

Build a Diorama

1. **Question** the situation for your diorama.
   - **Subject:** What scene do you want to show? What is its focus? What background should be shown?
   - **Purpose:** Why are you building the diorama? What effect do you want it to have?
   - **Audience:** Who will see your diorama? What do you expect them to learn?

2. **Plan** your diorama using a planning sheet. (See page 245.)

3. **Research** the subject.
   - **Learn** all about your subject. Look for pictures and diagrams.
   - **Gather** the materials you will need: models, a box, felt, clay, Popsicle sticks, glue, paint, brushes, markers, and so on. Print a background photo if you wish or paint a background.

4. **Create** your diorama.
   - **Start** with the background. Then paint the floor or cover it with grass, sand, or wood.
   - **Build** the structures with cardboard, toothpicks, Popsicle sticks, or other materials.
   - **Add** people or animals to tell your story. Use toy figures or make your own from clay or cardboard.

5. **Improve** your diorama.
   - **Evaluate** your diorama.
     - ▶ Does it clearly show your subject? Do the figures and background tell a clear story? Do viewers appreciate it?
   - **Rework** your diorama.
     - ▶ **Remove** parts that don't look right or don't help tell the story.
     - ▶ **Rearrange** parts to make the scene clearer.
     - ▶ **Rebuild** parts that need work.
     - ▶ **Add** missing parts that could help.
   - **Perfect** your diorama to make it look as good as possible.

6. **Present** your diorama to your family, class, or community.

Diorama

The first photo shows a student's Native American diorama. The second and third photos show examples of professionally made dioramas that you might see in a museum.

From Flickr by jillallyn

This student diorama is made from a shoe box. It uses cutouts of photos to set the scene.

This museum diorama shows Christopher Columbus studying a map.

This professional diorama uses miniatures to show a shipping and rail yard.

Inquire to...

Build a Scale Model

1. **Question** the situation for your scale model.
   - **Subject:** What does the model represent? What size and scale should be used?
   - **Purpose:** Why are you building this model?
   - **Audience:** Who will see your model? Will it be graded or judged?

2. **Plan** your scale model using a planning sheet. (See page 245.)

3. **Research** your scale model.
   - **Learn** about your subject. Look at the original item, photos, drawings, and other sources for help.
   - **Decide** on the best scale for your model (converting meters to centimeters or feet to inches).
   - **Gather** materials. For buildings, you might use cardboard or foam sheets. For vehicles, you might buy a model kit. For a prototype machine, you might use an Erector set or other building kits.

4. **Create** your scale model.
   - **Building:** Study a drawing of your building. Create a scale model of the drawing.
   - **Vehicle:** Follow the directions to build the kit. Or combine parts from different kits to make your own vehicle.
   - **Machine prototype:** Make each piece to the proper scale. Then connect them and test the movement.

5. **Improve** your scale model.
   - **Evaluate** your scale model.
     - Does it accurately depict your subject? Are all the parts scaled properly? Do moving parts work correctly?
   - **Revise** your scale model.
     - **Remove** parts that don't look right. **Add** any missing parts.
     - **Reposition** parts to make the model look better or work better.
     - **Rebuild** parts that are not sized right.
   - **Perfect** your model, providing final details.

6. **Present** your model to your family or in class.

Scale Model

The first model on this page represents an antique car. The second model helps the audience understand helicopters. The third model helps people imagine what a finished building would look like.

This model car includes moving parts.

This model helicopter actually flies.

This model cottage is a prototype. It shows what the full-sized cottage will look like when built.

Other Design Projects

You can try other types of design projects besides those shown in this chapter.

■ More Types of Cartoons

Multi-panel cartoon strips aren't the only types of cartoons you can make. You can also make a gag cartoon, which is a funny single-panel picture with a caption beneath it. You can draw a vocabulary cartoon or a comic strip to show the meaning of a word. Or you can add a caption or word balloon to a photo to make a photo cartoon.

■ Booklets

Fold several pages like a brochure. Then add a folded cover and staple or stitch them all together. This way you can make a booklet full of short stories, poems, essays, and artwork.

■ Rube Goldberg Machines

Rube Goldberg machines are crazy devices that use many odd steps to achieve a simple goal. Designing one will put your inventiveness to work.

This book is too good to eat!

Chapter 28
Performing Projects

When you must perform in front of an audience, you naturally want to do well. Good performances are practiced and polished until they are smooth and perfect. So whether you are acting in a play, giving a speech, or playing a solo, both you and your audience will appreciate a performance that shines. This chapter can help you prepare.

You will learn . . .

- Reciting Poems
- Giving Speeches
- Debating Issues
- Staging Plays

Project Overview

Here is a quick overview of the performing projects in this chapter.

Poem Recitals

Many schools host live poetry competitions. So do many other organizations. A poem recital can also add to holiday parties and other social events. (See pages 348–349.)

"Hi. My name is Foster Porro. My poem is 'Eletephony,' by Laura Elizabeth Richards."

Once there was an elephant,
Who tried to use the telephant—
<u>No! no!</u> I mean an <u>elephone</u>
Who tried to use the <u>telephone</u>—
(Dear me! I am not certain quite
That even now I've got it right.)

Howe'er it was, he got his trunk
Entangled in the telephunk;
The more he tried to get it <u>free</u>,
The louder buzzed the telephee—

Speeches

A speech is a formal presentation of information to an audience. Some speeches are informative, while others are persuasive. (See pages 350–353.)

Owning a Dog

Ladies and gentlemen, distinguished judges, and fellow students. I'm Lily Chen, and I would like to talk to you about the value of owning a dog.

When I asked my parents for a puppy, they said, "Puppies grow up to be dogs. And caring for a dog is a lot of work."

They were right. You have to feed your dog, provide it with water, wash it, clean up after it, train it, and play with it. Even when you don't feel like it or think you don't have time, your dog needs attention. Dogs thrive when they get a lot of attention.

Having a dog is worth all the work. Playing with a dog is better than playing a video game because you get exercise. Walking a dog means you get fresh air. Teaching a dog tricks means you have to think hard and work together. You and your dog become friends. Your dog can make you feel better when you're sad or ~~

So parents, if yo~
think about the worl~
And kids, remember~
so be your dog's best~
Thank you.

Caring For Your Dog

Debates

A debate is a formal discussion of an important topic. Debaters must research the topic fully and deliver their message persuasively. They must also respond to their opponents' positions. (See pages 354–355.)

Plays

Staging a play can be a big project. First a director chooses a script and selects a cast. Actors learn their lines and rehearse the play. Other people sew costumes and build sets. Once all the pieces come together, the play is ready to perform! (See pages 356–358.)

Moderator (*Teacher*): Today we will hear a debate about the following proposition: *Books do a better job of telling stories than films do.* The first team will argue for the position, and the second team will argue against it.

We will start with speaker one for the affirmative side, followed by speaker one for the opposition. Speakers will each have two minutes to present their arguments. Please give each speaker your full attention.

Calvin Waldoch, the podium is yours.

Calvin Waldoch (*first speaker for the affirmative*): Thank you, Mr. Kohn and my fellow classmates. For several reasons, books are the best way to enjoy a story.

For one thing, books are less passive than films. In a film, you see just what the director wants you to see. But in a book, you more actively imagine the scene. In this way, a book is a shared experience between the author and the reader. That alone makes books

The Tortoise, the Elephant, and the Hippo
By Clifford Bucio

Cast of Characters

ELEPHANT, lord of the grasslands
TORTOISE, a slow but clever animal
HIPPO, a neighbor to both

ACT I: Scene 1

(*African grassland with trees at stage right. TORTOISE slowly trundles from the trees. From stage left, we hear the thunderous approach of ELEPHANT.*)

ELEPHANT: (*Stomping on*) Get out of the way, Tortoise! You don't want to be stomped by a stomper like me.

TORTOISE: My shell's built for stompers like you.

ELEPHANT: Look out! One side! Gang way!

TORTOISE: Slow down! Ease up! HALT!

(*ELEPHANT tries to stop and stumbles onto TORTOISE, accidentally stepping on him before jumping back.*)

ELEPHANT: Ouch! Your shell hurt my foot.

TORTOISE: In a world of stompers, it's good to have a strong, sturdy shell.

ELEPHANT: (*Embarrassed*) You have a str
all right, but you're not a strong

TORTOISE: Is that so? I
war.

ELEPHANT: Nons

TORTOISE: M

ELEPHANT

Inquire to...

Recite a Poem

1. **Question** the situation for your recital.
   - **Subject:** Is there a specific topic for the occasion?
   - **Purpose:** Is the recital intended to entertain, educate, or persuade?
   - **Audience:** Who will hear the recital? Will it be graded?

2. **Plan** your recital using a planning sheet. (See page **245**.)

3. **Research** your poem recital.
   - **Choose a poem** that you enjoy and that works for the occasion.
   - **Learn** about your poem's history and meaning.
   - **Understand** any special circumstances for the recital.

4. **Create** your performance.
   - **Read** your chosen poem aloud.
   - **Note** places for emphasis. Give them extra volume or pauses.
   - **Include** gestures and facial expressions to help convey meaning.
   - **Memorize** the poem.
   - **Practice** reciting the poem.

5. **Improve** your recital.
   - **Evaluate** your performance.
     - ▶ Does it suit the situation well? Does it bring the poem to life? Is your pronunciation and delivery smooth? Does a test audience respond as you expect?
   - **Revise** your performance.
     - ▶ **Cut** gestures and expressions that aren't needed.
     - ▶ **Rework** your delivery to make a stronger impact.
     - ▶ **Add** emphasis to parts that need it.
   - **Perfect** your performance until it is both natural and effective.

6. **Present** your recital. Follow these tips for a successful performance.
   - **Take a calming breath** before you begin.
   - **Introduce yourself** and the name of your poem.
   - **Speak loudly** enough to be heard by everyone.
   - **Look out** across the audience to make them feel included.

Poem Recital

For a poem recital, the student below chose a funny poem. Notice how he marked the poem to help him recite it.

The **beginning** introduces the speaker and the name of the poem.

"Hi. My name is Foster Porro. My poem is 'Eletephony,' by Laura Elizabeth Richards."

The **middle** presents the poem itself.

Once there was an elephant,

Who tried to use the telephant—

Underlines show emphasis, dashes show pauses, and parentheses show confusion.

No! no! I mean an elephone

Who tried to use the telephone—

(Dear me! I am not certain quite

That even now I've got it right.)

Howe'er it was, he got his trunk

Entangled in the telephunk;

The more he tried to get it free,

The louder buzzed the telephee—

(I fear I'd better drop the song

Of elephop and telephong!)

The **ending** includes a pause before a "thank you."

"Thank you."

Inquire to...

Give a Speech

1. **Question** the situation for your speech.
   - **Subject:** What should you talk about? What should your focus be?
   - **Purpose:** Should your speech inform or persuade?
   - **Audience:** Who will hear your speech? What do they know about the subject? What do they need to know?
2. **Plan** your speech by using a planning sheet. (See page 245.)
3. **Research** your speech.
   - **Topic:** Gather information about your topic.
   - **Tools:** Prepare any visuals. Make sure you know how to use any electronic equipment such as a microphone or projector.
4. **Create** your speech.
   - **Beginning:** Get the listeners' attention and present your main idea.
   - **Middle:** Provide details that support your main idea. If you are arguing a point, remember to answer any objections.
   - **Ending:** Summarize your point and give a final thought.
   - **Visuals:** Make sure slides, props, or handouts are well made.
5. **Improve** your speech.
   - **Evaluate** your speech and your delivery.
     - ▶ Does the content focus on the topic? Does the speech achieve its purpose? Does a test audience get the point? Are they interested?
   - **Revise** your speech.
     - ▶ **Remove** extra words and ideas.
     - ▶ **Rearrange** parts to make things clearer.
     - ▶ **Rework** parts that need improvement.
     - ▶ **Add** quotations, statistics, or stories that support the main point.
   - **Perfect** your speech. Make a clean copy. Practice your delivery.
6. **Present** your speech in person or as a recording. Follow these tips:
   - **Take a slow breath** before you begin.
   - **Greet your audience** politely.
   - **Speak slowly** and loudly.
   - **Look at your audience** and connect with them.

Persuasive Speech

In this speech for a school contest, a student explores the value of dog ownership.

The **beginning** greets the audience and gives the main point.

The **middle** supports the main point.

The speaker uses a pro and con approach. She chooses to list problems first, then benefits.

The **ending** ties everything together.

Owning a Dog

Ladies and gentlemen, distinguished judges, and fellow students. I'm Lily Chen, and I would like to talk to you about the value of owning a dog.

When I asked my parents for a puppy, they said, "Puppies grow up to be dogs. And caring for a dog is a lot of work."

They were right. You have to feed your dog, provide it with water, wash it, clean up after it, train it, and play with it. Even when you don't feel like it or think you don't have time, your dog needs attention. Dogs thrive when they get a lot of attention.

Having a dog is worth all the work. Playing with a dog is better than playing a video game because you get exercise. Walking a dog means you get fresh air. Teaching a dog tricks means you have to think hard and work together. You and your dog become friends. Your dog can make you feel better when you're sad or angry.

So parents, if your child asks for a dog, don't just think about the work. Think about the benefits, too. And kids, remember that your dog will depend on you, so be your dog's best friend.

Thank you.

Other Speech Formats

The speech on the previous page was written out word for word. This is called manuscript format. It is best for a formal situation, like a classroom speech or a competition. For less formal situations, you can speak from an outline or list.

Outline

An outline gives the main points of your speech in order. It may also include some full sentences. Here is a modified outline of the speech on page 351.

> **Speech About Owning a Dog**
> I. Beginning: Greet audience, judges, fellow students
>   A. I want to talk to you about taking care of a dog.
>   B. My parents said, "Puppies grow up to be dogs. And caring for a dog is a lot of work."
> II. Middle: Give pros and cons
>   A. Cons: You have to feed, provide water, wash, train, and play with your dog, even when you don't feel like it.
>   B. Pros: A dog makes you exercise and get fresh air; teaching it tricks means thinking hard; and a dog is a good friend.
> III. Ending: Stress main points
>   Parents, don't just think about the work. Kids, be a good friend to your dog.

List

A list is great for informal situations. It gives just key words or phrases as reminders of what to say. Here is a list from the speech above.

> **Speech About Taking Care of a Dog**
> 1. Greet group
> 2. Quote parents
> 3. Cons: feed, provide water, wash, train, give attention
> 4. Pros: good exercise, tricks, friendship
> 5. Conclude

Your Turn Make your own speech. Use a list, outline, or manuscript.

Adding Visuals

Speeches often include visuals. Visuals add interest and help communicate ideas. You can use handouts, slides, and props.

Handouts

Handouts help an audience understand facts and reference them later. Here is a handout about the exercise benefits of having a dog.

	Before Getting a Dog: 4 ½ hours of exercise	Since Getting a Dog: 9 hours of exercise
Weekdays	• Walk to school 5 minutes • Recess 20 minutes • Walk home 5 minutes	• Walk to school 5 minutes • Recess 20 minutes • Walk home 5 minutes • Walk dog 30 minutes
Weekends	• Play outside 60 minutes daily	• Play outside 60 minutes daily • Exercise dog 60 minutes daily

Slides

Slides make great visuals. Here's a slide from Lily Chen's speech. (See also pages 324–325.)

Props

Props make your message more concrete.

Caring For Your Dog

Inquire to...

Debate an Issue

1. **Question** the situation for the debate.
   - **Subject:** What is the topic to be debated? Who will argue for it? Who will argue against it?
   - **Purpose:** What is the goal of the debate?
   - **Audience:** Who will witness the debate? Will they be able to ask questions? Will they choose a winning team?

2. **Plan** your debate by creating a proposition. A proposition states that a certain position is true or a certain action should be taken. One team will argue for the proposition, and one will argue against it.

3. **Research** the issue.
   - **Topic:** Learn both sides of the issue.
   - **Support:** Pay special attention to support for your side. A pro-con chart can help.

4. **Create** your side of the debate.
   - **Decide** as a team your best arguments and evidence. Also discuss how to answer objections from the other team.
   - **Develop** each team member's presentation.
   - **Practice** your side's presentation. Then practice again with someone arguing the opposing view.

5. **Improve** your team's performance.
   - **Evaluate** your main arguments.
     - ▶ Are your points strong enough? Are you prepared to counter opposing arguments?
   - **Revise** your presentation.
     - ▶ **Remove** any weak points.
     - ▶ **Rearrange** details for a stronger argument.
     - ▶ **Rework** parts that are unclear.
     - ▶ **Add** main points and supporting details that may be missing.
   - **Polish** your delivery.

6. **Present** your debate.

Debate

The following text shows the first part of a debate about the value of books and films.

In the beginning, a moderator sets the scene for the debate.	**Moderator** *(Teacher)*: Today we will hear a debate about the following proposition: *Books do a better job of telling stories than films do.* The first team will argue for the position, and the second team will argue against it.

Moderator *(Teacher)*: Today we will hear a debate about the following proposition: *Books do a better job of telling stories than films do.* The first team will argue for the position, and the second team will argue against it.

We will start with speaker one for the affirmative side, followed by speaker one for the opposition. Speakers will each have two minutes to present their arguments. Please give each speaker your full attention.

Calvin Waldoch, the podium is yours.

In the **middle**, the first speaker for the proposition states his team's position.

Calvin Waldoch *(first speaker for the affirmative)*: Thank you, Mr. Kohn and my fellow classmates. For several reasons, books are the best way to enjoy a story.

The first speaker makes a point supporting this position.

For one thing, books are less passive than films. In a film, you see just what the director wants you to see. But in a book, you more actively imagine the scene. In this way, a book is a shared experience between the author and the reader. That alone makes books better. . . .

The opposition's first speaker offers a counter-argument.

Haydee Seroka *(first speaker for the opposition)*: It may be true that books make the reader more mentally active than films do. But books require so much more time and effort. A film tells a complete story in just a few hours, while a book may take a number of days to read.

The opposing speaker continues with a claim for her team's position.

This fact shows that films tell stories more effectively than books. You don't have to remember what you read before or wonder what things look like. Instead, you can concentrate on what unfolds in the story. . . .

Inquire to...

Stage a Play

1. **Question** the situation for the play.
   - **Subject:** What is the subject of the play? Will it be serious or funny? Modern or historical?
   - **Purpose:** Why are you putting on the play? Is it to entertain? To inform? To persuade?
   - **Audience:** Who will see this play? What will they expect from it?

2. **Plan** your play using a planning sheet. (See page 245.)

3. **Research** the play.
   - **Topic:** Read the play or write your own.
   - **Tools:** Note any props and costumes you will need.
   - **Team:** Choose a director. Cast the actors. Assign crew members to build sets, make costumes, manage lighting and sound, create posters, and handle tickets.

4. **Create** your play production.
   - **Read** the script together.
   - **Block** scenes by deciding where actors enter, stand, move, and exit.
   - **Run** scenes to help actors learn lines and blocking.

5. **Improve** your performance.
   - **Evaluate** your play.
     - ▶ Does the performance meet your goal? Do the performers create the right mood? Does a practice audience respond well?
   - **Tighten** the performance.
     - ▶ **Remove** awkward pauses and unneeded actions.
     - ▶ **Rearrange** blocking so that speakers can be seen and heard.
     - ▶ **Revise** scenes that aren't working well.
     - ▶ **Add** emphasis to words and actions that need them.
   - **Perfect** your performance.

6. **Present** your performance. Continue to improve each new show.

Play Script

Here is the first part of a play script. Note how the script identifies characters, stage direction, and dialog (lines spoken by characters).

Title	**The Tortoise, the Elephant, and the Hippo** By Clifford Bucio **Cast of Characters**
Cast	**ELEPHANT,** lord of the grasslands **TORTOISE,** a slow but clever animal **HIPPO,** a neighbor to both
Act and Scene	**ACT I: Scene 1** *(African grassland with trees at stage right. TORTOISE slowly trundles from the trees. From stage left, we hear the thunderous approach of ELEPHANT.)*
Dialog	**ELEPHANT:** *(Stomping on)* Get out of the way, Tortoise! You don't want to be stomped by a stomper like me. **TORTOISE:** My shell's built for stompers like you. **ELEPHANT:** Look out! One side! Gang way! **TORTOISE:** Slow down! Ease up! HALT!
Stage direction	*(ELEPHANT tries to stop and stumbles onto TORTOISE, accidentally stepping on him before jumping back.)* **ELEPHANT:** Ouch! Your shell hurt my foot. **TORTOISE:** In a world of stompers, it's good to have a strong, sturdy shell. **ELEPHANT:** *(Embarrassed)* You have a strong shell, all right, but you're not a strong as me. **TORTOISE:** Is that so? I could beat you in a tug-of-war. **ELEPHANT:** Nonsense! **TORTOISE:** Meet me at the rubber trees tomorrow. **ELEPHANT:** I'll be there.

Act and Scene

Setting Description

Stage direction

ACT I: Scene 2

(The next day beside a stream where HIPPO is bathing. Rubber trees stand stage left.)

TORTOISE: *(Enters from trees and drags a long, thick bungee cord.)* Good morning, Hippo. I challenged Elephant to a tug-of-war today.

HIPPO: *(Laughing)* What a foolish challenge! Elephant is much too strong for you.

TORTOISE: There are different kinds of strength. My shell was too strong for Elephant yesterday, and my brains will be too strong for him today.

(ELEPHANT arrives stage right, stomping and snorting, lifting a barbell in his trunk.)

ELEPHANT: I hope you're ready to lose, Tortoise. . . .

Puppet Shows

A play doesn't have to include live actors or a full stage. You can also do a play as a puppet show. Paint a cardboard box as a stage, or stand behind curtains. Use finger puppets, marionettes, paper puppets on sticks, or even sock puppets.

Chapter 29
Web Projects

The World Wide Web connects computers, people, and ideas. All across the world, billions of people send words, photos, videos, songs, stories, products, services, and so on . . . back and forth. And every day, the Web gets bigger and more complex. You can grow this network of information by creating your own Web projects.

You will learn . . .
- Designing a Glog
- Making Digital Stories
- Creating Wikis or Blog Posts
- Sharing an Electronic Announcement

Project Overview

These two pages give a quick overview of Web projects in this chapter.

Glog

Glog stands for "graphical blog." You can think of it as a digital poster. Like a poster, a glog shows information graphically. Because it is digital, the glog can include audio and video as well as links to other information online. (See pages 362–363.)

Digital Story

A digital story is like an electronic slide show. Each slide can also include audio-visual elements and links to other resources. (See pages 364–365.)

Platonic Solids

The five Platonic solids are named after the Greek philosopher Plato. He lived about 400 years B.C.E. Each Platonic solid is an object with identical sides.

⚠ **Tetrahedron** means "four faces."
⚠ Each face is an equilateral triangle.
⚠ Though many call it a "pyramid," pyramids usually have a square base.

▱ **Hexahedron** means "six faces."
▱ We usually call it a cube.
▱ Each face is a square.

◇ **Octahedron** means "eight faces."
◇ Like a tetrahedron it has triangular faces.

⬡ **Dodecahedron** means "twelve faces."
⬡ Each face is a pentagon.

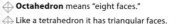

History of the Piano

The Clavichord

The Harpsichord

Wiki or Blog

Wikis and blogs are each ways of building a Web site. *Wiki* is a Hawaiian word for "fast." A wiki program allows you to create and link pages that other people will see as a Web site. *Blog* is short for "Web log." It is like an online diary with categorized entries. (See pages 366–367.)

Electronic Announcement

There are many ways of making announcements online. You can post a message on a trusted Web site or social-media account. (Always ask for your parent or guardian's approval.) Or you can send an email or text message to friends and family. (See pages 368–370.)

Book Reviews
by Ms. Wiggens's Class

The Slant Book
By Peter Newell

The Slant Book is a rhyming story about a little boy in a runaway cart. Each left-hand page has two rhyming stanzas. Each right-hand page has a matching picture. What makes this book so much fun is that the pages are slanted so that the words and pictures both run downhill toward the middle.

When the book was first printed in 1910, it was actually shaped with a slant. (See the picture above, or visit *The Slant Book* on the Library of Congress site.) The publisher even patented that layout. Nowadays, the book is shaped like any other book. But the words and pictures are still slanted.

The story in the book is exciting, and the pictures are funny. Some of the words are old fashioned, though. That makes some pages difficult to understand. Ask an adult or two for help. Better yet, have them read the

@KalaVandermolen|Chris: Hey, everybody! My brother Charles's birthday is tomorrow. Be sure to say "Happy Birthday" if you see him at lunch or recess. I'm sure it'll make his day great!

Graduation

| Helvetica | 12 | B | I | U |

To: desanctis@yahoogroups.com
Subject: Graduation
Attachment:
From: Randolph Desanctis

Dear family and friends,

I have graduated from fifth grade!

The graduation ceremony will be at 6 p.m. Friday, May 25, in the Ahluwalia Elementary School auditorium.

Afterward there will be a potluck celebration in the school gym.

Please come if you can!

Yours truly,

Randolph Desanctis

SMS

Inquire to...

Design a Glog

1. **Question** the situation for the glog.
   - **Subject:** What information will your glog cover?
   - **Purpose:** What do you want your glog to accomplish?
   - **Audience:** Who will see your glog? What do they need to know about the topic?

2. **Plan** your glog by making a sketch on a big sheet of paper.

3. **Research** your topic.
   - **Gather** information to use in your glog. Look for facts to list and images to show.
   - **Explore** other glogs for inspiration.
   - **Organize** your facts and images in the best order.

4. **Create** your glog using images, text, and links.
   - **Images** present your ideas visually. Make sure your images are attractive and informative.
   - **The text** helps to define the images, but avoid using too much text. Limit your text to captions and definitions.
   - **Links** to other information can help viewers who want to learn more.

5. **Improve** your glog.
   - **Evaluate** your glog.
     - ▶ Does it look good as a whole? Is the overall idea clear? Are the details well arranged?
   - **Revise** your glog.
     - ▶ **Remove** images and text that aren't needed.
     - ▶ **Rearrange** parts to guide the viewer's eye more effectively.
     - ▶ **Rework** parts that don't look or feel right.
     - ▶ **Add** visuals, text, and links that make your glog stronger.

6. **Perfect** your glog so that it clearly communicates your ideas.
   - **Present** your glog online with an adult's help.

Glog

In her math class, Jewel Oliveros made a glog to explain the Platonic solids. She included a picture of each one and labeled and defined it.

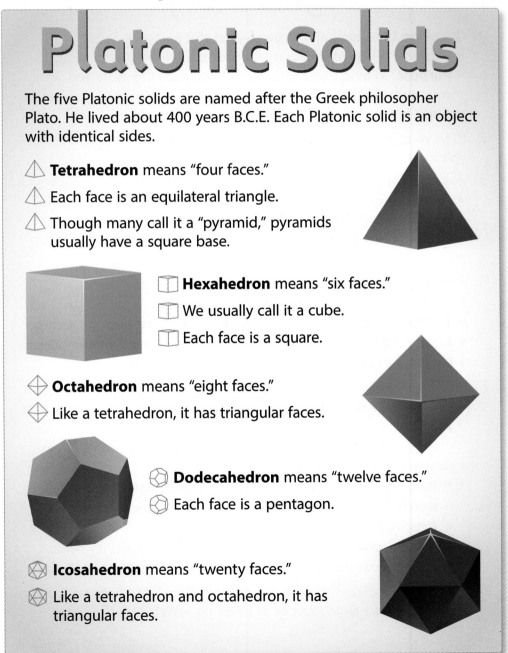

Platonic Solids

The five Platonic solids are named after the Greek philosopher Plato. He lived about 400 years B.C.E. Each Platonic solid is an object with identical sides.

△ **Tetrahedron** means "four faces."

△ Each face is an equilateral triangle.

△ Though many call it a "pyramid," pyramids usually have a square base.

◻ **Hexahedron** means "six faces."

◻ We usually call it a cube.

◻ Each face is a square.

◇ **Octahedron** means "eight faces."

◇ Like a tetrahedron, it has triangular faces.

⬡ **Dodecahedron** means "twelve faces."

⬡ Each face is a pentagon.

⬡ **Icosahedron** means "twenty faces."

⬡ Like a tetrahedron and octahedron, it has triangular faces.

Inquire to...

Make a Digital Story

1. **Question** the situation for your digital story.
   - **Subject:** What information will your digital story share?
   - **Purpose:** Why are you making a digital story? How do you want your audience to respond to the story?
   - **Audience:** Who will see it? What information do they need?

2. **Plan** your digital story. Organize your pictures, text, audio, and video.

3. **Research** your topic.
   - **Gather** information for your digital story. Collect images, audio, and video that can help tell the story.
   - **Explore** other digital stories to see what works well.
   - **Organize** the pictures for your story in the best order.

4. **Create** your digital story.
   - **Visuals** help users see the ideas in the story.
   - **Text** labels the visuals so that readers know what they are seeing.
   - **Audio** tells the story of the visuals and may provide mood music.
   - **Links** lead users to more information about the topic.

5. **Improve** your digital story.
   - **Evaluate** the presentation.
     - ▶ Is the digital story interesting? Is the subject clear? Are all the details helpful? Does it say what you want? Will people like it?
   - **Revise** your digital story.
     - ▶ **Remove** any images, text, audio, and links that aren't needed.
     - ▶ **Rearrange** parts so that the story flows more smoothly.
     - ▶ **Rework** any parts that are unclear.
     - ▶ **Add** images, text, audio, and links to make your story better.
     - ▶ **Perfect** your digital story, making each part the best it can be.

6. **Present** your digital story in person or online. You can present your digital story as a slide show or as pages on a Web site.

Digital Story

The screens below show the start of a digital story. Images and titles tell the basic information, and audio adds important details.

History of the Piano

From Wikimedia Commons by Charvex

 Audio:
[Piano playing] The first piano was invented in Italy about 1700 A.D. It was made by Bartolomeo Cristofori, who worked for Ferdinando de' Medici, the Grand Prince of Tuscany. Its name is short for *pianoforte,* which means "soft and loud."

 Audio:
[Clavichord playing] Earlier instruments like the clavichord weren't loud enough for performances. The clavichord was invented in the early 1300s. It hammered strings with metal blades.

Clavichord

From Wikimedia Commons by François Verbeek

Harpsichord

From Wikimedia Commons by Morn the Gorn

 Audio:
[Harpsichord playing] The harpsichord was invented at about the same time as the clavichord. This instrument plucked strings with picks. The harpsichord was very popular before the piano.

Inquire to...

Create a Wiki or Blog Post

1. **Question** the situation for your post.
   - **Subject:** What do you want to write about?
   - **Purpose:** Why are you making a post? Are you explaining something? Persuading? Entertaining?
   - **Audience:** Who will read the post? What will they gain from it?

2. **Plan** your blog or wiki post. Use brainstorming, clustering, or some other prewriting activity to help you.

3. **Research** your topic.
   - **Gather** information about your topic. Note any links you can make for more information.
   - **Focus** your ideas about the topic. (See page 301.)
   - **Organize** the details with a list.

4. **Create** your post.
   - **Beginning:** Get the reader's attention and introduce your topic.
   - **Middle:** Support your thesis with details.
   - **Ending:** Wrap up your post and offer a final thought.
   - **Visuals:** Include at least one helpful, attention-getting image.
   - **Links:** Include links to additional information online.

5. **Improve** your post.
   - **Evaluate** the post.
     - ▶ Does it fulfill your purpose? Is it interesting? Is it clear? Do readers respond well?
   - **Revise** your post.
     - ▶ **Remove** ideas and details that aren't needed.
     - ▶ **Rearrange** ideas into the best order.
     - ▶ **Rework** parts that have problems.
     - ▶ **Add** missing details.
   - **Perfect** your post, checking for errors.

6. **Present** your post on a school or personal Web site.

Blog Post

The blog post below was written by Vanessa Mannschreck for a language arts blog. It is meant to be informative and persuasive.

The title identifies the subject and draws interest.

A picture shows the book.

The **beginning** introduces the subject.

The **middle** adds supporting details.

Links lead to more information.

The **ending** gives a final thought.

Book Reviews
by Ms. Wiggens's Class

The Slant Book
By Peter Newell

The Slant Book is a rhyming story about a little boy in a runaway cart. Each left-hand page has two rhyming stanzas. Each right-hand page has a matching picture. What makes this book so much fun is that the pages are slanted so that the words and pictures both run downhill toward the middle.

When the book was first printed in 1910, it was actually shaped with a slant. (See the picture above, or visit *The Slant Book* on the Library of Congress site.) The publisher even patented that layout. Nowadays, the book is shaped like any other book. But the words and pictures are still slanted.

The story in the book is exciting, and the pictures are funny. Some of the words are old fashioned, though. That makes some pages difficult to understand. Ask an adult or two for help. Better yet, have them read the book with you. They'll laugh too!

Posted by Vanessa on March 9, 2013

Inquire to...

Share an Electronic Announcement

1. **Question** the situation for the announcement.
   - **Subject:** What information are you announcing?
   - **Purpose:** Should your announcement inform, persuade, or amuse?
   - **Audience:** Who will receive the announcement? How do you want the audience to respond? What will they need to know?

2. **Plan** your announcement.
   - **Social media** are good for quick news updates.
   - **Email** is good for sending details to a group.

3. **Research** your topic.
   - **Gather** the details your audience will need.
   - **Organize** your details. Put the most important ones first.

4. **Create** your announcement.
   - **Start** with the main point, or grab the reader's attention first.
   - **Add** details that support the main point.
   - **End** with an invitation or a final thought.

5. **Improve** your message.
   - **Evaluate** your first draft.
     - ▶ **Purpose:** Does the message accomplish your goal?
     - ▶ **Audience:** Does the announcement tell the audience what they need to know?
   - **Revise** your announcement.
     - ▶ **Cut** any unneeded details.
     - ▶ **Rearrange** details that may be out of place.
     - ▶ **Redo** parts that are unclear.
     - ▶ **Add** any missing information.
   - **Perfect** your message. Make it attractive and correct.

6. **Present** your announcement online. (Get an adult's permission and help.)

SMS

Social Media Announcement

The following text announcement was posted on a class's private account. The teacher set up the account name, and students started each message with a "|" (a "pipe" symbol) and their own first names.

Although short, this message provides all the needed details.

> **@KalaVandermolen|Chris:** Hey, everybody! My brother Charles's birthday is tomorrow. Be sure to say "Happy Birthday" if you see him at lunch or recess. I'm sure it'll make his day great!

Email Announcement

The email announcement below was written to advertise a graduation ceremony. The student drafted the message and then asked his father to email it.

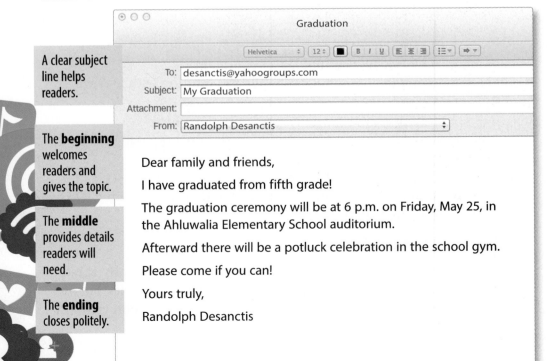

A clear subject line helps readers.

To: desanctis@yahoogroups.com
Subject: My Graduation
Attachment:
From: Randolph Desanctis

The **beginning** welcomes readers and gives the topic.

Dear family and friends,

I have graduated from fifth grade!

The **middle** provides details readers will need.

The graduation ceremony will be at 6 p.m. on Friday, May 25, in the Ahluwalia Elementary School auditorium.

Afterward there will be a potluck celebration in the school gym.

Please come if you can!

The **ending** closes politely.

Yours truly,

Randolph Desanctis

Formality in Web Projects

When communicating online, use the right level of formality.

Text Speak

Text speak has a long history. It was used as early as the 1800s, when toy printing presses were sold. For some messages today, text speak is still okay. "C U L8R" is text speak for "See you later." If your reader is unfamiliar with these abbreviations, text speak can cause confusion. Be careful even in casual use.

2day →	Today	**GR8** →	Great
ASAP →	As soon as possible	**HAND** →	Have a nice day
ATM →	At the moment	**LOL** →	Laughing out loud
B4 →	Before	**OMG** →	Oh my gosh
C U →	See you	**THNX** →	Thanks

Emoticons

Emoticons are almost as old as text speak. They are sideways "smiley" faces made of keyboard characters. In casual messages, they can be fun and convey your mood. Don't use them in more formal messages, though. Take the time to choose the best words instead.

:-) →	Smiling	:^) →	Smiling with a sharp nose
;-) →	Winking and smiling		
:-D →	Grinning	:o) →	Smiling with a clown nose
8-) →	Wearing glasses and smiling		
		:-(→	Frowning
B-) →	Wearing big glasses and smiling	:'-(→	Frowning with a teardrop

Note: Text speak and emoticons are too casual for offline writing. Do not use them in school papers.

Abbreviations

Abbreviations like "I'll" and "haven't" can keep a friendly message from sounding too formal. They're also great for dialog in stories. For more formal writing like school reports and invitations, avoid abbreviations.

How to Do Everything

One of the early titles that we brainstormed for *Inquire* was *How to Do Everything*. That title didn't stick, but it captures the idea of the book. If you can think critically and creatively, if you can collaborate and communicate and problem solve, you can do anything. Inquiry is the process for successfully doing everything from grocery shopping to landing human beings on Mars.

So, what do you want to do? Anything is possible. You have the tools in your hands and in your head. Use them to create the best possible future.

Your Turn Go out there and find your future. But when you touch down on some distant world, send us an email to tell us you have arrived safely: contact@thoughtfullearning.com. We look forward to hearing from you!

Index

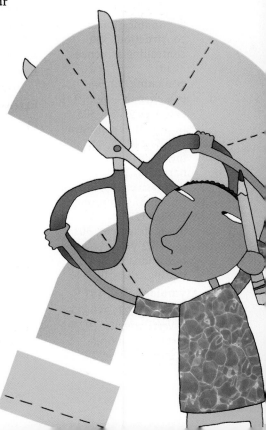

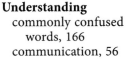